WHITE SPIRIT
ANIMALS

"Great Book! *White Spirit Animals* combines shamanism, trans-species telepathy, historic research, and native stories to show the reader why we must save the bear, lion, elephant, buffalo, wolf, and other species from extinction and how they have guided humanity in the past. A unique testimony to the close relationship between humans and animals and our ability to communicate and collaborate with each other."

JOHN PERKINS, NEW YORK TIMES BESTSELLING AUTHOR

"*White Spirit Animals* is a beautiful and deep work of art and heart. It provides a wealth of cross-cultural, historical, shamanic, and mythical information. It is likely to connect the reader with the symbolically deep realm where dreams come from. The images and stories resonate with that place of inner knowing in us. I am enthusiastic about this book—thank you, Zohara Hieronimus!"

JEAN SHINODA BOLEN, M.D., JUNGIAN ANALYST AND AUTHOR OF
ARTEMIS: THE INDOMITABLE SPIRIT IN EVERYWOMAN

"The traditional Haudenosaunee/Iroquois view is that those in the animal world are related to us. As humans we are within the same circle of life as animals as well as trees, plants, and the earth itself. Animals and birds serve as symbols for the family clans, and the bear and the wolf are part of that. These teachings are clearly covered in this book."

JOHN KAHIONHES FADDEN, COFOUNDER OF
THE SIX NATIONS INDIAN MUSEUM

WHITE SPIRIT
ANIMALS

PROPHETS
····· OF ·····
CHANGE

J. ZOHARA MEYERHOFF HIERONIMUS, D.H.L.

Bear & Company
Rochester, Vermont • Toronto, Canada

Bear & Company
One Park Street
Rochester, Vermont 05767
www.BearandCompanyBooks.com

Text stock is SFI certified

Bear & Company is a division of Inner Traditions International

Library of Congress Cataloging-in-Publication Data

Names: Hieronimus, J. Zohara Meyerhoff, author.

Title: White spirit animals : prophets of change / J. Zohara Meyerhoff Hieronimus, D.H.L.

Description: Rochester, Vermont : Bear & Company, 2017. | Includes bibliographical references and index.

Identifiers: LCCN 2017006924 (print) | LCCN 2017036738 (e-book) | ISBN 9781591432470 (pbk.) | ISBN 9781591432487 (e-book)

Subjects: LCSH: Shamanism—Miscellanea. | Animals—Miscellanea. | Human-animal communication—Miscellanea. | Parapsychology. | Occultism. | Prophecies—Miscellanea.

Classification: LCC BF1623.A55 (e-book) | LCC BF1623.A55 H54 2017 (print) | DDC 201/.44—dc23

LC record available at https://lccn.loc.gov/2017006924

Printed and bound in the United States by Lake Book Manufacturing, Inc. The text stock is SFI certified. The Sustainable Forestry Initiative® program promotes sustainable forest management.

10 9 8 7 6 5 4 3 2 1

Text design by Virginia Scott Bowman and layout by Priscilla Baker
This book was typeset in Garamond Premier Pro with Avenir LT Std, Hypatia Sans Pro and ITC Legacy Std used for display fonts

Cover images courtesy of *Wikipedia,* PublicDomain.com, iStock, and Pixabay

To send correspondence to the author of this book, mail a first-class letter to the author c/o Inner Traditions • Bear & Company, One Park Street, Rochester, VT 05767, and we will forward the communication, or contact the author directly at **www.WhiteSpiritAnimals.com**, **www.ZoharaOnline.com**, or **www.21stcenturyradio.com**.

For my mother, Lenore Pancoe Meyerhoff (1927–1988),
who nurtured my love and respect for nature.

For my daughter, Anna,
who continues this matrilineal caring tradition.

For all the animals who have shared or currently share
their lives with us, domestic and wild, captive and free,
may your voices be heard
and your love of the Earth become shared by all humans.

May Peace be our name
and plenty our gift,
coming home
Together!

Contents

ACKNOWLEDGMENTS   ix

PREFACE: THE CONVOCATION   xi

INTRODUCTION: WHITE SPIRIT ANIMALS   1
Prophets of the Wild

1   DREAMING SHAMANS   13
Telepathy and Trans-Species Psychology

2   BEAR   35
Protector of the Great Spirit

3   LION   82
The Golden-Hearted Alchemist

4   ELEPHANT   121
Teacher of the Buddhic Way

5   WOLF   167
Escort on the Threshold

6 BUFFALO RISING   207

Earth Guardians

7 THE SIGNS   265

Giants, White Dragons, and Other Stories
of Extinction and Restoration

◄ ►

NOTES   303

BIBLIOGRAPHY   312

INDEX   323

Acknowledgments

TO ALL MY TEACHERS, those present and those "not here now," human and animal, who have schooled me in the subtle reality of The All. To my husband, Bob, for his love and for his support of my multidimensional endeavors over the decades we have shared together and for his encouragement of this undertaking. To Hieronimus & Co.'s Laura Cortner for producing our talk show, *21st Century Radio,* and for facilitating the interviews of animal champions I selected to profile in this work. All of the animal protectors the reader meets— Gay Bradshaw, Charlie Russell, Carol Buckley, Tamarack Song, and Cynthia Hart, among others—are an inspiration to the world. They demonstrate how kindred relations with all species is possible. Writing this book would not have been possible without telling their stories, as well as those of the species they have devoted relations with: Bear, Lion, Elephant, Wolf, and Buffalo. Gratitude also to Meg Bowen for the details she assists with in our Hieronimus & Co. office and to Amy Ford for her wonderful, persistent diligence and patience in helping to source and format the illustrations in this book. A special "bow and a wow" to Gay Bradshaw for introducing me to trans-species psychology, a field she founded, and for her superb, collaborative editing of this book prior to the publisher's skilled and thorough additions.

To the Inner Traditions • Bear & Company community—Ehud Sperling, Jon Graham, Jamaica Burns, Anne Dillon, and others—thank you for co-creating this living prayer of mine: to write about animals using dream and waking telepathy as a primary process of gathering information. Few publishing companies in the world appreciate and support our natural psi aptitudes, such as telepathy, premonitory knowing, distant healing, or far seeing, which may be atrophied due to negligence in humans today but which are essential skills for us each to develop.

My deepest gratitude goes to Matata the bonobo matriarch for graciously showing me what is possible between humans and our animal kin—domestic and wild, captive and free—which is to come into loving rapport with them from "anywhere and anywhen." To our dogs Bella, Oxford, Omaha, Abbey, and our recently departed free-flying, sky-high Bailey, for being true friends and companions of joy in the daily routines of a loving life.

And humbly I wish to thank most of all the White Spirit Animal prophets and their species for taking me into their confidence and trusting me to tell their story in a way that they wanted it told. All of you have changed my life in ways no human could. To Bear, Lion, Elephant, Wolf, and Buffalo, may you thrive in the decades to come as humanity awakens to its purpose as stewards and companion kin of yours.

May we all together become peace on Earth.

PREFACE

The Convocation

I BEGAN THIS BOOK in the summer of 1960. I was six years old, communing with the trees and animals in the woodlands above the valley where our house was perched. We had a remarkable vista with a horizon line that stretched the imagination. My family's ten-acre site bordered hundreds of acres of pasture and corn fields that I would play and run in. It was a wonderful sunny July afternoon in Owings Mills, Maryland, where we lived. Birds were chirping and squirrels dashed about in post rain-shower excitement, a light mist rising from the heat of everything cooling off.

I was lying on the ground with my head tilted next to a rotting log, watching the industrious ants carrying eggs—and their own dead—to protective shelter. Our black mutt dogs of various sizes, Junior, Shag, and Blackie, were trying to decide whether to follow deer trails or chase squirrels nearby. It was a beautiful day and I was in my sanctuary.

Looking back on that moment, I remember with vivid clarity praying for the ability to "talk with the animals," wanting to know what they were thinking, what they needed, and what they felt and knew. I imagined that I would learn how to interpret a bird's song, a raccoon's haunting cry, or a dog's series of howls, not knowing that there was another traditional way to communicate, a way that went beyond words, barks, and caws. Today, this is called trans-species telepathy or interspecies communication, which is not only how humans can communicate with all forms of life, but also how all forms of life communicate with each other. The heartfelt request that constituted my prayer—that I would learn how to communicate with animals—became an activated longing in my soul's constellation (as are all things that we pray about). This wish became my Pole Star, the directional signatory in my childhood sky.

My youth was athletic and I was immersed in the natural world. Until I went away to camp for two months each summer, beginning at the age of eleven, I spent summers as an "insect paramedic," rescuing by hand as many drowning bugs as possible from our swimming pool, checking the skimmer daily for dead or struggling frogs, toads, or other unfortunate victims. I would also try unsuccessfully to resurrect the dead. Subsequently, in addition to my role as missionary nurse to heal other injured creatures, I became the master of funerary processions. Turtles, frogs, dead winged ones and such were the beneficiaries of these selfless ceremonies. I picked dandelions and red clover for their woodland burials and made small crosses out of twigs and bine stem. Then I would muster up the dogs to serve as pallbearers and we would head up the hill to bury the dead creatures in the woods, offering a prayer for their souls.

So began my lifelong pursuit of the practice of telepathy over a half a century ago. In those days my role models were Doctor Doolittle and Pippi Longstocking, for those fictional characters seemed to have the lifestyle that I desired most. Pippi Longstocking in particular appeared to have a most luxurious animal-centered life, without parents to tell her what she could or could not do, and relatively few boundaries between the outside and inside of her home. How splendid I thought that was! I imagined that my goat, Maria, could sleep in my bedroom instead of in her stall and that the blue jays that perched on my windowsill could fly in the house as well. (See color plate 1 of the author and her goat, Maria.) We cared for a trick horse named Sammy who could get out of his stall like Pippi's horse, and a semi-tame raccoon named Seymour who would come visit each summer and who my mother actually collared and leashed and then took with her to a costume party.

Looking back I now see that my mother must have had similar childhood dreams to my own, for we also had a woolly monkey that had the run of the playroom. Until, that is, the monkey passed on a virus to my mother from which she almost died, which sent Woolly packing. It was lost on us children that this monkey belonged in the South American rain forests. He would have lived there for seven to ten years in a large social group instead of being stolen and shipped to San Francisco, where my mother bought him as a "saleable pet."

Over the years, like my fictional role models, I have helped people find lost cats and dogs, reported what injured animals needed, and shared deceased animals' messages to an innumerable number of people. With others I have shared my communications with nature beings, from trees and rocks to angels who guard over buildings and mountains. Since the age of twelve, I have passed on messages from deceased humans to their families and friends. Animals and insects have warned me of earthquakes and tsunamis before they've happened, and I've been invited into animal convocations in both my dreams and waking life. I have also spent decades practicing nonlocal consciousness-related arts such as dowsing, radionics, healing at a distance, remote viewing, and I have conducted hundreds of soul readings for people. Now, fifty-six years after praying for the ability to do so, I can sometimes hear clearly the messages of wild and domestic animals, and through telepathy learn their personal stories.

When I was nine years old, I read *The Yearling* by Marjorie Kinnan Rawlings and I was inspired to become a writer. On my birthday that year I received my first typewriter, a beige Smith Corona that still sits, sacred, on my desk today. I remember it arriving in a big birthday box, shipped from my maternal grandpa Morris Pancoe in Illinois; he owned a stationary supply company. I had always hoped to author books about animals and more than half a century later I finally have. As the popular theologian and philosopher Thomas Moore once said to me, "The soul is always circling home."

This book answers two childhood dreams of mine: to communicate with the animals and to write about their lives.

Waking visions (which I have experienced during the day in contrast to nighttime dreams) have informed my career endeavors and all of the many books I've written. In the case of each book, I have been shown an image that reveals patterns of interface between other dimensions and our earthly lives, manifesting the axiom "As above, so below; as within, so without." One such life-changing experience occurred when a group of what are called White Spirit Animals came to me in a waking day vision, serving as the impetus for this book.

I was washing dishes at the time. As I looked out the window I was suddenly transported in my mind to a part of our property we call "the path." In a vision of myself, I was surrounded by numerous white-coated animals who gathered around me. Of these White Spirit Animals, there was a White Lion, a White Tiger, a White Wolf, a White Horse, a White Deer, a White Buffalo, a White Snake, a White Elephant, a White Whale, a White Shark, and a White Bear. (Other white animals such as mice, rabbits, and pigeons celebrated our convocation later.) These White Spirit Animals made it clear that they thought of me as a Lady of the Beasts, a name for an entire genre of goddesses in ancient Mesopotamia, Sumeria, and Chaldea. (Today, Artemis, of the Greek tradition, is the most well-known guardian of the animal kingdom, natural habitats, and children.)

The White Spirit Animals expressed a collective sense of urgency. Surprised by their arrival and their deliberate gathering in my presence, I asked, "Why have you come to me?" and "What can I do for you?" In unison, as if in a single voice that I could understand, they said, "We want you to tell our story." They made it clear that their stories should be told in a collective fashion rather than recounting one White Spirit Animal's story at a time. This was, according to them, "so that our message will be better understood and our purpose better seen."

It was another year and a half before I was able to commit to their request by submitting the idea for this book and several sample chapters to my publisher, Inner Traditions • Bear & Company, in September

2014. The journey from my waking vision to completing this book has been emotionally and mentally difficult. During much of it I was quite ill physically, which included a brief visit to a hospital's ER and ICU. These great beasts of the wild helped me to heal; however, that is a story for another day.

Learning about the terrible abuse orchestrated by humans against these wise animals has been heartbreaking, yet observing their forgiveness of humans has been inspiring. Their nobility and the perfect way each animal fulfills its divine purpose is a sacred testimony to creation. The wisdom these animals offer to the world demonstrates that they are true teachers.

As I concentrated on each of the White Spirit Animals in turn, each one expressed a concern for the survival of their species, the natural kingdom, and human beings. The purpose of each species is clear and their roles are of cosmic proportions. These wise animals highlighted the suffering of the world and told me that our survival depends on opening our hearts and expanding our awareness—birthrights we have ignored. Cultivating these natural gifts leads to experiencing the interconnected and interdependent reality of life.

The indigenous communities' traditional teachings of the White Spirit Animals indicate that close human-animal interaction can be traced back through the generations. These interactions have been recorded in story since the end of the last ice age, ten to fourteen thousand years ago.

Currently we are experiencing what scientists refer to as "the Sixth Extinction" and the Maya call "the flowering of the sixth sun." These wise animals, who like us are facing extinction, today call out, imploring us to "Save as many of us as you can." The White Spirit Animals and the cultures that honor them offer us wise guidance for the times we live in. As I have learned in this journey with them, the ancient past and impending future meet us for our challenges of today. It is with great humility and gratitude that I thank these wise prophets of the wild for asking me to join them in their Earth-saving efforts.

I invite you to hear their stories and honor their wisdom teachings.

White Spirit Animals

Prophets of the Wild

THIS BOOK IS A JOURNEY through the lands and cultures where several animals called White Spirit Animals live. These sacred animals are white-coated, unlike the rest of their species, and each is revered in the locale where they have existed for centuries. They are found among the black bear in the British Columbian rain forest, the lion in South Africa's savanna ranges, the elephant in the African, Indian, and Thai forests and fields, and the wolf and buffalo in many parts of the plains and woods of the United States. Each species is the hierarchal apex of their ecosystems, meaning the environments in which they live will disassemble without them. These illustrious White Spirit Animals are special due to their white coats, which make them highly visible and therefore vulnerable. However, they are also rare in number and humans make infrequent contact with them. If we are fortunate enough to see a White Spirit Animal, it changes us as people. Because they stand out, we pay more attention to them than their kin. All of the White Spirit Animals teach humanity about the species they are members of—and this explains, in part, why they are all mythologized and revered by the human cultures surrounding them. Simply put, White Spirit Animals are rare yet they represent millions of animals among them. Each White Spirit Animal is important to the Earth's well-being and, while precious to indigenous cultures dating back thousands of years, they are all endangered species, but also part of prophetic teachings about these emergent times.

Just as great civilizations, whether in Africa or India, built their holy centers in geographically central locations, these animals are found in central roles figuring prominently in shamanic ritual and in the psychological gestalt of Native peoples. As our partners, they take part in human development. Traditional teachings in the world speak of the human-animal bond as one of collaboration between sentient beings whose cultures, communities, and families have purpose together. Humans and animals are kin—sisters and brothers.

The esoteric Chassidic Jewish tradition of Kabbalah (received teachings), of which I am a lifelong student, were codified in a book by Rabbi Schneur Zalman of Liadi (1745–1812), in imperial Russia. (He is also known as Baal HaTanya or Alter Rebbe.) In this book he not only explains how to unite the mind and heart, he describes the human as having a divine soul and an animal soul, which work in consort in a person's life. The divine soul, which is already perfected, is unique to each person; it attaches us to the Creator. The other, the animal soul that is primarily within the physical body, is a biochemical, bioelectric, and biomagnetic synapser that uses informed light for functions such as breathing, eating, mating, and sleeping.

The animal soul and our physical bodies allow the divine soul to have sentience, which is experienced through the faculties of thought, feeling, sight, hearing, smell, taste, touch, speech, and action, making our animal soul a holy entity, our ally in co-creation. We live, as Rabbi Schneur Zalman describes, in numerous worlds beyond the densely physical one. Our souls reflect these worlds and function in the realms of emanation, creation, formation, and action. This hierarchy of interfacing realities is detailed in two of my three prior books published by Inner Traditions: *Kabbalistic Teachings of the Female Prophets* and *Sanctuary of the Divine Presence*. As explained there, the animal soul is on its own path to perfection, helping us overcome the need for immediate gratification, the fight-or-flight impulse, and uncontrolled anger, among other emotions. Animal sacrifices in biblical times were symbolic of people refining themselves—for example, water rituals to purify one's emotions and fire rituals to refine the will. The animal soul also gives us an innate drive and devotion to live, enabling every creature to fulfill its purpose when given the freedom to do so. Animals teach us about our animal soul and they do so beautifully when we watch them and listen.

We all look for meaning in our lives, and just as archaeological ruins point to other epochs in time that reveal how our societies were organized to meet basic needs and spiritual yearnings, mythologies and legends leave us a clear trail of the meaning each society places on its inner purpose and hidden architecture. Animals become gods, natural environments become holy landscapes of signs and symbols, and people become holy conduits for bringing wisdom, beauty, invention, and harmony to the world. In fact, all of life offers us knowledge, understanding, and wisdom.

Each of the animal wisdomkeepers in this exceptionally highlighted group is part of a much larger ecology of spiritual beliefs, agricultural and ecosystem principles, as well as prophetic importance. The way they all live on earth and their balanced use of nature's resources teach us about conservation, restoration, and preserving the future. They are a link between our present and our ancient past. They teach us about a proportionate use of power, the significance of communal sharing, the roles of female and male for humanity's greatest development, and respectful action relative to an economy of scale: "Take only what you need." Each is an epicenter of the location in which it exists. Each is part of elder lore and as such is of mythological importance, giving these animals potency in every age in which they are encountered physically, dreamt of, or spoken about.

Cross-culturally, the White Spirit Animals and the species they are part of utilize what today is called nonlocal consciousness. We know this because, as witnesses in this book will attest, we humans can enjoy what is at times a telepathic relationship with them. Nonlocal consciousness is the ability to experience phenomena that happen outside the normal constraints of time and space, such as farseeing (remote viewing), knowing things before they occur (premonition), understanding what any person, animal, or other life-form needs by hearing or seeing their images through distant feeling or thought transference (telepathy). Nonlocal consciousness also includes being contacted by someone who has died, which spiritists may see as an apparition of a deceased human or animal, or hear as a message from a deceased being who is trying to communicate with a living relative or friend. We also can recall other lives (regressive memory), see nature spirits (clairvoyance), hear spiritual messages (clairaudience), experience ourselves as outside of our own bodies (astral projection), heal others "at a distance," and know the future (prophecy).

Each of us is born with all of these supersensible capacities but we may not develop them. They are, however, all natural bio-systems, or what the late renowned psychic, author, and artist Ingo Swann (1933–2013) called "biomind superpowers" that are available for us to use for our survival as well as our evolution. The cultures that the White Spirit Animals bless with their presence use all of these and other faculties in their personal and communal lives. In indigenous cultures worldwide, animals, shamans, and medicine people work together in carrying out numerous tasks, such as healing others or locating missing people or lost parts of a human being's soul. In this process, some of the above practices may be utilized. In other instances, using dreams or contemplative vision, a person will receive information not otherwise available to them through the normal senses.

All Creation is embedded in the same life field connecting all of existence. If we listen we can hear all life talk. Learning to use these internal skills often gives birth to invention and creativity in any field. It is also why direct trans-species telepathy—the faculty for and enjoyed benefit of communication between all species and life-forms—takes place.

The Hebrew prophets retreated to natural environments—mountains, rivers, forests, deserts, and fields—in order to nurture, for similar reasons, their humility, courage, and imagination. To access and nurture this range of talents requires relaxing into the right hemisphere of the brain, suspending judgment, getting comfortable with not knowing, and staying open to the unknown emotionally and mentally. Like all skills, they require practice. A shaman or medicine healer practices their art throughout their lifetime as part of a lineage that is passed down through generations. These lineage traditions stretch from century to century, preserving cultural wisdom as well as ancestral beliefs, holy artifacts, and nonlocal "medicine bags."

Unlike the other books, newspaper and magazine articles, and television productions I have authored and produced, and the thousands of broadcast interviews I have written, hosted, and aired live, this book was formed using what is sometimes called whole brain thinking. This includes drawing on the processes of the left hemisphere of the brain in equal measure with those of the right hemisphere. The left brain concerns itself with logical and linear thinking. The right brain processes include those of intuition, dreaming, and vision-making.

The stories and perspectives of the White Spirit Animals that I have written about here were largely derived from my collaborative dreaming with these special animals, as well as learning about them from the Native traditions that honor them.

Another feature of some of the chapters is a cross-cultural perspective of the respective animal under discussion, and historical information about it as well. The implications of ice age origins of these animals are often featured, in addition to astronomical correlations that further indicate how important these animals were to ancient peoples. And because my interest is clearly in their conservation, many of the book's chapters contain the current status of the animal in terms of their population size and collective health and welfare, as well as a discussion of the challenges and abuses they face at the hands of human beings.

Most of the chapters are also characterized by the inclusion of experts' perspectives on the animal or subject profiled. This information is drawn primarily from the radio show that my husband, Bob Hieronimus, and I host. *21st Century Radio* has been on the air since 1988 and is the longest aired new paradigm radio program that we know of in the world. Unless otherwise stated or indicated by endnote, all of the quoted material in this book derives from live broadcast interviews I hosted between 2014 and 2016.*

As well, those readers whose imaginations are captured by the animals depicted may enjoy learning more about their respective species. Thus, basic facts and figures about each animal are provided. This compendium of information in each chapter provides, I hope, a vibrant portrait of our community of animal ambassadors.

It is also important to state that this book is not an anthology on animal biology or behavior, though these subjects are discussed, nor is it a historical study of the Native traditions mentioned. I am not an ecologist or even a symbologist. I am rather a lifelong phenomenologist, a person interested in various states of consciousness and how a person arrives at experiencing them. Specifically, in this case, I am referring to a phenomenological symbiosis with animals that is mutually realized by the animal and human simultaneously. This shared communication, known as telepathy, is repeatable and shows sentience and self-awareness in both animal and human.

I have been an environmental, social justice, and animal rights activist my entire life, as well as being a pioneer in the area of holistic healthcare. I am also one, like millions of others, whose spiritual search has been focused on alleviating suffering in the world. This is one of the reasons that in 1984 I founded the Ruscombe Mansion

---

*These portions of text are supported by one endnote at the outset of the interview-derived material. This is a form that prevails throughout the book. Interested readers may access any entire interview via the source URL in the endnotes section of this book, with the exception of one or two of them that were conducted "off-air" and thus are not accessible via *21st Century Radio*'s website, www.21stcenturyradio.com.

Community Health Center in Baltimore, Maryland, America's oldest free-standing out-patient holistic healing center, which still offers integrative services today. Also, to perhaps identify a shared quality of being that most telepaths evidence, I am a highly sensitive person. This is an actual psychological reference to people who have especially refined inner receivers, making them prone to not liking crowds, loud music, loud voices, or overstimulation as children or adults. Although these refined inner receivers may be deemed to be a liability, they are the very same inner receptors that help spiritual healers of all kinds do their work successfully. As a sensitive, many of us develop very strong wills and courage to overcompensate for and obscure the inner shudder that comes from almost imperceptible stimulus. Like a spider whose web detects anything anomalous near its home, we "sensitives" are constantly picking up signals from around us and even from far away, which makes us very good visionaries. My sensitivities were calmed and also strengthened by being around animals and in nature as a child, as they are to this day. I always have dogs of some breed or another by my side.

The American Lakota people teach that there are two basic forms of animal communication. One is a form of telepathy that animal lovers, myself included, seem to possess, and the other is through the Great Spirit that invigorates all life. I have had the privilege of experiencing both kinds of rapport.

While writing this book I practiced dream telepathy for three years, recalling dreams that imparted information, feelings, and wisdom teachings related to the animals discussed and the ecosystems they preside over. These dreams took place between August 2013 and December 2016 and are called incubated dreams. As I wrote about each animal I asked them to teach me what they wanted others to know. I prepared before going to sleep each night with a meditative focus and gratitude that such a process of sharing between species is possible. This form of communication is available to all of us and can be used to talk with any living or nonliving entity. Another type of vision, called waking visions, has been my own primary modus operandi for making important life decisions as well as career changes. They are images that appear less inside the mind and more as if someone were holding up a movie screen for me to look at. Like dreams, when we visit many places and an enormous amount of content becomes relevant, my visions all happen without expectation and come and go very quickly, as Spirit often does in our lives. These visions may show entire stories that would take days to tell orally. This book, as described in the preface, is the result of such a visionary experience that took place four years before it was written.

Just as imagery related to these animals may appear in our dreams or in waking visions of the psyche, so too do images correlated to these animals appear in the night sky. It's interesting to note how many of the White Spirit Animal species on Earth, great beasts of the wild, are named in the star systems above us. Each of these White Spirit Animals and their representative star systems is a focal point for millions of people on Earth, not just a few animal lovers. Each is part of modern-day prophecy and some are directly connected to stories about teachers from off-planet realms.

Sacred traditions of the world share a similar blueprint for humanity's highest calling—to create a peaceful and bountiful civilization of an awakened people, a prophesied golden age of illumination. Varied shamanic, indigenous, and spiritual traditions show that to accomplish this human destiny, we need to open our hearts in order to experience our divine natures. We are being urgently called by the animal kingdom to restore our reverence and care for the Earth, whose well-being depends on a collaborative sharing between created forms, rocks, plants, animals, humans, and spiritual beings of many dimensions, all taking part together in being and unfolding the manifest world. Systems of belief that ignore this reciprocal interdependence and intelligence give rise to abuse, greed, and the large-scale destruction that is manifesting on Earth today as a result of centuries of rational materialism.

In addition, a destructive belief in domination and exploitation of all that lives as a human birthright, a "species entitlement" rooted in this dogmatic fundamentalism of Cartesian materialism, has literally led to planet-wide loss and ruin. For five hundred years this philosophy in general has encouraged us to think of ourselves, our minds, and our existence as being separate from the rest of life—we are mechanical, dense physical entities that "end" when the body dies and whose awareness stops at our skin's edge. This point of view is barely more than one-dimensional relative to the multiverse we are actually part of. The good news is that we are leaving this "old paradigm" while the more challenging reality is that we can expect enormous and unpredictable changes as we do so.

One such change we can all be grateful for and assist in is the prophesied increase in human-animal telepathy, which this book honors. My efforts to share the meaning of each animal's ecological and spiritual impact on Earth and human nature is a theme that runs through each chapter of this book. Dreaming is core to shamanic activity, and in adherence with this ancient practice of dream reception and interpretation, it has been fascinating for me to learn about the animal kingdom in this manner. I encourage everyone to explore this dream process on their own.

The White Spirit Animals, as guardians of animal wisdom, are spoken of by cultures that revere them as being remnants of the Ice Age and each is said to have a special purpose on Earth. For example, White Buffalo is a harbinger of peace and abundance according to many Native American tribes. White Bear, the great Earth healer, teaches us about nurturance and patience. The White Lion is a sign that we are entering the age of the heart, according to the myths and prophecies of Zulu elders in Timbavati, Africa. The White Elephants of India and Thailand remind us, as they do those of Hindu and Buddhist faiths, of the meaning of good fortune, compassion, family, and nurturance. The White Wolf songs heard by plains, desert, and arctic peoples speak to our love of community and of our inbred need to cultivate independence as well.

The great whales, though not a focus of this book, are also mammals like the ones we are about to discuss further. Their acoustical sonar ranges miles in all directions, reminding us how thought waves reach worldwide even though we are not conscious of this. As adults, we are each 60 percent water beings (as babies we are estimated to be 75 percent water), thus it is wise to remember that water amplifies anything we put in it, like thoughts of love and healing or, unfortunately, words of anger—or more obviously, nuclear waste, plastic, and other wastes we dump into the Earth's water body. What we do to our Earth waters affects the entire planet.

We now know scientifically that consciousness functions outside of the constraints we attribute to the experience of time and space. We are immortal spiritual beings having physical experiences. That our prayers, our good thoughts and feelings, can affect someone else's well-being hundreds of miles away, as proven scientifically, reminds us to work toward self-awareness. It is a mandate for each of us to brighten our intentions with goodwill toward each other and the world. Even the loving joy of one person, it can be shown, literally improves happiness in the local environment—in the same neighborhood or building for instance.[1]

Love and joy are contagious energies, but so is fear. So sensitive are we as receptors that we react neurophysiologically to unsettling events even before they occur. Recognizing this "subquantum" interconnectedness between everything—where time and space are no longer constraints—is the axis about which most sacred societies, indigenous cultures, and mystical religious paths revolve and converge. Things can happen faster than the speed of light, while our regular practice of right compassionate action, rooted in humility, will always lead to beneficial change. Where our hands and hearts come together with joy, we improve the way other entities feel—be they in the mineral, vegetable, animal, human, or spiritual domains—because we are being in The All. If all of life is light at varying frequencies and amplitudes, then everything is connected, literally, not just metaphorically.

The White Spirit Animals and the species they belong to are bridge walkers between the visible and invisible realms. Their appearance in human awareness, especially in the past few decades, and the reverence for their well-being that their presence seems to awaken in us, has led to a worldwide movement for their protection, in part through eco-tourism and the growing animal sanctuary movement. The common goal worldwide is to prevent the hunting of them all, and foster peaceful relationships between humans, animals, and the Earth herself. For despite humanity's attempt to call the bear, lion, or wolf predatory and therefore justify their elimination, in fact, they are each essential to maintaining entire environments and cultures, as are the elephant and buffalo.

In *White Spirit Animals* we are asked by the animals to protect and bond with nature, to act upon our inner voice, and to perform intentional right action—all of which enables engagement in the purposeful and wise actions of everyone and everything. The message of the animals is simple, "Improve life around you," to which I add, "and the life within us." Westerners in particular have been focused on impacting the outer world and dominating the landscape. Adopting new ways of relating to the world is our task at hand. His Holiness the Karmapa, Ogyen Trinley Dorje, explains the link between our hopes and actions in his eloquent work *Interconnected: Embracing Life in Our Global Society*. As he shows, while we may be inspired to do good, following through with compassionate action depends a great deal on each person's inner qualities. "For compassion to blossom, we need to nourish our courage, our altruistic aspirations, our empathy, our sense of responsibility, our wisdom. . . . Bringing together the right environment within us allows us to respond well to the environment around us. Inner conditions and outer conditions interact; the interplay between them creates the reality in which we live."[2] The inner life of each person and the outer world we create together are interconnected and interdependent at all times, hence The All.

Another wisdom teaching these animals taught me is how our

own loss of matrilineal societies led to reckless brutality toward the animal, human, and natural worlds, and that protection of mothers and children, as a primary function of a species' survival, is also a moral imperative. Matriarchal societies are characterized by the practices of consensus, collaboration, and compromise, rather than competition and oppression. These White Spirit teachers implore us to create right relations among ourselves. They urge us to restore Mother Earth and to use our multidimensional capacity for dreaming a new world into being and, in so doing, to heal our own personal and collective wounds. Their teachings are universal, found among numerous cultures and languages. The wild messengers are reminders and speakers of the one language of unity. These prophets of the wild have come to teach humanity how to enrich the Earth, how to live in peace and shared abundance. May we be open enough to hear them, and wise enough to act on what we learn.

1
Dreaming Shamans

Telepathy and Trans-Species Psychology

IT'S ALWAYS NICE before going on a journey to read about where you're headed. The shape-shifters and talking animals you are about to meet in the world are not outside normative scientific or psychological understanding. In fact they are all quite normal, depending on where in the world you live, what you believe, and what you have experienced.

IVY LEAGUE MULTIVERSES

With the colorful addition of quantum physics to our vocabulary, consciousness has taken a driver's seat in many academic labs—whether they be at Stanford, Princeton, Harvard, Yale, UCLA, or the CIA. In these labs various studies are undertaken, which analyze such phenomena as how intercessory prayer effectuates healing or how focused awareness makes order out of randomness.[1] Other studies have shown the benefit of meditation in decreasing PTSD symptoms, slowing aging, and averting heart disease.[2] Remarkably, consistent group meditation by even 1 percent of the population has a notable impact. Called the Maharishi Effect, named for the external effects of Transcendental Meditation practice taught to Westerners especially by Maharishi Mahesh Yogi (1918–2008), it increases the safety of the areas in which the meditations occur by 16 percent.[3]

Various forms of laying on of hands have proven successful in reducing inflammation and trauma, to the point that subtle healers who practice Reiki are now operational in the emergency trauma care centers of some major cities. The protocols established by the late psychic Ingo Swann, with engineer and parapsychologist Harold Puthoff and physicist Russell Targ in the 1960s at Stanford Research Institute (SRI), then called the Star Gate Project (funded by the CIA), enables an average intuitive person to do what Native and ancient cultures historically depended on shamans, chiefs, prophets, and special visionaries to do: obtain information from outside their own physical territories.[4]

One part of the SRI research, and part of the larger psychic CIA spy program Star Gate (1978–1995), was a process called remote viewing, in which viewers were given only the coordinates (longitude and latitude) of the location of the target, subject, person, place, or environment that they then observed from a distance. The coordinates, like the name of an animal I do a reading with, acts as a beacon, much like a lighthouse does for ships at sea. In this manner, during the Iranian hostage crisis (which lasted from November 4, 1979, to January 20, 1981), looking thousands of miles away with only their "biological equipment," viewers were able to acquire relevant information about where some of the 444 students and diplomats who had been taken hostage were hidden, thereby saving their lives.[5]

Various studies having to do with premonitory physiology, such as reacting to events before they happen, near-death experiences and their impacts on adults and children who experience them, afterlife communication, before birth memories, spontaneous remissions, time travel, astral projection, miracles, and reproducing the Greek psychomanteum have been undertaken by parapsychology pioneers.[6] Raymond Moody, M.D., is one such pioneer. One of his special areas of expertise is helping people make contact with loved ones who have died.[7] Using a special environment Moody has created, replicating the Greek practice of communicating with the dead, his psychomanteum features a comfortable chair in a small, darkened, enclosed space, and includes the use of gazing into a water pool for visions, a form of scrying Moody replicated from the Greek Necromanteion.

All the aforementioned kinds of phenomena are localized in the shaman or medicine healer. Shamanistic phenomena is as ancient as it is modern. It can include premonitory dreams, visions, predictions, shape-shifting into other forms—animal or human—being consumed in visceral stimulus or ecstatic experiences, removing spirits or reuniting them, and talking to ancestors or off-planet intelligences that function in a psychological framework of holism in which everything is interconnected at all times and under all circumstances. Shamanism, dreaming, and numerous kinds of psychology schools are the expertise of my mentor and friend Stanley Krippner, Ph.D., of Saybrook University in Oakland, California, from where I received an honorary doctorate in humane letters in 2012 for my "substantial body of life work."

Stanley Krippner has helped thousands of students worldwide pursue studies in anomalous, paranormal, and supersensory experiences that are typically associated with the work of shamans. As well, he has helped other professional doctoral candidates learn how to facilitate the natural and vast capacities of each person. "Dr. Krippner, I presume?" seems appropriate to say when around him, as he is likely the only Westerner whose name is on the lips of indigenous shamans in Brazil, Ecuador, China, Russia, Costa Rica, and elsewhere, who are apt to ask other Westerners, "Do you know Stanley Krippner?" He's been everywhere. It's said that he's in the million-mile fliers clubs of both American and United Airlines and knows everyone in the many fields that he has helped to pioneer. I first met Stan in 1982 when my husband was pursuing his Ph.D. in humanistic psychology and he was Bob's faculty advisor.

A few years ago I called Krippner to tell him about my telepathic conversation with a matriarch bonobo by the name of Matata. She had bilocated (or what might be better known as astrally projected) into my bedroom one night at our river house, where I do most of my writing. This happened one week after I conducted an interview with world-renowned senior scientist Sue Savage-Rumbaugh, Ph.D., a primatologist and psychologist at the then-named Iowa Primate Learning Center in Des Moines, Iowa.* Rumbaugh helped found and run the research lab's multigenerational relations, including those between her own children, her sister's children, and the children of the bonobos that were being studied. She was the energetic link between Matata and me, the bridge we both used in order to meet.

In my waking encounter with Matata the bonobo, in which I could visibly see her, she greeted me in typical bonobo style by masturbating and smiling resplendently at me. I later learned that this is natural behavior among bonobos of all ages. I have seen many unusual things in my life but I wondered for a second, as funny as this will sound to some of you, if I was not in fact hallucinating her presence and her activity. I was not. Matata had obviously listened to my conversation with Rumbaugh on an invisible party line and knew how to find me. As I would later write in my report about Matata, "She has tagged me," and "She comes to have conversations frequently," and "She is in my orb a lot."

I saw her clearly during that first encounter, as did my white shepherd dog Bella, who was visibly afraid. After we said hello to each other, Matata would come to me "to have some talk'" as she put it. She would ring me up on the telepathic line and when she did I always tried to take her call. But sometimes I told her I would have to call her back!

I called Krippner for his advice about how to proceed with Matata, as I have about other projects I have undertaken. With hearty enthusiasm he said, "It's a wonderful and worthwhile effort," meaning the pursuit of our trans-species conversations, and then he told me about one of his recent graduates whose dissertation had focused on animal communication. "Just keep good records," he said, then added, "Good luck, keep me posted."

---

*This learning center was later called the Great Ape Trust and today is named the Ape Cognition and Conservation Initiative (ACCI).

MATATA SPEAKS

Matata and I had thirty-some recorded telepathic conversations in 2012, though there were others when Matata, whose name in Swahili means "trouble," would show up in my consciousness while I was grocery shopping or out with the dogs, to tell me about her day at the research lab. I always wrote down what Matata said to me because otherwise I would not have remembered her stories and concerns. I quickly recognized that she was a wondrous and wise mother and grandmother in bonobo clothes, and our friendship was deeply heartfelt. Much of her life she had been unhappy. After being taken captive at the age of five from her home in the Congo, being displaced and separated from a family she would have spent her life with, she was then imprisoned for the rest of her days. In captivity, where she lived for more than forty years, she experienced numerous unnatural separations from her own family whom she had given birth to while in shared captivity. In the case of Kanzi, she kidnapped him six months after he was born to another bonobo and adopted him as her own son.

After Matata failed at the task of being able or maybe willing to do what she called "stupid," referring to the lexigrams scientists were trying to teach her, Kanzi, having watched his mother's lessons, started using the lexigram board one day without prompting. Rumbaugh explained how Matata's children then learned of their own free will to use computers and symbols, to communicate "all manner of their thoughts and ideas."[8] This was heralded as proving the intelligence of the bonobos. Kanzi became so famous that he attracted the helpful attention of English rock stars Peter Gabriel and Sir Paul McCartney among others. But to me, Matata spoke not of Kanzi's fame or "advanced linguistic aptitude" nor his ability to make and use tools—including making a fire and roasting marshmallows—but of his "being spoiled and not having good understanding of how male bonobo should be."

Kanzi's father, Bosondjo, was not allowed to stay with Matata and Kanzi, an institutionally enforced policy for captive bonobos (and many other captive species) based on a "species survival plan" to prevent inbreeding. This policy is completely destructive to the bonobo family culture and the teaching of their young and is not based on observing the animals first to see if in fact they might harbor any unnatural mating desires. In fact, the policy has been labeled species "eugenics" by critics, as it prevents bonobos (or other animals) from having the autonomy to choose mates; many are relegated to nonbreeding clusters in their particular captivities. Kanzi had no male teachers. His father was sent to a "multispecies prison" (another term for zoo, employed by those who oppose them) in Jacksonville, Florida. Matata spoke repeatedly with a wistful hope about going home with her family to the Congo, as any immigrant does of a land they love and have been torn away from.

Months after Rumbaugh and I initially spoke, she left the primate center, due to the board of directors' change in direction. In our private conversations she explained that she was hoping to return the apes to a Congo sanctuary as a family and give them total autonomy in their daily lives while still in captivity. She formed a charity called Bonobo Hope as a vehicle for raising funds for their ultimate freedom. Matata made clear how radically her life and the lives of the other bonobos changed, even in captivity, after Rumbaugh's forced removal from their lives. They went from feeling loved and being part of a human family— having been raised with Sue's own son and niece, among the other bonobos—to being treated entirely like objects for research.

By the end of our conversations after almost a year, I had to be honest and tell Matata that some humans wanted to help her go home, and their "Suebono" (as Matata referred to Rumbaugh when talking with me) had been one of them. But Matata made clear, she would only go if her entire family could also "go home." She wasn't going to leave anyone behind. Her heart sighs were at times so grievous, her depression so palpable, that it would make me cry for her suffering and longing.

Matata's death six months after our last exchange did not come as a surprise to me, for during the time of our prior conversations, she told me, "I lay down soon, not get up. Here hurt," pointing to her chest.

Some of our conversations were focused on the bonobos' daily lives as she told me about the cold cement floors of her enclosure, which I was told were heated but not always working or warm enough for her. She talked about how her cracked feet or the bonobos' bottoms hurt and about their winter coughs. She didn't like the snow and rain in Iowa or the lack of diversity in her fruit (diverse by captive standards but not in the wild). Matata wished her daughter Panbanisha had not died and often spoke of wanting her grandson Teko with her more, as would happen in the wild as his guardian and teacher. She spoke of other things and of other family members as well. Matata was one of the longest lived captive bonobos in the world. She is survived by her two sons, Kanzi and Maisha; her daughter, Elykia; and grandsons, Nyota and Teko. (See plate 2 of Matata and her family.)

Matata fondly recalled the sound of the Native people, and their singing and song in the night as well as their drumming, which she said the male bonobos liked a lot. She also told me other stories about the ancient past. One was about "the land of the giants during the Ice Age when bonobo and human lived together to survive." Matata's stories would captivate any audience as they did me. I credit her with taking me by the hand, leading me into her life through telepathic communication, and showing me what is possible.

She died on the summer solstice of 2014. I imagined her rolling in the grass or sitting in the woods and picking at the sticks and stones, which she liked to do. But I learned she was in lock-down, alone in her cage, shut in each day by 5:00 p.m., unlike Rumbaugh's practice of letting the bonobos stay outside until sundown, because, as she says, "they love the sunset, and watching the sun go down."[9]

I hope Matata is in the presence of her "not here now" kin, which was how she referred to deceased family members and wise elders whose permission she had to secure before telling me "bonobo secrets." Her heart, like some distant drum, just stopped beating. Matata offered me her trust and her story, which is exactly what people do when seeking therapeutic help from shamans, medicine healers, and healthcare professionals. It is also what humans do with animal spirit helpers or other life-forms when we ask them to help us. It is an irrevocable trust.

WELCOME TO THE MAGIC SHOW

I have had the great pleasure of knowing Stanley Krippner, Ph.D., for several decades and interviewing him a number of times. In several hours of interviews with him, I learned how his lifetime of investigating the paranormal began as a childhood fascination with magic, and then developed into his interests in hypnotism and precognition. Having experiences as a child in extrasensory perception also contributed to his professional pursuits, ultimately leading Krippner to an examination of the world's medicine men and women, shamans, spiritists, and other people who employ nonlocal consciousness as a normal modus operandi in their lives.[10]

"I certainly was quite interested in magic and I did perform magic shows for friends and relatives from time to time," Krippner explains. "I was always eager to watch magicians at work, knowing that everything I saw was an illusion. However, that got me thinking. How did they use optics and perceptual misdirection to create these illusions? And so from a very early age my interest in magic also led to my critical thinking. I have tried to maintain that critical stance throughout my career."

Having interviewed thousands of new paradigm thinkers and doers during almost thirty years of broadcasting, I've found that there are repeating patterns in their lives. Most had a childhood involving nature and many had a near-death experience, or recalled telepathy, precognition, out-of-body travel, and other phenomena, just as I experienced in my own childhood near-death from drowning and numerous other anomalous experiences I've had, such as seeing the future, being asked in 1985 by the Blessed Mother (Mary) to create the New Order of the World Mother, or, more basically, finding a contact lens in four acres of grass. Other individuals were also exposed to a variety of cultures and environments at a young age. Simply put, new paradigm mavericks tend to come from a soul group of adventurous people looking for the truth about human capacities, and they show great reverence for all of life. When I asked Krippner what "aha" moments sparked his interest in shamans and medicine people, he shared these wonderful stories.

"I was growing up in the middle of the Depression. My parents had a farm without much money, and I wanted very much to buy a set of encyclopedias from my aunt who was selling a group of books that was called *The World Book*. And for an unheard-of sum of one hundred dollars you could get this entire set and of course my parents couldn't afford it. So I got to thinking, *I have one rich relative and that's my Uncle Max. Maybe he will lend me the money.* And then I thought, *No he can't lend me the money because he's dead.* I then reflected, *That's a strange thought to have in my mind.* However, a moment later the telephone rang and it was my cousin in tears, telling my parents that indeed her father had just died of a heart attack."

As I was wondering out loud if he had told his parents about his premonition, he said, "It was one of those instances where I really hesitated to say anything about it because I didn't know what the repercussions would be. Later when I did tell them, it was accepted in a matter-of-fact way. In the meantime, there were any number of stories that were floating around in the neighborhood and among my family and relatives about unusual happenings. One of the most unusual events was a mirage that my parents called me out to see. We were looking at the sky and there was actually a desert scene, with animals and people that looked like cowboys [or Arabian shepherds Krippner later told me], maybe even cattle, and it took me years to figure out that this was a very unusual optical illusion: a scene [from one location on Earth] can be reflected in the sky and be seen at a different place on the planet."

"Also in my younger days," he continued on as if these events happened yesterday, "I was at a family party and then again, they called me out and we looked toward the sky and saw a blue moon. There it was, very rare and very deep blue. I found it was a rare occurrence that is based on gases that coalesce. Years later in Hawaii, I actually saw a green flash that seemed to explode as the sun was going down. I was told that it was another rare but natural occurrence. These 'aha' moments all have natural explanations. So we can't describe them as being something not natural or from another world or another dimension. They have rational and scientific explanations." This led Krippner to look for natural, science-based explanations in the fields of his study, including dream telepathy.

Stanley Krippner's enormous contributions have covered the entire spectrum of planetary shamanic traditions in which the White Spirit Animals and their species play a large role. Krippner highlights the fact that "Shamans appear to have been humankind's first psychotherapists, first physicians, first magicians, first performing artists, first storytellers, and even the first timekeepers and weather forecasters. Shamans not only represent the oldest [healing] profession but are 'the world's most versatile specialists.'"[11] All of this is true and, as performers of many dimensional functions, they show us what all humans are able to do. As with any other talents, as we practice using these aptitudes in our lives, our nonlocal awareness and interspecies telepathy, among other skills, improve.

Krippner clarifies the tricky area of defining what a shaman experiences phenomenologically. This is my main interest as it was in the study of the tabernacle tradition explored in my book *Sanctuary of the Divine Presence*. I wanted to know just how the Israelites brought down the presence of the Creator and the Holy Spirit into the Tent of Meeting, and the conditions under which this phenomenon and others had happened.

In Krippner's book *Demystifying Shamans,* coauthored with Adam J. Rock, a senior lecturer in psychology at Deakin University in Australia, he helps to clarify this issue of a "phenomenological field" as being "absolutely anything that is in the total momentary experiencing of a person, including the experience of the self."[12] This precision is important and the authors replace "the use of terms like shamanic states of consciousness" with "shamanic patterns of phenomenal properties. . . .

We get a more precise picture of the subject."[13] Their work is a tremendous contribution in that it provides a way to discuss and study these phenomena, which are consistent, verifiable, and repeatable by each person who taps into this other way of being in the manifest and not-yet-manifest worlds. The phenomena are not the contents of the states of consciousness per se, but rather the phenomenal field where we see our varied subtle faculties in action.

Another significant contribution in *Demystifying Shamans* is rooting the shamanic capacity in prehistoric life or, as I discovered from the White Spirit Animals, in the last ice age. As Krippner and Rock explain in their book, "For the shaman, the totality of inner and outer reality was fundamentally an immense signal system, and shamanic states of consciousness were the first steps toward deciphering this signal system. We point out that Homo sapiens were probably unique among early humans in the ability to symbolize, mythologize, and, eventually, to shamanize."[14]

SHAMANIC DREAMING

The Greeks venerated dreaming and used dreams for healing and prognosticating. As director of the Dream Laboratory at the Maimonides Medical Center in Brooklyn, New York, from 1964 to 1973, Krippner conducted extensive research on the history and potential of dreams. (See plate 3 for a photo of Stanley Krippner.) "Certainly in traditional cultures," he explains, "dreams were highly valued and are one of the high arts practiced by the shamanic healer. So we might ask, Why has dreaming been devalued for so long in the Western civilization?"

A misinterpretation of the Bible in St. Jerome's translation from Hebrew/Greek into the Latin Vulgate led to "dreams being taboo by the Catholic Church for over a thousand years. . . . Secular literature didn't begin to include dreams until the Renaissance, then literature and then the scientific research blossomed. The situation that we are in right now is a slow recognition that dreams might be valued again. Thirty years ago the International Association for the Study of Dreams was created . . . so there is hope." Krippner concludes "that perhaps dreams will reach the place they had back in ancient Greece when people would incubate dreams and would dream about their health and their futures."

Shamans as well as other medicine men and women use their own dreams to make decisions about if or when they should take action at the behest of persons, places, or creatures, as well as to retrieve other information about what action to take. Dreams are an ancestral inheritance that give every person entrée to the wisdom of their soul and the collective unconscious. Dreams are sacred enablers.*

Dreaming is a component of human evolution. Dreams are a primary tool used by shape-shifting healers and are one way in which spirit animals and other animals can help us. "Dreams," Krippner says, "have a purpose in sleep. It's to consolidate memories, throwing out the useless memories and keeping the important ones. Also dreams help us to regulate our emotions. We can't deal with many of these feelings during the day, so we do it in our dreams. So when people have unpleasant experiences in their dreams, it is actually positive, as it helps a person resolve issues. In addition, people can use their dreams to incubate a solution to a problem."†

There is a direct link, reveals Krippner, between shamanic practices and contemporary hypnosis, another curative art he has studied and mastered. He employed hypnosis to help Grateful Dead drummers Mickey Hart and Bill Kreutzmann improve their rhythmic timing.

---

*In Judaism it is said that sleep is 1/60th of death, and that a dream is 1/60th of the world to come, meaning that in sleeping and dreaming we are literally experiencing a small portion of what afterlife states of being are like.

†Dream incubation is the purposeful preparation for an answer to a question or need. If a person wants to make contact, as an example, with a deceased relative, concentrating with love on a photo of them before going to sleep and asking them to visit during a dream is part of such a process. Basically, incubating dreams means preparing for them consciously. We establish our intention or question, and then use our dream content for the answers.

"Shamans use a lot of ritual, and a lot of suggestion, a lot of focused attention when working with the people they help. Sometimes they are working with the whole community. Taking a look at human evolution, the shamans conduct rituals that activate the immune system."

"Shamanism is an ancient tradition," explains Krippner. "Of course there are still shamans in the world today and most of them are doing good work for their community. But hypnosis and many of the other topics I investigated really have their roots in shamanism." He then clarified. "The shaman is a man or woman who is designated by their community, who is able to get information in unusual ways, ways that other members of their community cannot do on command: telepathy, remote viewing, out-of-body experience, to name a few. And when they get this information they bring it back to the community and they help and they heal people in the community. The shaman is actually a public servant in many ways, and if the community is smart and picks the right person to be a shaman, this is to the community's benefit." One fascinating perspective Krippner has is about the power of the placebo effect. A shaman's medicinal herbs and other healing agents might not be the vital component of a person's healing. Rather, the healing might be due to the afflicted person's belief in the shaman's powers.

"People who did not respond to suggestion," he points out, "people who did not respond to placebo, and people who did not respond to imagination died out and couldn't pass on their genes. As a result of this we can use all of these tools from our primeval ancestors such as imagination, such as expectation, to do some self-healing. . . . People who didn't dream and didn't have this function also dropped out of the gene pool. This is adaptive, this is part of evolution." (See plate 4 of an oil painting by the great Western artist George Catlin entitled *Medicine Man Performing His Mysteries over a Dying Man.*)

Some of Krippner's research shows our ability to communicate through dreams, using telepathy on the part of a "sender" who concentrates on an image, which the dreamer is intended to receive in their sleep. Many "receivers" successfully accomplish this task. This has long been the Native people's practice worldwide as they communicate with each other as well as their animal helpers and other nature helpers. This talent can save lives at times and at others facilitates the sharing of love in quiet ways at a distance. In the case of this book, the animals primarily sent me messages in my dreams.

Krippner's dream telepathy experiments are world renowned and show that all thought is interconnected and is especially accessible when focused intention and attention are involved, and this is why psychics and clairvoyants can do what they do. It seems to me that a person's intention acts like a beacon, shedding light in the field of its search. Our attention allows us to see what our intention has pulled into view. In Native traditions the unknown and unseen realms are a maximum potential, rather than being thought of as "empty" or "nothing."

Like human dreamers, animals also have rapid eye movement when they sleep. This is indicative of the dreaming experience and therefore proves some degree of sentience and self-reflection on the animals' part. Animal communicators will tell you that of course animals dream, and every pet owner will describe watching their dogs running great contests in their sleep or cats batting at something not visible to the observer.

Pertaining to the dreaming shaman's other powers, we learn from Krippner that "The more animals a shaman has under their command, the more powerful they become." Eagle, for example, allows one to fly above an area to survey it. Bear gives the skill of finding healing herbs or underground information. Wolf offers stealth and power to one's walk in Spirit. All of the animals a human establishes rapport with confer on the human being the animals' particular skills and awareness. These are not casual affiliations, but deep associations of shared spirit and purpose done in complete conscious agreement between human and animal, or human and trees, or human and rivers. Humans are offered this relationship with all of life. All we need to do is accept it.

As an authority in humanistic, transpersonal, Jungian, and other

Fig. 1.1. The author performing a blessing of deer (June 2015) and a deer burial ceremony (July 2016)

forms of psychology, Krippner has demonstrated that the psychological and psychiatric communities have so often misjudged what people describe as being a deeply authentic spiritual experience by calling it pathology instead. That is not to discount serious mental psychosis or other illnesses. He shows that often the judgments made by psychiatrists and psychiatric facilities investigating or treating people who have supersensible experiences reveal their own lacks and limited frame of reference.

"The basic question," Krippner clarifies, "would be why are these experiences outlawed? Why are they considered pathology by many psychologists and psychiatrists? If I were to name my most important contribution it's been to indicate that these experiences, whether they are verified or not, are part of mainstream experience. For the most part they are not pathological, they are part of the human potential." It is also noteworthy that they are all life-affirming ways by which we can make our world and ourselves more whole.

In vivid contrast to the life-affirming use of our supersensible faculties (farseeing, clairvoyance, clairaudience, clairsentience), often ridiculed or dismissed in the Western culture (though this is changing), the modern world in general suffers from ignorance or cultural prohibition of these birthrights. Yet these abilities are needed to creatively address some of the serious issues we face in the world.

THE MODERN PLAGUE OF DISSOCIATION

It is good to ask ourselves how we as people consciously or unthinkingly participate in acceptable though immoral behavior such as polluting our shared natural resources, voting for candidates who wage war as an economic enterprise, or "looking the other way" when we see someone or some other entity being hurt or, even worse, taking part in doing injury to others. In 1963 Stanley Milgram of Yale University studied this very question as it pertained to Nazi war trials at the time. Milgram carried out one of the most famous psychological studies of obedience. It focused on the conflict between obedience to authority and personal conscience.[15]

A film of his studies was released two years later with the title being, naturally enough, *Obedience*. What he found in general is that when an authority figure tells a person, almost any person, that they must do something to inflict pain on another person, most people, having had little experience with complete autonomy and self-directedness, will commit acts of abuse on others to some degree. Milgram argued that obedience can lead to genocide.

Dissociation is a break from our ordinary flow of consciousness by which we permit ourselves to do something we might later regret, or which we know from the outset is wrong but we do it anyway. Dissociation is the most unreported psychological condition we must overcome, a spiritual poverty impacting the entire world. Dissociation is also a survival skill of the psyche. "It was once a useful defense mechanism," Krippner underscores, "because it helped people dissociate from their own pain. But now," he adds, "it is too often used for people to dissociate themselves from the planet's pain."

The whole world suffers as a result, and we all must work to change ourselves, each one of us. Instead of ignoring the health of the planet, we need to face her weakened condition and work to restore her. One example of how we are conditioned to dissociate from the world around us is worth showcasing because it helps to better identify other instances of this process when it happens.

We often hear about the military's "collateral damage" that occurs during or after a bombing campaign. Using these two words, *collateral* and *damage,* obscures the reality of places that are destroyed—places where people live, work, pray, and go to school; hospitals where people go for help; homes where people and animals are left maimed or dead; bridges blown up, power stations darkened, news outlets bombed. Collateral damage? When food and water become more scarce, lives are turned upside down and inside out. Using dissociative mind control, a term like *humanitarian aid* can actually take the form of dropping bombs. Collateral damage arrives in our presence, its bloody glory masked by antiseptic euphemism, and it barely makes a ripple on the surface of conscience. We dissociate from the pain and suffering of war, and a term like *collateral damage* helps us do so. We then repeat the process of making war century after century, accepting it as a natural activity for human beings. I argue that the act of making war is artificially promoted and inspired and is a very unnatural activity to participate in. Ecosystems, human and animal lives, whole cities and towns on all sides of any war are left in shambles. At this point in Earth history, we should be beyond war and be working together for the well-being of our world.

The distressing planet-wide environment and the declining state of its resident species are the collateral damage of centuries of scientific and intellectual materialism, without our heart intelligence having been cultivated as an equal partner. This great divide is as serious as any other in the world of social ecology, today often referred to as a gulf between the "haves and have nots." This sort of severe and life-threatening chasm and its associated impoverishment of spirit is also why, in part, much of humanity is in psychological crisis, suffering—as either victim or perpetrator or both—from varying degrees of post-traumatic stress disorder (PTSD) and its dissociative components.

THE IMPACTS OF DISSOCIATION AND HOW TO REMEDY THEM SHAMANICALLY

Gay Bradshaw, Ph.D., has authored a seminal book, *Elephants on the Edge,* in which she details PTSD and multigenerational trauma that is a result of human brutality in the elephant species. Having doctorates in both psychology and ecology, and as the founder and director of the nonprofit Kerulos Center in Jacksonville, Oregon, Bradshaw's expertise covers a wide range of disciplines. Understanding emotional and psychological dissociation is part of her work. "Dissociation," Bradshaw explained in an interview,[16] "is where a person cuts off from their emotions, cuts off from even their own thinking, and becomes detached. We have defined ourselves as separate from all of nature. In a sense, dissociation defines our culture. We see this in many manifestations. One of them is intellectually, such as scientific objectivity, where the scientist is expected to be dissociated and not emotionally involved" in what they are doing. The observer effect in physics, however, proves irrefutably that anything anyone focuses on is changed by that "attention."

There is no such thing as total objectivity. Everything is subject to the lens of the viewer and interpretation given to what is being observed. Bradshaw reminds us that "Fifty years ago, Jane Goodall began calling chimpanzee subjects by name instead of by the institutional practice of giving them numbers and this really upset everyone, because she was showing that we are not separate from the animals that we use in any way we choose."

Trans-species psychology, Bradshaw highlights, "is the scientific recognition that all animals, including humans, are understood using the same unitary model of brain, mind, and behavior. Brain morphological differences mean that while information may be distributed and processed differently as a result of adaptation to specific physical environments, there are no qualitative differences among species," hence the capacity for trans-species telepathy.[17]

Bradshaw's approach of trans-species psychology is an enormous help in explaining why humans can communicate with animals as we do with each other. It is also why I use the term *trans-species telepathy*. It rests solidly in science and cultural history.

When Bradshaw founded the field of trans-species psychology she "had never intended for it to be anything other than a convenient, temporary label to bring attention to the fact that the entire body of science shows that all animals, humans included, are basically the same. We are variations on a theme. Species differences are really leveled down to the cultural differences, but this fact is ignored and denied and the reasons are very clear. One reason is economic interests, the billions of dollars spent in research and pharmaceutical development, biomedical research, in the biological sciences overall, and of course in psychology too. You know, the academic industry of 'academia' relies on being able to exploit animals. This goes on in agriculture, industrial farming, vivisection, and most other modern endeavors. So when you look at the entire spectrum of what you are calling 'animalcide,' nonhuman animals provide the engine for the entire Western civilization," she concluded. Bradshaw was using the term I invented in 2010, *animalcide,* to refer to humans' relentless systematic abuse and mass killings of animals.

I hadn't thought about the scale of our exploitation of animals in quite this way before. Bradshaw argues the case for all animals in that "they deserve to be given self-determination and sentient autonomy." (See plate 5 of Gay Bradshaw with her dog.)

Her revolutionary work is further explored in our journey with elephants in chapter 4.

WE HAVE MORE IN COMMON
WITH THE ANIMALS THAN
WE MIGHT IMAGINE

Humans and animals experience pleasure, joy, pain, excitement, fear, hunger, anxiety, family bonds, grief, contentment, community belonging, and self-purpose. We should stop pretending that this is not so.

PTSD—which Stanley Krippner has researched, treated, and found hypnosis to be helpful in treating—is experienced by victims of abuse, both animals and humans. Soldiers and civilians of war, police, fire fighters, first responders, emergency room personnel, and people who survive traumatic break-ins or displacement also experience PTSD, as do people who are in car accidents or who see them, and the millions of variations on this theme. There is another set of influences often overlooked but which play an enormous role in our society's dissociative behavior. Anyone of any age who watches tragic news, broadcast events, or excessively violent movies and TV shows repeatedly, or plays online video or other games with content where death, loss of life, and violence in general are promoted as entertainment, is not only desensitized from their own feelings, but is put into a perpetual fight-or-flight pattern, exciting the adrenal glands and hypothalamus, both of which are regulators of our inner bio-systems. This neuro-excitement and biochemical stimuli leads to neurophysiologic and psychological overstimulation, eventually having consequences in people's behavior elsewhere. Irritability, depression, addiction, lack of concentration, mood swings, tantrums, road rage, domestic violence, animal abuse, aberrant mass shootings, murders by juveniles—all are fed by this kind of violence diet.

Just seeing or hearing the pain and suffering of others, or playing at domination through cruelty, slowly does its colossal and hidden damage. This damage seeps into the heart, which we then have to flee and dissociate from in order not to the feel the pain we are experiencing in a very real though perhaps unconscious manner. The chronic bullying we now see online and in schools, which has led to tragic suicides, is part of this complex societal illness. At its simplest, when we violate the golden rule "Do unto others as you would have them do unto you," we flee to the comfortable room of denial.

This dissociative mind control, perfected by the military, the media, and Hollywood, lessens our sensitivity to life around us. In such a narcotized state, domination becomes the prevalent norm, silencing the wise soul in each of us. What ultimately saves us from totally ignoring sensible and life-sustaining values is that we are empathic beings. We are designed to function by riding the waves of love most of all, washing in and out of our hearts with the tide. *We feel, therefore we are.*

Helping in the recovery from this addictive and often facilitated dissociation is a primary part of the shaman's healing work. In each instance of dissociation we leave a part of ourselves behind, a part of our soul. Shamans help regather these lost fragments of the self or the shattered vessel of each person, group of people, or other life-forms. For kabbalists, the shattered self and missing of soul parts mirror the cosmic events when Creator first made the world. The vessels he created broke from containing too much light.

The kabbalistic Tree of Life's ten-dimensional structure and its ten varying qualities or spheres of experience reflect our own physical and spiritual anatomy. They give a proportionate measure of light to the world and each person in gradient degrees. Humans have the essential job of rectifying Creation by elevating the sparks from each fragment that fell from the original godly endeavor and purposeful shattering of the vessels. We are all asked to be shamanic. Loving acts and heartfelt prayers wherever we are do just this. While it is fun to joke that even the Creator makes mistakes, kabbalists will say this breaking of the vessels was a purposeful event, giving humanity free will *to be of service or not to be of service.* That is the question of our lives. Raising the sparks is another way of saying, "Let us shine, let us shine, let us shine." When we allow life without any requirements to surprise us, meeting it with open wonder, we are nurtured by delight.

With this as backdrop we join the White Spirit Animals and their species, as well as the wonderful communities of human beings who value and collaborate with them. The animals' stories are sobering and enlightening. So gather up your walking stick and compassionate heart, allow your mind to relax and open, and come with us on a fascinating wilderness excursion with the prophets of the wild as our guides. They will show us our inherited ancient past, the work we must do in the present, and their hopes for our future.

2
Bear

Protector of the Great Spirit

The Great Spirit is in all things; he is in the air we breathe. The Great Spirit is our Father, but the Earth is our Mother. She nourishes us, that which we put into the ground she returns to us.

BIG THUNDER (BEDAGI) WABANAKI ALGONQUIN

OUR JOURNEY into the shared human and animal world begins with Bear. Bears populate myths, literature, art, and music in cultures worldwide. Children of the West likely meet Bear first in the nineteenth-century fairy tale "Goldilocks and the Three Bears." In this tale, one day a little girl named Goldilocks shows up in the bears' home and samples their three bowls of porridge; the three chairs of Papa, Mama, and Baby Bear; and their three beds. When Papa, Mama, and Baby Bear all return home they remark successively, "Who's been eating my porridge? Who's been sitting in my chair? Who's been sleeping in my bed?" Finally throwing back the covers of Baby Bear's bed, they see the little girl, Goldilocks. She jumps up and runs back into the forest from whence she came.

The Goldilocks story is a bit scary, even though the manner by which the bears are depicted is charming fiction. The free-living bear society is matrilineal and lacks any stay-at-home Papa Bear. But the tale of the three bears is enduring and has imprinted generation after generation of children in the West with the image of an angry "in charge male bear" who growls and controls the "man cave." However, bears in most or many other children's stories in the United States are very different. The popular bear is friendly and neighborly, which is true to their nature.

In 1944 the United States Department of Agriculture (USDA) Forest Service began using Smokey Bear to educate the public about the dangers of forest fires. His smiling and instructive presence on signs still adorns campgrounds around the country. Then there was the loveable Yogi Bear cartoon character that started out in 1958 as a member of *The Huckleberry Hound Show.* Yogi became so popular that the animation studio Hanna-Barbera gave Yogi his own spin-off show three years later. Yogi's huge influence on baby boomers assured a long-lasting love of bears for years to come. Yogi's down-home, "I'm

Fig. 2.1. American black bear, *Ursus americanus*
From *Brehms Tierleben (Brehm's Life of Animals)* by Alfred Edmund Brehms (1829–1884)

smarter than the av-er-age bear" conversations with his ever-present sidekick in Jellystone Park, little Boo-Boo Bear, went straight to the hearts of fans.

These two animated characters show us that bears aren't the scary bears of Goldilocks but are our *pals*. As an example of how deeply Yogi and friends entered the American unconscious, I actually gave the endearing nickname of Boo-Boo to my daughter Anna as a toddler. I did not consciously associate it with Yogi, and, interestingly too, I recently learned that *boo* is the word for a Mongolian shaman.

There are even more examples of bears in American lore. After Yogi and Boo-Boo came the Berenstain Bears who arrived on the scene in 1962. The cartooning couple Stan and Jan Berenstain, and later their son Michael, enchanted new generations of children with Bear, once again as a trusted companion. This image of Bear is not far from the truth. People today may be surprised to know that it was only a few decades ago that you could see families of people picking berries or sunning yards away from lounging black bears, as a number of my radio guests have shared with me.

And then there is Teddy. He is the soft and cuddly bear that millions of children turn to for security and protection, tell their secrets to, and with whom they share their most cherished dreams. The soft brown, golden, or white plush bear is treated by children as a gentle being—courageous, curious, playful, patient, loving of its young, intelligent, forgiving, compassionate, and a solitary being. He was modeled after a black bear, parent of the White Spirit Bear. In the early 1900s the Ideal Toy and Novelty Company, founded by the American couple Morris Michtom and his wife Rose, and the German Steiff company, apparently unaware of what each other was creating, simultaneously made stuffed toy bears. Bear was in the air.

The Steiff bear was based on Richard Steiff's drawings of bears that he had seen at the zoo, while the Ideal Toy and Novelty Company named their bear Teddy in honor of American president Theodore Roosevelt (1858–1919). In 1902, on a Missouri bear hunt, Roosevelt refused to shoot a bear that had been run down by dogs, cornered and clubbed by the president's aides, and then tied to a tree. When told he could shoot the bear as his day's trophy, Roosevelt refused, calling it "unsportsmanlike." Instead, he asked that they shoot the black bear to put him out of his obvious pain and misery. The Michtom's Ideal Toy and Novelty Company, which flourished during the post–World War II era and was the largest doll-making company in the nation,

Fig. 2.2. President Theodore (Teddy) Roosevelt on a hunting trip (1902)
From the *Washington Post* original cartoon by Clifford Kennedy Berryman (1869–1949)

named their bear Teddy to commemorate this event, having asked the president for permission to use his name for their bear creation. The incident and the teddy bear were celebrated by conservationists. Even the *Washington Post* printed a cartoon, which was the inspiration for the "Teddy Bear," showcasing the event to highlight Roosevelt's ethical inclinations toward animals. In addition, Roosevelt would become the presidential force behind saving the buffalo as free-roaming animals in Yellowstone National Park, literally keeping *those* American icons from becoming totally extinct.

CROSS-CULTURAL PERSPECTIVES OF BEAR

On the global stage in days past the ancient Greeks called the top of the world "the land of the Great Bear." In Finnish paganism and among most Native tribes the word for Bear (in each of their own languages) is not spoken for fear that a bear will manifest at the mention of its common name. In general, Bear is spoken of by North America's Native traditions as the "brother to the first people." According to the Cherokee, indigenous to what is now the southeastern United States, Bear is the greatest and first created Earth being. The Creator used Bear to anchor down the northern quadrant of the sky and the north wind, the direction from which Spirit comes. The Navajo of the southwestern United States refer to Bear as "a fine young chief" and the Sami people of northern Finland, Norway, Sweden, and Russia speak of Bear as the "wise one." Siberian custom identifies Bear as the "owner of the Earth." The Japanese Ainu call Bear "the divine one who rules the mountains."

In terms of seasonal designations associated with the bear, the Great Lakes Potawatomi people call the January full moon the "moon of the bear." The Tlingit people of the Pacific Northwest coast call February "the Black Bear moon," and July "the salmon moon."

Until the early twentieth century and reminiscent of Paleolithic bear cults, members of the Ainu people, an indigenous culture in Japan's Kurile Islands and on Sakhalin Island in the North Pacific Ocean, maintained their own bear cult. They believe that bears in their physical bear form are deities making their appearance for the benefit of the people's welfare, providing meat to eat in the winter and furs for warm clothing. The bear that willingly gives up its body and is killed by hunters is prayed over, thanked, and honored for its body parts—its flesh and fur—which are used to meet valuable physical and ritual needs. Through the bear's self-sacrifice it gains tools for its spirit journey as protector of people and its own kin, earning the right to reincarnate as a human. Purposeful self-sacrifice is believed to be an honor that elevates the soul of both animal and human.

For the Cree in North America and Canada, Bear is ruler of the hunt. Performing bear-related dances, hanging bear skulls, and singing chants to induce dreams of bears are all aspects of asking Bear for a good hunt, for essential prosperity and protection.

In the cultures of Central Asia and North America, Bear is the fierce mother guardian protecting her cubs and the woodlands, fishing the world's waters, and eating off the world's lands. To the people who identify with her, "Bear Spirit" confers dream vision, courage, healing powers, inner resourcefulness, patience, and an understanding of what freedom is—all of which is gained through humility, generosity, self-restraint, and nonviolence. This awareness comes from a wholesome respect for boundaries and fulfilling one's purpose.

THE ICE AGE FACTOR

Bear is regarded as a shape-shifting being when called by a shaman, medicine man or woman, or a bear clan member. In these instances, Bear can appear as if from thin air, a phenomenon associated with the large hominid referred to as Yeti, Sasquatch, or Big Foot. These creatures range in height from eight to fifteen feet, suggesting they may be survivors of the last ice age. They are comparable in size to hominids

Fig. 2.3. Petroglyph of Bear (1600 BCE to 1300 CE) at
Potash petroglyphs site in eastern Utah
Photo by James St. John

of the same time period, including giants that stood eight to thirty feet tall and date back twelve to twenty thousand years. At that time the giant *Arctodus simus,* a short-faced bear, stood eight to ten feet on its hind legs and weighed a ton. They lived eight hundred thousand to eleven thousand years ago but went extinct.

The White Spirit Animals survived the last ice age, during which time they helped our species survive. What caused the termination of the ice age has been open to debate, but the most accepted theory today, and one that is consistent with diverse historical and Native stories worldwide, is described in Graham Hancock's masterful *Magicians of the Gods: The Forgotten Wisdom of Earth's Lost Civilization.* Specifically, the theory posits that extraplanetary events caused cataclysms on Earth.

"Near the end of the last Ice Age 12,800 years ago," Hancock explains, "a giant comet that had entered the solar system from deep space thousands of years earlier broke into multiple fragments. Some of these struck the Earth, causing a global cataclysm on a scale unseen since the extinction of the dinosaurs. At least eight of the fragments hit the North American ice cap, while further fragments hit the northern

European ice cap."[1] Matata the bonobo described this in very similar ways using her own details about Earth changes being associated with the original giants who possessed monstrously large animals under their command. "Thankfully," she said, "the sky gods helped to eliminate them [the giants] using meteorites and comets, saving bonobo" and other, smaller bipedal life-forms from extinction.[2] To the bonobo, this was a war between the "sky gods" and the first race of giants who had not interbred with humans.

After the comet struck, the subsequent tsunamis, earthquakes, and sudden melting of ice sheets resulted in a global flood. This account can be found in all cultures. These cataclysmic changes on Earth led to a tremendous variation of new or adapted life-forms as well as a massive die-off of ancient and larger scaled species. By 8000 BCE, the climate was very much like ours today, and similar to what it has been over the past ten thousand years. As legends recount, shamans, priests, magical people, people of the sky, and their animal equals—the White Spirit Animals—helped restore life using transspecies telepathy, another development that occurred with these Earth changes.

The prophecies and mythologies associated with White Spirit Animals, including the White Bear, originated not less than ten thousand years ago. For the Cherokee people, White Bear is guardian of the North and is credited as being the source of inspiration and knowledge as he climbs toward heaven up a ladder of arrows. On this ascent, he gathers snow and ice on his fur, gradually becoming completely white by the time he reaches the Pole Star. There White Bear resides to remind us of the past and future glacial ages.[3] Of course, the polar bear is a white bear familiar to many people, but it is the rare white black bears we are coming to know that are the "White Spirit Bears." They are genetic relatives of both the polar bear and the magnificent brown grizzly bear.

Legends worldwide describing the Ice Age make sense when we look at the actual geographic extent that ice intruded—from Iceland as far south as the British Isles. Northern Europe was swallowed in ice south to Poland and Germany. Further to the west, Canada was entirely engulfed by ice as well. Ice sheets in North America stretched as far as the Missouri and Ohio rivers. The Southern Hemisphere—Chile, Argentina, and Africa—and parts of the Middle East and Southeast Asia also experienced mountain glaciations.*

Between twelve thousand and ten thousand years ago the last of the five major ice ages ended, leaving behind great lakes and enormous ice sheets that remain today in the Arctic, Canada, Alaska, California, parts of Asia, and on Mount Kilimanjaro in Tanzania. Recent climate change has reduced the size of these ice sheets significantly. In the past, of the Earth's 197 million square miles, an estimated one-third of the Earth was covered by ice. According to the International Union of Geological Sciences, the most recent period had its last glacial maximum thirty thousand years ago, in the Pleistocene epoch that began 2.58 million years ago. Our current Holocene epoch is also part of the Quarternary period. In fact, it is now being called the Anthropocene epoch, which we examine in our journey with Elephant.

In Eurasian history, Neanderthals date back forty thousand years ago when humans lived in caves. This was, according to matriarch Matata, how and where humans and bonobo lived together and even interbred. "Bonobo are between the lines. We are close to human and close to ape. We are a mixture," she explained. Although at first this statement, given during one of her "elder lore" story hours with me, sounded fantastic, it turns out that it is likely true. A 2010 *Science* magazine article on this very issue claims that "Neanderthal DNA is 99.7 percent identical to modern human DNA and a chimp's [which is similar to a bonobo's] is 99.8 percent identical to humans."[4]

---

*There are glacial and interglacial periods within each major ice age. Currently we are in the interglacial Holocene epoch following the Pleistocene glaciation, both part of the larger Quaternary Ice Age.

PERTINENT PERSPECTIVES OF MATATA
AND OF THE INDIGENOUS PEOPLES

With Matata's disclosure, I learned that Matata knew history a lot better than I did. She also spoke about humanity's disconnection from the Earth. "We do not judge humans," she said. "We understand their weakness of not feeling part of the Earth. They are separate [those with power] . . . from the Earth. They lost their feet when they got wings [airplanes]."

It is clear that when tribal peoples of the world speak of the White Spirit Animals' origins, they are talking about history, uniformly, as remnants of a former ice age that humanity survived with the animals' help. But these cultures also claim that assistance came from off-planet societies who gifted humanity with agriculture, medicine, and advanced technologies worldwide. The Cherokee say that their stories go back to the beginning of time and the reappearance of these white-coated animals is the fulfillment of prophecy about this century's Earth changes.

Just as Matata's stories about her own DNA are scientifically accurate, so are her colorful stories of prehistoric events, which include accounts of several races of giants, discussed in the closing chapter of this book. The same can be said of the "Little People" as mentioned by the Iroquois, Inuit, Cree, Crow, Comanche, and others. Cherokee medicine men were said to confer with the Little People. The medicine men would sing to Bear as part of their ritual convocation, which elicited healing information from the Little People.[5]

The following story is a good representation of these stories in general.

The Little People Impart Wisdom
to the Cherokee

In the old days Cherokee medicine men would travel to the rock caves each
year to meet with the Little People and share in their secrets. The medicine

men would stay in the mountains for seven days and nights telling stories around the campfire. On the first night they would tell the story of Bear and sing the songs Bear had taught the Cherokee. The songs were for good hunting. On the second night, they would dance the green corn dance for good crops, singing and dancing all night long. On the third night a song was sung to invoke the deer spirit to be kind to the Cherokee hunters. The fourth, fifth, and sixth nights were spent on more storytelling, dancing, and singing. Each medicine man told about a sacred formula that the Little People had entrusted to him.

On the seventh night, at the darkest hour, as the drums beat louder and louder, the Little People, or Yundi Tsundi, danced into the circle. They danced and chanted sacred songs. Then the Little People told the medicine men to return the secrets that had been shared with them that year. One by one the medicine men placed the secret formulas in the hands of the Little People. One by one they left the cave and rejoined their tribes with new healing information, going back each year to return and receive the spirit gifts of the Little People.[6]

According to many Native traditions, the condition of Bear is the indicator of how any world age will fare. The bear on the mountain is like a "canary in the coal mine." Lion, Buffalo, Elephant, and Wolf are also regarded as barometers of human fate, making their importance equal to that of Bear.

"As a very young child, maybe the age of three or four," Judy Tallwing, Apache elder and medicine painter, recalls, "I can remember my grandmother telling me a story about the White Spirit Bear in the North. You see we lived way down in Arizona. But she said that this White Spirit Bear is very sacred. And if this White Spirit Bear should ever disappear from Earth, all human beings would disappear as well. Can you imagine how scary it was for a little kid to be told this?"[7] As Tallwing's memory showcases, White Bear is teaching us that we are precious to each other's survival and that Native legends regarding these special animals and our relationship with them have their roots in history. They are part of spiritual theology and cultural beliefs based in generational experience.

BEAR SYMBOLISM IN THE HEAVENS ABOVE

Following the hermetic axiom "As above, so below," when we look to the star systems as the tribal and other sacred traditions do, we can see in what ways bears and other animals have been venerated. Bear is around all of us at night. Indeed, in a dream of mine in which Bear appeared, he explained that they were "leaving their spirit trail in the night sky."

There are many varying explanations as to how the star systems that have bear names—Ursa Major (Great or Large Bear) also known as the

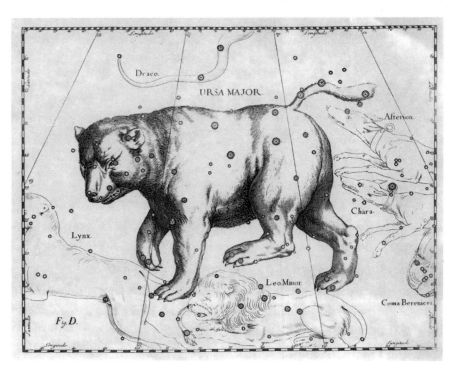

Fig. 2.4. Ursa Major, the bear
By astronomer Johannes Hevelius (1611–1687)

Big Dipper, and Ursa Minor (Small Bear) or Little Dipper, came into existence. Here is one account.

The Creation of the Big Dipper

The Wasco tribe of the American Northwest describes the creation of the Big Dipper contained in Ursa Major as a story about wolves, coyotes, and bears. There were five wolves who would share their food with Coyote. The wolves were staring at the night sky one night, so Coyote asked them, "What are you looking at?" to which they replied, "There are two animals up there but we can't reach them." Coyote said that was easy and he shot an arrow into the sky and it stuck, and then he shot another that stuck to it until he had created an entire chain of arrows that reached the ground, whereupon the wolves and the coyote climbed up the ladder of arrows to the sky.

The oldest wolf had his dog with him and when they reached the sky they could see that the animals there were grizzly bears. The wolves stayed there looking at the bears and the bears looked back at them. Coyote thought they looked so good sitting there in a group that he removed his ladder of arrows from the sky, leaving the bears, wolves, and dog together.[8]

Most of us learn about Ursa Major's well-known Big Dipper in grade school. The constellation is visible to the naked eye in the night sky from anywhere above the 41st parallel. Ursa Minor, whose bright star lies at the end of its Little Dipper handle, is the de facto North Star, also called the Pole Star or Polaris. The North Pole itself is known among Western children as the place Santa Claus comes from. The Earth's celestial North Star marker will change its location in the centuries to come as a result of the equinox precession.

The precession of the equinoxes takes place over a cycle of twenty-six thousand years, shifting about one degree every twenty-seven years. As noted in one of my earlier books, *The Future of Human Experience,* plasma physicist Paul LaViolette notes that this twenty-six-thousand-year periodicity is the same time span (thirteen thousand to twenty-six thousand years) between recorded galactic core explosions that tend to upend civilizations with violent extraplanetary impacts. LaViolette maintains that galactic explosions caused the end of the last glacial age. These cycles of impact on our terrestrial and cosmic weather last for generations, not just a few years.[9]

The figure of twenty-six thousand years shows up in the calendar cycles of the Hindu and Maya traditions as well as the Western astrological systems of calculations. Hopi, Cherokee, and other First Nation people and other ancient civilizations like the Egyptians and Babylonians use the Pole Star, or the North Pole Star signatory, as a cosmic clock as well as terrestrial guide.

The faint star Thuban in the constellation Draco (Latin for *dragon*) held that role in 3000 BCE, the Middle Bronze Age when sage kings in imperial China came to prominence until 1793 BCE. Beginning in 3942 CE (approximately 1,926 years from now) and again in 5200 CE, this inheritance will go to Gamma Cephei or Alrai. This name Alrai is derived from Arabic, meaning "the shepherd," or "the shepherd's dog." It sits at the knee of the constellation Cepheus, the king. One could posit that this event may signify the time period of a prophesied thousand years of peace that traditions worldwide predict: the age of a cosmic king or alliance with a royal lineage or a messianic consciousness when a shepherd will come and guide humanity into unity consciousness.

The Pole Star position returns to the Little Bear in 27,800 CE.[10] I suspect that any prominent Pole Star position within any star signatory affects the culture on Earth below because of the meaning we assign to the pattern of the stars above and all around us. Just as Ursa Major and Ursa Minor as the mother and cub of bears have affected humanity for thousands of years, the star of the shepherd, or shepherd and dog, may do the same in the future.

As is seen by the naked eye, the Ursa Major and Ursa Minor constellations share global importance among humans everywhere. They are also vital for any outdoor adventurer, mariner, or traveler because they provide orientation north. The Little Bear's northern Pole Star, or Polaris (the brightest star at the end of the Little Dipper's handle), stands at the foot of Orion, whose belt stars point to the galactic center. The North pole region and the Pole Star are the bears' domain, which makes Bear a sacred steward of cosmic proportion. All longitudes on Earth come together here. Our predecessors worldwide understood and honored this, as do many living tribal people, spiritual seekers, and animal preservationists today. Bear is a point of physical and spiritual unity.

THE UN*BEAR*ABLE ROOTS OF WESTERN DISSOCIATION

The numerous tales from Greek lore regarding the origins of Ursa Major and Ursa Minor are well worth exploring because these mythologies show up in culture as behavior and values. In general, the elements and themes in the various myths are the same, although who does what to whom and when changes depending on the given source. The main players are Zeus; his wife, Hera; Zeus and Leto's daughter Artemis, the goddess over the wild and protector of animals, children, and childbirth; Callisto, Artemis's virginal hunting devotee and Zeus's conquest; and their son Arcas who is born out of wedlock.[11]

In a general telling, Zeus, the god of sky, rain, and thunder, the Supreme Being in the pantheon of Greek gods who is also a serial rapist, takes for himself a virgin named Callisto. She is the daughter of Lycaon, the king of Arcadia. In one version, Zeus, who has a history of turning himself into animals to take his conquests by surprise, turns himself into a bear to seduce and impregnate Callisto. In a second version it is Hera who throws Callisto to the ground in a rage after discovering her pregnancy and changes Callisto into a bear.

One day Callisto's young son Arcas goes out hunting for a bear and shoots Callisto. As the bear lies dying, Callisto begins to return to her human form and is saved by her son. They are then cast out together to their place in the northern sky.

The tale of Callisto is a banishment tale of a woman who becomes a bear and a bear who becomes a woman.

Another classical telling of this story features Zeus turning Callisto into a bear to disguise his rape and her pregnancy. In order to save Callisto's life from his avenging wife, Hera, Zeus places Callisto in the sky for eternity as the constellation Arctos or Ursa Major, the Great Bear. At Zeus's instructions, her son Arcas is rescued from her womb by Hermes, another of Zeus's sons born with a nymph named Maia (a sister in the Pleiades cluster), who saves the baby from Hera's command to kill the bear. Hera is well aware that the bear is in actuality Callisto.

Obviously the Greeks were familiar with shape-shifting but what I find so interesting about these stories is that, according to the scholastic literature about the time period, Artemis and her huntresses could and would also change themselves into Bear and Deer. Giving Zeus or Hera or even Artemis the credit for Callisto turning into a bear may be a reinterpretation of a deeper truth. Knowing the natural inclination of earthly bears to protect their offspring, the story of these two heavenly bear keepers of Earth's "mother and child" suggests that in fact it may have been Callisto herself who changes into a bear, whether literally or symbolically, in order to save her own child. This is much like mother and cub hibernating together in the cosmic den. Bear, whether of sky or Earth, embodies the ferocity and gentleness of the protective mother. My interpretation makes the tale of Callisto an elevation tale rather than one of banishment—honoring Callisto and the female bears' empowerment in a way the Greeks did not.

In any case, although the story of Callisto and her son is told in many different ways, I believe that these Western patriarchal tales reflect and have had significant influence on society's view of unwed mothers and their historic banishment from families and communities. This has contributed to the mindset of holding a rape victim culpable and punishing the orphan for being orphaned. In contrast, the all-powerful dominator "rapist" Zeus has historically been championed by the legal system and the culture, while the victims—primarily women and children—are penalized. This gender-based assumption that ruling males have the authority to dominate and destroy is found worldwide.

In today's human slavery cartels, "At least 12.3 million people are in forced labor worldwide. . . . 600,000–800,000 men, women and children are trafficked across international borders each year. Approximately 80 per cent are women and girls. Up to 50% are minors."[12] Bears are treated similarly to virgin girls; unwed pregnant women; victims of rape, whether male or female; and those individuals who are imprisoned or enslaved in abusive situations. What animalcide perpetrators do to bears—entrap them, hunt them, kill them—is no different from the murder and torture performed by captors and cartels who enslave and murder people. Paying a fee, the "hunter" (read "murderer") is permitted to take the life of a bear with bullets or arrows for the pleasure of killing.

Blood lust in sexual and violent assault and human or animal murder shows our human capacity for dissociation between our inner self and our outer actions. It also reflects the extraordinary entitlement that some humans feel, which provides a justification for them to enslave and murder others. Again, this kind of violence is born from a deep inner disconnection from life and one's authentic innocent self within. From a cultural perspective, the story of Callisto and Bear captures a deep sense of powerlessness and impotence felt by many men and some women, which is expressed in their aggression—but also these stories reveal the victimhood that is ascribed to sentient life that is female or nonhuman.

Brutal physical assault, exploitation, and rape are military as well as personal weapons of domination and ruination. They are the forces responsible for so much of the pain and suffering in our world today. This same sense of prerogative enables the mass clear-cutting of life-preserving, sacred rain forests, and the extraction of oil and gas from vitally undeveloped areas. Such a distorted sense of entitlement leads to wanton killing of people in war worldwide and the extinction of wild animals essential to any given ecosystem's hierarchy of life. The story of Zeus reflects the same attitude responsible for the decimation of the natural world through an increasing carbon footprint, amplified use of nuclear power and arsenals, genetically modified organisms, and other life-threatening developments that are negatively impacting the entire planet and all its inhabitants.

As explored in chapter 1, dissociation is a psychological process for repeating actions we consciously know cause harm, pain, and suffering. Dissociation is a method for dealing with all kinds of behaviors that seek to destroy rather than beautify, harmonize, and elevate life. To claim that our civilization's power structures behave sociopathically is not an exaggeration.

In the tales of the Great Bear and the Little Bear, Native matrilineal traditions elevate the bear and cub to life *bear*er, the preserver, guide or way-shower, spirit guardian, healer, teacher, peacemaker, and reminder of ancestral life. In stark contrast, the Western patriarchal mythological tradition reduces the mother and child to banished outcasts. Male domination is institutionalized, sowing a conscious separation in gender and rights, and rooting inequity in Western civilization's philosophy and behavior. Its impact is the dark side of the White Spirit Animals' story and that of our own.

SHE BEARS AND THEIR VENERATION

Despite the grim scenario outlined above, we have begun to move toward an ascending arc in consciousness. Increasingly, human beings and sentient life-forms, including the White Spirit Animals, are meeting and working together for a renewed consciousness with a unified purpose.

There are many local cultures in the Western world that prove this point. In these communities, veneration and honor of the female bear is still in place. This demonstrates that while a dominant patriarchal culture continues to control society today, the divine feminine is active and alive. It is unfolding with women's movements and child and animal rights movements that are growing in every country of the world. Increasingly, humans are wide-awake and working to create a balanced world, made whole through compassionate action and the cultivation of our minds and hearts.

According to Marija Gimbutas, Ph.D., professor of European archaeology at the University of California, vestiges of the maternal lineage of the bear culture remain in many European communities today. For example, a pregnant woman is still referred to as "the bear." When she walks toward a group, others may call out loudly, "Here comes the bear!" This reference to Bear, Gimbutas writes, is reminiscent of an ancient pagan chant.[13] Pregnant women do indeed sway like bears at times, lumbering from side to side, particularly as they approach term. Certainly most mothers are as ferocious as a bear when it comes to protecting their children, something that I can attest to from personal experience.

Gimbutas provides numerous examples of bear rituals involving women donning bear masks. The lead figure at Artemis's temple in Sparta wears a bear mask and to this day, on February 2 in Crete, there is a celebration of the Virgin Mary as the bear. Crete's Minoan bear culture thrived until about 1450 BCE. When a volcano erupted there between 1627 BCE and 1600 BCE, the blast was so great that it is thought to have caused a tsunami. This eruption is spoken of as the last major volcanic eruption to occur in the past ten thousand years. It destroyed much of the advanced, decentralized culture of this island civilization—yet to this day, the Bear remains a revered species there.

Further north Bear was venerated by the Celts as the bear goddess Artio. The city of Bern, Switzerland, still honors the bear on its emblematic coat of arms. Russia has been called the Great Bear at various times since the sixteenth century due to its size and power. This image is conserved in language today. When we "bear down" on something, are we not becoming "Bear," staying firmly in place with great focus and strength? An Ojibwa woman in menses is called Mako-wii,

"Bear Woman." Women "bear" children with great and enduring effort. And do we not "bear" witness to life?

THE BEAR DANCE

The oldest surviving dance of the Ute people is a ritual called the Bear Dance. These Native people of Colorado, Utah, Wyoming, eastern Nevada, northern New Mexico, and Arizona say they have lived in these locations since the beginning of time. The Bear Dance, apparently their oldest surviving dance, celebrates a bear's natural inclination to stand on his/her hind feet while rubbing up against a tree to scratch where paws can't reach. To a human, this looks like dancing.

Once a year Bear Spirit is honored by the Ute by corralling men into an area where woman are then allowed to ask a man to dance, which no man can refuse. "Legend has it that two brothers were hunting when one of them noticed a bear doing a dance while scratching a tree. The bear taught the hunter the dance, along with songs, to take back to his people. The songs showed respect to the bear spirit, and respect to the bear spirit makes one strong."[14]

Not all cultures revere the bear, however, and as a result, these species suffer from many atrocities. Trophy hunting businesses, where animals are held captive in order to be shot for a fee, hold bears in parameterized captivity or in cages for people to kill. Thirty-one American states still allow this practice of canned hunting, which will be discussed more fully in our journey with Lion. Also, bears are stolen from their homes in the wild to be put into zoos and other captive environments.

The bear's nose is the most sensitive part of its body, yet for centuries thousands of bears have had their lips or noses pierced with a red-hot metal poker through which a rope or chain is then passed. This is a method of control to force them to dance or be led around for other entertainment purposes. The innate sensitivity of the nose and lips, and the fact that an infection often settles in there, means that the bear lives in constant pain. This leads to traumatized cubs, many of whom die of shock or dehydration and starvation. If they do manage to survive, the cubs spend shortened lives in commoditized slavery, much as human indentured servants and sex slaves do today.

Beaten and abused with sticks, the orphaned cub eventually submits to standing on its hind legs or performing other tricks. Bears' teeth are knocked out or broken and their nails are pulled out, all so that they can't fight back and harm their abusers. Many bear owners are poor and can barely feed their enslaved animals, and the ensuing poor nutrition and abuse may lead to a loss of fur and blindness.

Typically in Russia, Europe, India, and Sri Lanka, mother bears have been killed in front of their infants. The cubs become prisoners and are forced to live a life of servitude as dancing bears. This "dancing" is the result of systematic torture. "The Roma training method involved greasing the bears' paws and having them stand on hot plates while music played; the bears hopped on the plates to avoid the burning pain, which became associated in their minds with the sound of the music. Eventually, just hearing the music caused the bears to repeat this 'dancing' movement."[15] It was as late as 2007 that the last three conscripted dancing bears in Bulgaria were freed from the Roma gypsies.

These performances have nothing to do with Native bear dances. Bear dances such as those of the Ute people are healing rituals, not traumatizing ones. Dancers wear feather plumes that they leave behind in the dancing area to represent the sorrows and worries they wish to shed, which will be carried away by the healing spirit of Bear. The Ute illustrate how the horrendous ways in which Bear has been exploited can be replaced with nonviolent rituals, celebrating Bear's contributions to society.

In 1972, when bear dancing was outlawed in India, the government provided funds to the Kalandar peoples to help them start new businesses; often these took the form of small shopping stalls. This is an example of how replacing animal exploitation with other life-affirming practices works very well. It's win-win all around. Today, the Agra Bear Rescue Facility just north of the Taj Mahal in northern India and the

Bannerghatta National Park near Bangalore provide refuge to emancipated "dancing bears" and other formerly imprisoned black and sloth bears that are now able to live out the remainder of their lives in safety. These are a few examples of steps toward right relations with the animal kingdom.[16]

For centuries in Romania, dancing bears were common. Since 2005 World Animal Protection has funded the Asociatia Milioane de Prieteni (AMP), the largest bear sanctuary in the world. They legally remove bears from captivity, giving them a safe sanctuary life. As of 2016 they care for more than eighty-seven formerly abused and neglected captive bears.[17]

OTHER HORRORS THAT BEARS ENDURE AT THE HANDS OF MAN

At least twelve thousand bears in China, North Korea, Vietnam, Laos, and Myanmar are imprisoned so that their bile may be extracted as part of a two-billion-dollar-a-year industry. While bear bile is made into powders, pills, and ointments for medical and folk healing, not only are there alternative, non-bear substances that can replace bear bile's claimed purpose, there is no scientific proof that the purported benefits of bear bile is anything more than cultural fiction. Historically, a bear was killed and its gallbladder removed for its bile. But in the 1980s this historic practice was turned into an industry, conscripting thousands of captured bears to a lifetime of suffering, pain, and slow death. While it's been claimed the bile has curative powers to address a broad range of maladies such as "trauma, sprains, fractures, hemorrhoids, conjunctivitis, severe hepatitis, high fever, convulsions, and delirium,"[18] scientific studies have been unable to show any benefits and Chinese doctors often refute the popular notion, claiming that this century-old practice is not scientific.

Animal protectors around the world understand that bear bile farming is a barbaric form of animal torture. These bears are kept in "crush cages," aptly named because the enclosure is typically so small that the bear cannot stand up in it. If imprisoned when young, the bear's body can grow into the cage itself, embedding the body into an immoveable metal straightjacket. These bears live with permanent medical catheters, body drains, and other objects implanted in their bodies. Such apparatuses are used to extract the bears' liver bile that is stored in the gallbladder. In addition, some bears have one or two hands amputated, which are sold for profit. These bears often die due to the additional trauma and infections. Himalayan black bears (*Ursus thibetanus*), better known as Asiatic black bears, and also called moon bears, are the species most often used in the bear bile business. In the wild, they live up to the age of thirty-five, but these individuals, whose life essence is farmed and harvested like corn, have significantly shortened five-year life-spans, full of disease, pain, and suffering.[19] Fortunately people like Jill Robinson and the organization she founded in 1998, Animals Asia, promote compassion and respect for all animals and work to end the barbaric bear bile trade and bring about long-term constructive change through initiatives like the bear sanctuary she founded in Vietnam.*

Despite the indignities, immeasurable suffering, pain, and abuse heaped upon them, bears and other commodified species nonetheless show restraint and a purposeful use of power—even forgiveness. Sociopathic behavior is a global illness in human beings and is at the heart of our global psychosis. Disturbingly, animal exploitation as well as the indentured labor and sex slave industry are growing exponentially given the alarming rate of displacement from historic homelands due to war, poverty, and climate change.

---

*Animals Asia also works to end the trade in dogs and cats as a food source in China and Vietnam, and lobbies to improve the welfare of companion animals, promote humane population management, and prevent the cross-border export of "meat dogs" in Asia. In addition, Animals Asia campaigns for an end to abusive animal practices in zoos and safari parks in Asia, and works closely with governing authorities to improve animal management and increase awareness of the welfare needs of captive animals. You can learn more about this wonderful organization here: www.animalsasia.org.

BASIC WHITE BEAR FACTS

Approximately one in ten black bears born in the British Columbian rain forest is white. The white coat, often with a yellow tinge, is caused by the recessive gene *MC1R*—a genetic wrinkle. The gene is associated with the human gene that controls the appearance of fair skin and red hair in humans. Similar to the case of humans, a bear carrier need not be white-haired itself to have white-furred offspring, but a white-haired black bear needs to receive the recessive gene from both parents. This shared genetic link between human and Bear makes the Scandinavian or Celtic image of the red-haired maiden riding the White Bear that much more intriguing, perhaps suggesting an intuitive awareness of a common inheritance.

The average weight of a White Spirit Bear (and/or a female black bear) is approximately three hundred pounds, compared to a male grizzly bear, which can weigh as much as twelve hundred pounds. White Bears live about thirty years, much as their Neanderthal brothers and sisters did.

As an apex species—animals who occupy the top of the food chain in their habitats—bears function as ecosystem epicenters. Bears are omnivorous, feasting largely on berries, grasses, roots, and other vegetation, with pulses of fat-rich pine nuts, salmon, and the occasional rodent. The British Columbian rain forest, where White Bears live, provides a bounty of food for the animals, for it is abundant with rich vegetation and wild salmon.

Mating occurs during the late spring and summer months. Winter hibernation, depending on location and weather, can last from six to eight months. The bears sleep until spring when they awaken and start eating until they mate; then winter hibernation returns again. (See plate 6 of a White Bear fishing.) When bears come out of hibernation in the spring, although they lose body weight over the winter, they do not lose muscle and bone mass as humans do in long-term sedentary situations.

Female bears that have accumulated enough fat before hibernation are able to birth healthy offspring in January (up to three cubs at a time, weighing only one pound at birth). The mother bear will go without food through the entire winter, while at the same time nursing her cubs. Mother and cubs will share the den for the first two to three years of a young cub's life. As the cubs grow the mother teaches them how to live—how to forage, fish, and hunt, how to defend themselves, how to nurse, how to prepare for winter hibernation, how to keep the den clean, how to stay safe from both human and animal predators, how to share and play, and how to be a curious but discerning bear.

As with any animal that lives as a member of a larger group in order to survive—whether a lion pride, an elephant herd, a wolf pack, or even a whale pod—the male bear does not remain with the female bear and her cubs. He leaves shortly after impregnation in the summer. Some bears remain in close proximity to each other their entire lives and have bonds that one could loosely call a community, but these are not monogamous relationships.

Bears establish and maintain social positions by communicating with a variety of sounds as well as with what appears to be mental telepathy. They mark with scent, huff, clack, groan, and growl. Cubs hum when nursing. In hibernation, their heart rates slow to as low as eight to fourteen beats per minute. Breathing can become as slow as one breath every forty-five seconds, in contrast to that of the waking fifty-five breaths per minute. This ascetic accomplishment surpasses that of a yogi, who can breathe two times a minute (our normal breathing rate is twelve to twenty breaths per minute). Scientists are still trying to unlock the bears' secret of hibernation and the physiological benefits of this genetic programming that many mammals have, which is triggered by changes in temperature and food sources. Researchers hope that the mechanism of hibernation might be adapted to the treatment of strokes and other brain injuries where slowing down metabolic rates, breathing rates, and other body functions can help restore a person's health.

MY INTRODUCTION TO BEAR IN
REAL TIME AND IN THE DREAMTIME

When Bear is in someone's life either physically or in dreams or in other imagery, it's a sign that that individual has a deep love for the Earth, enjoys a healthy level of independence or needs to develop it, and harbors a mothering and healing instinct. Bear has graced my own life with her presence.

I met Bear through a book that I still own. Called *The Biggest Bear,* it was written by Lynd Ward and published in 1952. As a four-year-old, I was horrified to learn that people killed bears or locked them in cages at a zoo, which the book explained was a way of protecting the bear from being shot as a trophy. From then on I was one of Bear's champions. Among the dozens of stuffed animals that slept on my bed each night, a yellow bear was my favorite. He was the size of a one-year-old toddler, and I adored him from the age of six on. I sewed Bear up a few times until my mother secretly and unceremoniously discarded him while I was away one summer.

The street where my family lived was called Caves Road and the stream that runs through the Dogwood Farm property where I live today is called Little Bear Run. From nursery school through senior year, I attended the Park School, a private school near Baltimore where the mascot is a bear, specifically a brown and white bruin.

I have dreamt of brown and black bears my entire life. Once, when I was living in the Colorado Rockies, I saw a black bear up close. My stepdaughter Maré and I, in July 2012, were on a road trip following the historic trail of the Cherokee vision quests and active North Carolina mineral springs. Our cabin in North Carolina was circled by a bear whose rummaging around made enough noise, along with the pelting rain on the cabin's metal roof, to wake us both up in an alarmed state in the middle of the night. The mind accelerates quickly, searching for an explanation when frightened. The words *middle of the night, bear, rain?* ran through my startled-awake mind, knowing most animals don't like to be out in the rain. This thought made our situation that much more frightening because it raised the possibility that *human* predators might be outside our door. A bear seemed much less worrisome.

It is worth saying that Maré and I both woke up at precisely 3:45 a.m. when I whispered to her, "Are you awake?" upon which I grabbed a heavy metal lamp as my weapon and she the flashlight, because we both had an overwhelming feeling of being watched. I felt we were being watched not by just one presence, but it seemed to me, by thousands of little eyes. Of course, when we turned on the inside and outside lights, we saw nothing moving. After we laughed a bit too hysterically we eventually did get back to sleep.

The next morning I reflected on the psychic message that I had received upon arriving at the remodeled tobacco-drying hut where we were staying: that "a slave woman had been raped and murdered there." In the chalet cabin guest book others had written of their "romantic getaway in the cabin" and of the "beautiful snow and wood fireplace." Before leaving, I added our entry, which read, "This cabin is haunted and Mothman is at the door."

Overnight, the outside light had attracted the wildest array of the most gargantuan moths I had ever seen—orange, yellow, brown, and red moths. But Bear pacing outside our door was decidedly the big story. I recounted our experience to the proprietor in the main lodge house. However, I left out that we'd considered packing the car in the driving rain at 4:00 a.m. just to get out of there, but had decided against it because we were too afraid to dart back and forth between the cabin and car under the dark and wet horror-tale conditions.

After finishing our story, the proprietor looked at me and Maré with a glint in her eye, a smile on her lips, and a just-lit cigarette dangling from the corner of her mouth. "Ya'all see Bear last night?" she asked in her southern drawl. This was followed by a light laugh as she puffed on her cigarette while making omelets for the guests. (I watched to see whether ash got mixed in with the eggs.) Evidently, this black bear must have been a regular camp resident who went trashing at night, looking for anything that anyone had left on the cabin's front porch.

BEAR MEDICINE DREAMS

The abilities possessed by a tribal or community member who mediates between the physical and the spiritual worlds, so-called "bridge walkers," give every awakened person—whether they are a medicine man, shaman, or anyone else—the capacity to reach the limits of their own identity and be subsumed by the totem animal with which one is working. Some say that this talent, when used for the betterment of others, is a positive form of dissociation from one's own identity. I prefer not to confuse terms and instead highlight that this empathetic capacity is engendered in any of us, over time, as a result of self-nullification, sincerity of heart, and love of service.

Dreams of Bears and Their Healing Roles

While writing this book I experienced a wonderful series of dreams with Bear and its healing role. In one dream, Bear stood inside a tipi. Outside there was snow on the ground and the air was cold enough to make an exhaled breath visible. She knelt by the fire and then smudged with burning sage above her head toward the sky seen through the tipi's top. In another dream, it was summer and Bear was walking slowly around outside as I followed along. She was foraging in the woods and fields, pointing to plants to be used for eating and others with which to create smoke medicine, to be used in smudging, pipe ceremonies, and healing.

In my dream, Bear explained that smudging with sage or sweet grass and cedar or other plants "is to prepare for Spirit, to invite Spirit in," suggesting that nothing impure can tolerate the vibration of these medicinal smoke plants. Pipe medicine, she emphasized, "unites an individual or the entire community in oneness with the Great Spirit and brings healing and vision." Bear said that these two

Fig. 2.5. Fool Bull, Lakota medicine man (1849–1909)
By John Alvin Anderson, taken on the Rosebud Indian Reservation, South Dakota, 1900
(Library of Congress)

rituals of smudging and pipe sharing, when used together, "make for complete spiritual and physical well-being among human brothers and sisters." Both dreams were enchanting. In each case I woke up feeling that Bear and I had touched in the ethers: Bear knew me and I knew Bear.

As a healing guide, Bear seeks out plants for its own needs as well as for others. Our North American brown bear and bears of the Kodiak Archipelago dig up *Ligusticum porteri,* also known unsurprisingly as bear root. Bears chew on it and then rub it on their fur. The plant is known to have antibiotic properties and helps to aid stomachaches and repel insects. Alaskan brown bears, grizzlies, are known to chew on grasses like water chestnut, nut grass, and white star sedge to rid themselves of tapeworm and parasites, before retiring to their dens for winter hibernation.

Other plants reflect a connection to Bear in their names: bear's paw, bear tongue, bear's clover, and bearberry. The red fruit of the bearberry is a bear favorite and, like the bear, bearberry is well adapted to arctic and subarctic climates. I found it of particular interest that when dried, this plant is used in medicinal smudging as an incense to purify, sanctify holy space, and establish scented boundaries between influences, shapes, and dimensions. It was the kind of smoke medicine that Bear had shown me in my dream.

BEAR DREAMTIME

My own three years with Bear and all the other wonderful animals written about here allowed me to experience what others have experienced for millennia: humans can dream with Bear and come into rapport with bear consciousness. If one is respectful of Bear's being and culture, patient and humble as well as kind and trusting, these animals will answer an honest request for help as they did in my dreams. In one dream, which I had on Halloween, they showed me that if we turn the world upside down and cut it in half, "What do you get?" they asked out loud and then answered, "A bowl of bears." Their story, revealing their gentle sense of humor, reminded me of a commercial for a children's bear-shaped cereal. What they were showing me was that their star-scape of Ursa Major and Ursa Minor would now be at the bottom of the world bowl.

It is absolutely true to say that bears govern dreamtime and journeying in dreamtime in amazing ways. Bear showed me, as if showing a conservationist's drawing, that conservation must begin as a plan from the outer edge of a geographic area toward the inward center of that ecosystem's physical mass, so as not to disenfranchise any species to the water's edge or cliff's edge or edge of not having life. Meaning, when we define an area for restoration and conservation, they suggest identifying the entire ecosystem's range and devising plans based from the outer boundaries to its center.

In a vivid dream one night, I was shown that in every case a bear story is told, Bear is present in spirit and is capable of avenging any human, but refrains. The offending individuals include people in zoos, laboratories, "entertainment prisons," and who hunt in the wild. The fact that Bear is aware of the common human viewpoint that bears are violent predators, yet bears do not kill every human they encounter or by whom they are held captive, tells us that their nature is a spiritual one. As Bear said in my dream, "We could kill every human being we wanted to, even while the story is being told, but we do not. We listen." This statement reflects bears' capacity to affect the spirit world, not just the physical world. Bears are bridge walkers and bring us into contact with the spirit worlds whose Great Spirit Bear protects. (See plate 7 of the White Spirit Bear in Great Bear Rain Forest.)

White Bears, like all bears, are related to the canine family genetically. From DNA mapping it is said that the brown cave bear and dog are 92 percent identical, having separated into two species 50 million years ago. This adds context to animal communicator Dawn Brunke's own beautiful story as told in her book *Dreaming with Polar Bears:*

Spirit Journeys with Animal Guides. She tells of meeting polar bears through dreams, first through a white dog guide in her toddler and adolescent years, and then of a White Polar Bear whom she walked beside in the dreamscape of the Arctic, where she became an intimate member of the bears' council. Bears, she discovered, were dreaming her into their dream as much as she was dreaming about them. This is the realm where Bear and human unite in a seamless web of trans-species communication. To be drawn to Bear as an ally is to seek Bear wisdom—Earth's medicine—to know what ails a soul.

SHAPE-SHIFTING SHAMAN AND BEAR PHENOMENOLOGY

Bear, we now know, is a foundational guardian of sustenance, a protector of the Great Spirit's abode and an Earth healer. In Native stories humans can become bears and bears can become powerful men or beautiful women. However, at times, Native cultures remind us that seeing Bear become a person or a person become Bear may be a case of mistaken or temporarily shared identity. This particular "bear act" of "shape-shifting" highlights the use of consciousness to exhibit temporary material forms and is practiced worldwide. As in the case of all White Spirit Animal work with shamans, medicine healers, and human elders, shape-shifting is one of the common forms of communication exhibited when human and animal come into magical rapport.

One historic explanation of this recorded and witnessed phenomena is that the soul transmigrates from one species to another after death. This is described in numerous sacred writings, mythologies, and folk tales. However, this does not account for the more common shape-shifting when the shaman later returns to normal consciousness and does not die. Another perspective is that when a human being shifts consciousness into a realm of being associated with but different from the material world of which we are also part, the witnesses are also shifted. In physics, this is akin to entrainment between the facilitator (the shamanic doer), the community participants, and witnesses, who are all brought into attunement with each other, making acting and witnessing, seeing and doing, collaborative. This subtle experience would be described as an interchange between the realms of action, the dense material world and body, and the next level that is outside but interpenetrating, the realm of formation.

Western esotericism calls the latter the astral or emotional body with which one can connect. A good example of this would be the appearance of Matata in my bedroom when she and I first met. Regardless of what words or systems one uses to describe the phenomenology of experiencing multidimensionality, we basically operate as biocapacitors and receivers, and this is one way to appreciate that we actually do connect with our "spirit cell phones" to all of life, and why we are able to communicate telepathically via the cosmic light satellite. All of us are in a state of constant emanation and reception, sending and receiving messages via our thoughts, feelings, and actions.

THE WHITE SPIRIT BEAR

The beliefs of Native tribal peoples about White Bears express a fundamental awareness of the bears' glacial-age origins, their realized sacredness, and an understanding of the vital interdependence between humans and bears. This relationship is mutual, having equal importance for both species and the balance of the manifest world and intradimensional spirit worlds we inhabit together. If a tribe is associated with a bear clan, its members are forbidden from killing a bear of any color. Bear is the sacred animal guide of Native people, and similar to humans, bears have ancestors and collective memory.

Because they have been isolated for so many generations, the White Spirit Bears have been able to live in virtual obscurity on the Princess Royal and Gribbell islands of British Columbia. The White Bears, also called Kermode bears or *Moksgm'ol* by Tsimshian coastal First Nation people, are part of the *Ursus* genus of bears (*Ursus americanus kermodeii*) in the family Ursidae (bears). This family includes brown bears (also called grizzlies), polar bears, and black bears. There are an estimated four hundred White Spirit Bears living on the two islands, where fourteen hundred or more black bears live as well.[20] Indigenous peoples have known of White Bear's existence, but divulging this information to outsiders has been taboo. There is a fear, as dreams of my own suggested, that hunters would come to kill the White Bears much as they have done to the grizzly bear, which is now at risk of extinction.

The Tsimshians have a very long story that has several versions describing their respect and honor of this White Bear. Here is one that I recount in abbreviated form.

A Meeting on the Ice

The story centers on Asdiwal, a young man who provides food of his own free will to a starving chieftess and her mother. Both of their husbands have died from famine. In one of at least four versions of the story, after having taken care of the two women, Asdiwal sees a White Bear and follows it up the mountain. However, in order to keep following the bear, he must go even further up a very tall ladder to the sky. Climbing high up into sky he looks through a window and sees that the bear is actually a beautiful woman dressed in a white bearskin. Consistent with the archetypal nature of a hero's journey, when a person discovers their purpose and destiny, Asdiwal discovers his and ends up marrying this she-bear. In some bear legends, removing a bearskin cover is code for shape-shifting back into human form. The main point is that woman and bear are like each other.[21]

Asdiwal's betrothal represents the blessing of plenty and the honor of Bear Spirit that is conferred on those who serve others in need—those who follow Spirit from Earth to sky without knowing where Spirit will take them, but yet retain faith and sufficient self-nullification to stay close to Spirit. Bear, as Spirit's guardian, can see into the invisible, premanifest realm of formation and creation. It can feel impulses before humans do, such as when they and other animals detect the onset of a forest fire or an earthquake prior to the event, hours and even days before it happens. Much more attuned to their feelings than most humans, animals are the quintessential multidimensional travelers. Sensitive to infrasound and seismic activity, they are often able to escape tsunamis, earthquakes, and other natural disasters, whereas humans are caught off guard. Spirit Bear may know the seismic activity before it occurs and know the Spirit that causes such activity.

THE GREAT BEAR RAIN FOREST

Rain forests cover less than 10 percent of our Earth's surface yet they provide up to 70 percent of the oxygen needed for existence on Earth. British Columbia's temperate rain forest of the White Spirit Bears encompasses one-quarter of the world's coastal rain forest ecosystem. The fact that the White Bear is called the great healer and medicine chief is understandable given that these rain forests also hold as much as 80 percent of the medicinal plants humanity can benefit from, most of which remain unknown to date.

Rain forests are dense with foliage, creating a microcosm unto themselves. In the British Columbian coastal rain forest the preponderance of coniferous (evergreen) trees is a statement of ecological sustainability. Western hemlock, yellow cedar, western red cedar, Douglas fir and amabilis fir, and Sitka spruce fill the forests. They do not break under the weight of snow and they seed themselves with the cones that drop to the forest floor. Some of the largest trees, coveted by logging companies, are near the water's edge. Their shading branches keep the waters cool enough for the salmon to thrive, which in turn feeds so many other species, including humans. Without the trees, the rivers and the life they support would all die. Birdlife is diverse and includes the bald eagle, common raven, trumpeter swans, as well as countless shore birds, harlequin ducks, and sandhill cranes. The largest concentration of grizzlies resides here and the gray wolf numbers up to eight thousand individuals. However, similar to the bear, rain forests worldwide are endangered.

THE MAN WHO WALKS WITH BEARS

There is perhaps no one who knows as much about the Spirit Bear as Charlie Russell, whom I call "The Man Who Walks with Bears." Russell is a real bear man in the deepest sense of those words. The bears love him and he, in turn, loves them. He enjoys and honors the outback and the solitary life. He is patient, consistent, dedicated, loyal, hearty, and at home in nature and in the love and fellowship of bears, animals, and other nature-loving humans.

Russell is a naturalist, former rancher, and pilot who even built his own light plane. He's been a Canadian wilderness guide and a wild-life photographer and, as such, has lived among the bears in Siberia, the Rockies, Alaska, and Canada. He spent a decade in Russia rein-troducing brown bear cubs to the wild. His lifelong presence among bears has been the subject of various documentaries. One was made by the BBC in 2006, entitled *Bear Man of Kamchatka*. A second one is entitled *Walking with Giants: The Grizzlies of Siberia* made by PBS in 1999. Russell is also the author of three books about bears. They are *Grizzly Seasons: Life with the Brown Bears of Kamchatka* written with Maureen Enns; *Grizzly Heart: Living without Fear among the Brown Bears of Kamchatka*; and *Spirit Bear: Encounters with the White Bear of the Western Rain Forest*.

Charlie Russell is a wonderful storyteller, and one story he shares in its short version is a legend of the White Bear, which he learned from an Indian of the Pacific Northwest.[22]

The Legend of the White Bear

At the beginning of time, so the legend goes, the whole world was white with ice and snow. Then the raven came from heaven and the world turned green, as it is now. But he also wanted to make something to remind himself of the beginning and its whiteness. So on this island, the one where people have never lived, he went among the bear, the black bears, and one-tenth he made white. That way he could look at them and remember the world as it was. And then the raven issued a decree: "The White Bears would live here forever in peace." This is called "the raven's decree."

Going back to his own beginning with Bear requires that Russell describe his childhood home. "We lived right on the edge of what was a national park, on a ranch that's been in the family for over a hundred years." This is the same ranch where, as his father, Andy, recounts in the foreword to Charlie's book *Spirit Bear* "Charlie Russell, my second son, has been destined to be associated with bears from the time he was born. When he was about a month old, his mother left him sleeping in his carriage on the verandah of our cabin one fine morning. While she was inside, a black bear came out of the trees close to the house and went up on the porch. It didn't disturb Charlie but retreated back into the bush leaving some dirty tracks on the step."[23] When I learned about this incident, I wondered if it wasn't an instance of a bear mistaking the cries of baby Charlie for one of its own cubs, a known phenomenon.

Being with Bear is what Charlie Russell does. Bears know that he respects them and he has befriended many of them. As he shared with delight in our interview, a White Bear tried to body wrestle him once, chest to chest, standing upright on both legs, actually throwing Russell to the ground with sheer bear power. "I learned," he said with a chuckle, "that this kind of play was not possible, as they are so much stronger and bigger than me." But he found other ways to play with Bear, with less roughhousing between the human-bear brothers. (See plate 8 of Charlie Russell with a grizzly bear that befriended him over the years.)

In a slow-paced drawl, as if taking slow and steady steps across the thousands of miles he has ridden on horses or walked—many of them behind bear, in front of bear, alongside bear, higher than bear, lower than bear, sitting with bear—Russell makes it simple to understand why living among bears has been his life's work. "I have been interested in bears all my life," he shared so sweetly. "It's something about how they are perceived and misunderstood." In 1961 his father was making a film about grizzlies. "I was about twenty years old, and my father wanted my brother and me to be cameramen. . . . What I saw was an animal that was so different from the animal we depicted in our stories all of the time. To me, it was a beautiful intelligent animal and yet the stories were all about violence and how they wanted to kill us all of the time. And so that really caught my attention. How could an animal appear and act so differently around myself and my family and yet nobody told nice stories about them?"

Bears are called predators, but their behavior is not predatory. They do not hunt for sport any more than an ant does, and they seldom kill smaller mammals. On the contrary, they largely eat vegetation and prefer to eat the carcasses of animals already killed. When they do hunt and kill another animal, it's for food or self-defense, nothing else. Charlie Russell is in the position to know under what conditions humans do encounter bears in the wild. It is clear, he detailed in our discussion, that when there have been bad situations between bears and humans the cause is a serious lack of food or because there is the sense of threat. "They come into towns to get human food, and some of them have no fear of humans and get up real close. . . . But the notion they are our enemies is a modern invention," he insists.

Russell's own first encounter with a White Bear occurred in 1991 when he was hired as escort and guide for the wildlife filmmakers Jeff and Sue Turner. The Turners were creating a PBS sponsored film called *Ghost Bear,* about the White Bears of British Columbia's rain forest. Having been around bears his entire life, nevertheless, when one came within inches of Russell's own camera, he was filled with joyful amazement. "As I was digging the film out, the White Bear scrambled down over the edges in the stream toward me. I quickly lifted the back of my camera, but before I could change the film, he stood up on hind legs and looked down into the camera. His nose was only inches from it! I could scarcely believe what I was experiencing! Here was a wild bear, of fearsome lore, examining me and my trappings as though I were a novelty, a cousin from the big city come to visit—an object of curiosity but definitely not something to fear, or to eat for that matter."[24]

Bears have other wonderful traits in addition to their obvious curiosity for novel things in their environment. As Russell explains, "They seem to want to be social, but it's to their advantage to be solitary [also among themselves], and because of their size they are able to do that. They can dominate the landscape. They are so strong that if they run into trouble they can usually get out of it with their strength. There aren't many other animals around who can push them around, except each other. So when they have to be social, they are. Because they are drawn to certain food sources like salmon and berries, and these food sources can be in small areas, it crowds them together, and in these situations, they can get along quite well." But as Russell emphasized, "They don't choose to be there. When they can spread out they usually do spread out. I noticed that with the cubs I rescued and raised—these were cubs that had been in a zoo. And I learned by buying those cubs and taking them out to my very remote cabin, where they would learn to become independent."

As a bear preservationist, Russell emphasizes that he never fed bears human food, "but they were never discouraged from being around me if they wanted to be." When he raised the zoo cubs in Russia, he had to feed them initially so that they could learn how and where to feed. However, he only fed them the plants and fruits that a bear would naturally want. They did not become aggressive when the food was withheld. As Russell explains, he just stopped feeding them and would tell them, "No food today" when they came for their twice-daily feeding. He did this until they simply stopped coming for food, having learned from their shared walks where to find food on their own. "Don't feed them human food, never let them taste the clothing of humans," as they may then associate eating with humans as a source of food.

Russell weaned the bears at a time when there was plenty of food around for them to forage. However, as a general rule, due to the fact that humans have not abused the White Bears, they do not have the fear that other bears have. Subsequently, there is some concern that too much interaction with humans could interfere with their natural way of nonaggression with us.

Knowing the challenges the bears face for survival in an ecosystem besieged by the timber and oil industries, Russell appreciates the hardships of bear life. Every time he speaks of Bear, there is love in his voice and it sweetens with a tone of reverie as he retells a story. "It was amazing to walk with them every day and see what they did. It was year after year. They were so close together themselves, attached to each other, that initially they wouldn't separate. They would look out for each other. But then as they got a little older they eventually would break up. They don't stay siblings together for very long. These stayed together till about three years old and then they'd get in a row over salmon along the lakeshore, and then they'd fight over another one and pretty soon they would go around the lake in different directions from each other. They didn't have to do that, but that's the way they separated themselves . . . but when it came to pine nuts they would join up and go eating pine nuts together because there was so much in a small area."

Bears have personal and communal feeding areas during seasonally specific times. So do all people who live off the land.

My many dreams about Bear consistently identified Bear as Chief Medicine Guide or, in modern hospital parlance, Chief of Medicine. In one dream there were black, brown, and White Bears. Brown bear said to me, as if I were in a class, "Now, when any of us are wounded, the first thing to do is to stop the bleeding." He showed me their techniques of being still and licking the wound and then rolling in certain grasses. Indeed, Bear has an ability to take care of another bear's wounds and to stop the bleeding by using the previously discussed bearberry.

It's interesting that bears are not territorial in the way that wolves and lions are. Although they do need a certain amount of space around them wherever they go, they share resources with us well, though most humans are too afraid of them to share with them as Russell does. He lets bears roam his cattle ranches and leaves dead cattle on the edge of the woods for the bears to eat. He frequently watched bears walk among cattle and they were undisturbed by them. "But occasionally you would see the cattle move due to an encroaching male bear they did not trust." Unlike other ranchers, Russell is unique in this practice. He has shown that bears and other animals, along with their human herders, can coexist well in the same area without them killing other bears, wolves, coyotes, or other animals of the wild.

When we talked, I felt I could hear Russell's heart in his words and commented that he seems "to love the bear's lifestyle—the relative isolation in the outback and the very quiet winters and rambunctious summers." "Yeah, I think that's true," he answered, and then continued with his major concern. "Again, the biggest problem that bears have with humans is being misunderstood. . . . Continually, we are so afraid of them that we make up stories about them that are usually not very favorable to the bear. That's why I went to Russia. I wanted to find out a few things about them. I wanted to show that bears weren't unpredictable, that they weren't dangerous, and that they have lost their fear of people. These ideas were the excuse to kill so many bears around national parks, for instance. We have never done well at living closely with them and sharing our land with them, because we are so afraid. I wanted to demonstrate that these ideas were incorrect. I think I have but I still have some trouble with bear managers and other people, that these animals can be trusted, that there can be a very strong trust built between humans and bears."

Most bears are active from dawn to dusk. They only become

nocturnal hunters to avoid humans for the most part, while some become habituated to people in order to gain access to the plentiful buffet of improperly stored garbage and other attractions, as in the case of the black bear that visited our cabin near Asheville, North Carolina. Like other preservationists, Russell doesn't advocate our intruding on their habitats; quite the reverse. Ecotourism offers humans an opportunity to see bears without harming them.

The issue of finding ways to protect bears from hunters is personal with Charlie Russell. One tragic story unfolded when, returning to Russia to spend the season watching the grizzly bears he had raised and released into the wild, he found that they had vanished. These were bears he had fished with, was friends with, and loved. Eventually he discovered one of the bear's eviscerated organs hanging on his cabin, where it had been left with a note. As Russell shared with us, "It was heartbreaking. To try to deal with the violence that was visited upon these wonderful bears was one of the most devastating moments of my life. It was clear that the hunting culture was giving us a message—when we want to kill bears, we will kill bears." Though a bear can run up to thirty-five mph, these bears couldn't outrun human predators. Their trust of some humans may in fact have prevented them from knowing whether to run or to hide from the people who killed them. In wildlife conservation work, this is an unintended consequence: the confusion of some of the animals about who is friend and who is foe.

"There was a time when we ate black bears especially, but that time passed a long time ago. So we kill cougars and wolves and bears just for our own egos. We've developed a whole industry around it. But even before that, Bear in particular was considered a very heroic animal to kill, so somehow," Russell opines, "we borrow strength for ourselves from this strong animal by killing it. I have trouble with that. However, now people are going out to look at these animals rather than kill them. The hunting is such a strong part of our culture because it goes back so long, so we tend to keep doing it, but looks sillier and sillier all the time, and that type of hunter is having a more difficult time looking like a hero."

THE VALUE OF ECOTOURISM

Tim McGrady, founder of Spirit Bear Lodge in British Columbia, leads tours into the rain forest and helps show the importance of ecotourism as a way to not only protect the White Bear population but also the largest intact temperate rain forest on Earth. In this case, White Bear is the guardian of our medicine and the Earth's oxygen-enriching power. This power is called "the spirit," or Ruach in Hebrew. It is the living process of respiration associated with the plant kingdom and the breath that is breathed into our bodies at birth. White Bears protect the spirit of the Earth, and their rain forest habitat highlights this prominent role beautifully.

McGrady has seen the positive impacts of ecotourism, though many wildlife animal enthusiasts object to even this type of interaction between humans and wild animals. As he explains, "ecotourism enriches and supports the local economy," or what I call the "life economy," which seeks to elevate all parts of any situation. Its opposite is our prevalent death economy of exploitation and ruination. As he notes, recent studies show, "more money is made from ecotourism than is made from the seasonal killing of wildlife."[25] However, it is argued that even this tourism is an encroachment on the animal's well-being and is simply a lighter form of exploitation. Nonetheless, observing an animal in its natural habitat, which is what ecotourism is all about, is a vast improvement over killing it.

Killing or cruelly exploiting other sentient life, as though it has no inherent value unto itself for being what it is, is the grossest kind of arrogance and selfishness and leads to destruction of families, ecosystems, and planets. Cultures change when we redefine our own sense of responsibility, when we articulate clearly life-affirming ideas, when we identify the most basic challenges and respond to them properly.

Behavior also changes, along with the meaning we give to life around us and within us. Bear comes to heal humankind by showing us this.

I was motivated to write this book in the spirit of hope and love. My search has been to find out about these amazing beings, the White Bears and other bears, and what they have been trying to teach us in our journey on Earth together. Bear mother and bear cubs teach us about our deepest calling and obligation to protect and guide all of Creation. They call to us and remind us to preserve our rain forests, to save our great medicinal resources, to be patient, to use only what we need, to rest, to dream, to practice economy of scale, and to guard freedom—as it is sacred.

THE GREAT BEAR INITIATIVE

The Great Bear Initiative is a beautiful example of how the White Spirit Bear, the Native people who cherish them, and the British Columbian government have all come together to protect the Great Bear Rain Forest and its inhabitants. "On February 1, 2016, the final Great Bear Rainforest Agreement was signed between First Nations and the British Columbian government, permanently conserving 19 million acres of Pacific coast between Vancouver Island and southeast Alaska. About 9 million acres are off limits to logging, with the balance managed under some of the world's most stringent harvest standards."[26] The Great Bear Initiative is comprised of almost two dozen different coastal First Nation communities working in concert with the British Columbian government in what is referred to as a "government to government" relationship. In recognition of First Nation lands and values, the signatories to the agreement intend that all future generations of revenues and decision-making will be collaborative in practice.

It's nice to believe that here in the land of the Spirit Bear, the master of the natural world, the healer of mankind, polar guide of humanity, guardian of the Great Spirit, the shape-shifter is shifting our own awareness into one of love and care for the Earth.

WHITE SPIRIT BEAR LESSONS

Like dogs, bears are curious and defensive animals. They are not aggressive as our cultural stories, hunting fables, and private fears may insist is true. Bears will sooner run from humans than approach us if they sense danger. They may come into close contact with a human when running away from another bear as Charlie Russell recounts does happen, or they may use a human as a shield between themselves and another bear, as also takes place when humans walk with Bear. Bears acculturate to humans in their midst who are not aggressive and they preserve in memory our once-pristine alliance. They teach us about loosely associated communities, whose needs are addressed in seasonal ways based on what the environs offer naturally.

Bear wisdom is strong, confident, grounded, gentle, and long lasting. Bear instructs us on the importance of having clear boundaries, self-restraint, and gratitude. Bears' unswervingly kind respect for humans, the very species that has done and continues to do them the most harm, reflects Bear wisdom as a healer, not just of physical bodies but also of beating hearts.

Bear wisdom includes the need for resourcefulness, resting much of the year, and breeding well to perpetuate the species. Bears are called chiefs in the animal kingdom, healers of the Earth. As the "bear-er" of life, being at the northern pole of the planet, they teach us love for Mother Earth and her living spirit, recalling that the Great Spirit issues from the North. They are masters of the natural world and have a predilection for shape-shifting with human partners.

Bear is a peacemaker and teaches all of us patience, endurance, and the importance and value of walking, standing, sitting, and lying down, actions that in traditional Taoism are compared to the Four Dignities.

Meditation in any of these positions is of value. Indeed, Bear has a quiet, ascetic respect for the life around her. Bear teaches us that we should share resources and avoid conflict when possible, though Bear is able to command ferocious and powerful forces when needed.

Bears exemplify the holy art of mothering, putting the welfare of their young over all else—a simple formula that has made it possible for them to live and thrive for millions of years and that has engendered the well-being of all species. For their protective stewarding of their young, they are called the great givers of life. They teach us the natural way in which mothers guide their offspring before they go out into the world as individuals. This is wisdom in action.

Bear medicine is ancient Earth medicine, and as such it is based in listening to the voice of Spirit that tells one what to gather, where to gather it from, and what it is for. Bear medicine includes drumming and vision quests, dream incubation, pipe and smudge ceremonies. Bear teaches us the value of dreamtime, showing us the importance of learning from our nighttime dreams, waking visions, and meditation. As guardians of Spirit, bears guide peace-building between humans on Earth and animals in our midst. Peace between animals does not mean they have overcome their differences or that they have won a territorial war. The majority of the time it means sharing resources when needed, avoiding conflict altogether, or walking the other way around the lake to avoid confrontation—all the while listening to the call of raven overhead.

The White Bears' message is one of hope and concern and serves as a promise of their well-being on Earth as well as our own. Of course the degree to which we change our individual, cultural, and economic practices will determine the state of our shared future. Reflective of their obvious Earth care, which is executed with amazing gentleness despite the great force available to them, bears teach us the proper use of power. They show us the fundamental truth of survival, the primary need of sentient life for food and shelter, and that when either is threatened violence may easily be provoked. In fact, they advocate preparing for Earth changes now, regarding housing and food for millions if not billions of people who already are in need of such basic provisions. White Spirit Bear, as a bridge to our past and future, appreciates the round and cyclic hoop of life by which all is connected and sustained, reminding us of this inherent unity of The All in the cave of life we share together.

3
Lion

The Golden-Hearted Alchemist

No matter who we are, no matter in which part of the world we dwell, we are one. We are one with each other. We are one with the Earth. We are one with the moon, the sun, and the stars.

VUSAMAZULU CREDO MUTWA,
ZULU LION SHAMAN AND *SANGOMA*

IN THE LAND where trees are called "growing people" and ancestral spirits (*amadlozi* or *abaphasnsi*) are consulted in community decisions, we meet the White Lions of Timbavati, South Africa. Here along the 31'14" meridian, also referred to as the "Nilotic meridian," which stretches from mineral-rich Zimbabwe to Giza, Egypt (where the enigmatic Sphinx was built), and beyond, is the home of these magnificent animals. Some reside within the 7,523 square miles of Kruger National Park, South Africa. The White Lions live a world away from the Great White Bear of British Columbia, Canada.

POINTS OF ALIGNMENT WITH A COMMON, SACRED CENTER

Sacred centers, sacred cities, and commercial civilizations all utilize a geographical center. As the late Jon Michell pointed out in his book *Sacred*

Center: The Ancient Art of Locating Sanctuaries, one most often finds an axis along which sacred sites were situated. Sacred sites hold the timekeeping stoneworks of a community, be they stone circles or other methods of timekeeping.1 Applying this premise to the White Lions of South Africa, it's been determined that Timbavati sits on the African Nilotic meridian. This is the only place where the White Lion is native and acts as an axis for numerous periods of time and societies of the past.

The discovery that the birthplace of the legendary White Lions aligns exactly with the meridian on which the resting place of humankind's greatest lion riddle, the Great Sphinx of Giza, stands is the work of a South African woman, Linda Tucker. The foundation in her name and her organization the Global White Lion Protection Trust are dedicated to preserving these great sacred felines. Their vital and important efforts, recognized worldwide, are well profiled elsewhere.*

Like indigenous leaders in whose homeland other White Spirit Animals are born, here too, in Africa, Zulu elders teach that there is vital significance in the appearance of the White Lions in Timbavati at this time. As with all the other White Spirit Animals, the White Spirit Lions have come to warn us of dramatic Earth changes, encouraging us to work together in these perilous times. Protecting the Earth, as Lions have protected humans throughout time, is our noble-hearted duty.

LION IN THE HEAVENS ABOVE

Bear, Chief of Medicine and Pole Star guardian, accompanies us on our journey, calling forth Spirit and the power of Earth healing. The pointer stars of Bear's Big Dipper direct our eyes to Leo, the lion constellation, who shows how we can illuminate our hearts with golden rays of purified intention. Lion sits astronomically near Bear and is most visible in March in the Northern Hemisphere when spring comes in with a roar.

---

*In her books *Mystery of the White Lions: Children of the Sun God* and *Saving the White Lions: One Woman's Battle for Africa's Most Sacred Animal* and on her websites www.lindatuckerfoundation.org and http://whitelions.org.

Fig. 3.1. Star system Leo
From the *Celestial Atlas* by Alexander Jamieson (1782–1850)

Cancer, the crab constellation, is situated in the heavens to Leo's west while Virgo, the maiden constellation, lies to the lion's east.

Leo, as an astrological sign of the zodiac, is a fire sign endowing those born under it with a larger-than-life showman-like personality. These individuals are often the center of activity and attention. They like to make friends and are eager to bring people together for playful enterprise. At social gatherings, people rely on the fiery Leo to liven things up. However, just like their namesake, Leos can be demanding and insist that others see things their way. They ask for loyalty from their friends and children, and they are fierce in battle. If Leos find fault with anyone's behavior, they may respond with lion-like growling.

CULTURAL HISTORIES OF LIONS

Lions are found in every culture on nearly every continent: Africa, Asia, Australia, North America, and Europe, and every culture has its own name for Leo. The Persians called the lion constellation "Ser" or "Shir"; the Turks, "Artan"; the Syrians, "Aryo"; the Jews, "Aryeh"; the Indians, "Simha."

Lions are historically associated with royalty, power, the ruling class, and protection. Their likeness is found guarding temples, thrones, and cities throughout the world. Belgium, Luxembourg, Norway, Sierra Leone, India, and Sri Lanka are only a few of the world's nations that have a lion as part of their coat of arms or national emblem as well as featuring Lion in national folklore. All cultures regard Lion as the bearer of bravery and nobility, whose mission is to protect the royal family or warrior. The emblem of Judah's tribe and that of King David was a lion, as were the forms decorating King Solomon's throne.

The ancient Greco-Roman story of Hercules also involves a lion.

Hercules and the Nemean Lion

Hercules's first task in the series of Twelve Labors was to slay the immortal Nemean lion, whose pelt was impervious to man-made weapons and whose claws could cut through any human armor. In this ancient shape-shifting story, the lion would capture women and bring them to his cave for the purpose of luring men who would venture forth to save the damsels. When the men arrived, the women turned into lions and killed and ate their valiant rescuers.

Hercules foiled the Nemean lion's plans by blocking off one of the two cave exits. He then clubbed the lion and strangled him. After killing the lion, Hercules fashioned the pelt to use as a magical cloak of invincibility and invisibility, protecting him in battle and assuring his victory. For centuries this victorious legend set the trend of killing lions as a sign of bravery. According to Herodotus and Aristotle, "real" flesh and blood

Fig. 3.2. Historical etching of *Panthera leo melanochaita*
From *Brehms Tierleben* (*Brehm's Life of Animals*) by Alfred Edmund Brehms (1829–1884)

lions existed in Greece until around 480 BCE and became endangered by 300 BCE. The species became extinct by 100 BCE.

The Nemean lion is said to have been the offspring of Zeus and Selene. Selene was a Titan, the race before the generations of Olympian gods, who carried the moon each night in a chariot pulled by white horses. The Nemean lion fell to Earth from the moon. Other traditions also describe lions falling from the sky or coming from other planets.

Another prominent lion motif is found in the representation of female figures in the form of a lion or women sharing an association with lions. "The Lady of the Lions is an image that extends across time for more than 6,000 years and across a wide geographic region as far as Minoan Crete to the west, Anatolia (Turkey) to the north, and Mesopotamia (Sumer, Babylon, modern Iraq) to the east. More than 40 goddesses in Egypt were associated with lions or other felines."[2] The largest sculpture to survive the prehistoric Aegean and Mycenaean civilization is the lion gate of the Bronze Age in present-day southern Greece. The two lionesses facing each other adorn the citadel's entry gate on the northwest side of the Mycenae Acropolis. A lion patrols the wall of the Ishtar Gate in modern-day Iraq, which was built by the Babylonian King Nebuchadnezzar II in 600 BCE.

Asherah (or Anu), the consort in the Sumerian pantheon of the gods, mother goddess in numerous Semitic cultures, and connected to the Tree of Life, is called "the Lion Lady." She was worshipped by the Canaanites and later, prior to 6 BCE, by some of the Israelites. The Lion Lady has also been referred to as the "Queen of Heaven" for whom cakes are made to prevent her from meting out her wrath on the Earth. In earlier times, Inanna the Sumerian goddess of love and war and later Isis of Egypt were also considered the Queen of Heaven. The Hindu goddess Durga is often depicted riding a lion (or tiger) as she rides into battle to fight the demons. The powerful lion-headed Sehkmet of ancient Egypt was given province over birth

Fig. 3.3. The Mesopotamian goddess Ishtar (ancient Sumerian goddess Inanna)
seen here with a lion on a leash. From approximately 5300 BCE–1940 BCE,
this "Lion Lady" or "Queen of Heaven" was worshipped.

and death and was a fierce participant in the judgment of others. In Roman mythology, Cybele, referred to as "mother of all that exists," sat accompanied by two lions. She is also depicted being driven in a chariot pulled by lions.

The Queen of Heaven is partnered with female lions as protectors and givers of spiritual power. The fact that in other parts of the world lion shamans use lions as psychic partners, or use cats to divine the future or present the situation of a person, suggests that perhaps the goddess employed her telepathic abilities to enter the minds of the great female huntresses. Are they, as some ancient lineages submit, reminders of a human-headed lion race of people from another planet who came to Earth one million years ago, when lions are said to have first appeared?

Five thousand years ago, the Sumerians lived in advanced cities. They wrote extensively and used the wheel, among other inventions and innovations. Their Queen of Heaven is said to have stolen tablets of wisdom from the wisdom god Enki, who was part of a much larger cosmic drama involving sky people or beings who descended from heaven almost two hundred thousand years earlier.

The late scholar Zecharia Sitchin (1920–2010) spent his life investigating Creation stories of the ancient Near East. Based on readings of original cuneiform and manuscripts in Assyrian, Babylonian, and Hebrew, Sitchin's fourteen-book series, The Earth Chronicles, posits that about two hundred thousand years ago the Anunnaki people came to Earth searching for gold. They picked the perfect area in South Africa to land, according to Sitchin. The general area has, to this day, underground deposits of gold following the Nilotic meridian, some calling it a river of gold, which is connected with many archaeological discoveries concerning the prehistoric origins of *Homo sapiens* and is where the White Lions live. It is this gold that purifies the waters of Egypt and all of Africa. The Nile is not only the longest river in the world, it is one of the few rivers to run due north along the geographical meridian. This impressive stretch of water extends southward into Laetoli, Tanzania, and the ruins of Great Zimbabwe, ending near the Sterkfontein caves of South Africa, close to Timbavati.

THE WHITE LIONS OF TIMBAVATI: VESTIGES OF THE LAST ICE AGE

The White Lions are part of the ancient prophecy of the Zulu people, the largest tribal group of sub-Saharan Africa. They refer to themselves as Amazulu, "people of the sky" or "people who travel through the sky of space." Consistent with other cultural origin stories of the lion, the White Lions of Timbavati are revered by African wisdomkeepers as star children who fell from the heavens.

Zulu beliefs are based on the presence of ancestral spirits who often appear in dreams, and a supreme being who is seldom involved in the affairs of mortals. The Zulu's great Earth Mother is Nomkhubhlwane. Her name means "she who chooses the state of an animal" and as such she is a shape-shifter whom shamans learn to emulate.[3] Nomkhubhlwane can take on the form of a lion or lioness and join a shaman to provide protection in his or her healing work or appear in the shaman's dreams. One traditional explanation given for the White Lion's stature stems from when, it is described, all of humanity suffered from disease and famine due to the "anger of Mother Nature," and the majestic White Lions helped us survive.

The African White Lions are regarded as animals from the last ice age and their white color is considered testimony to these conditions. During those desperate times, tradition teaches that the people prayed all night and day. In response, the gods sent down the White Lions to teach the people how to survive, how to hunt, and how to keep warm in the bitter, wild cold. Their mission of helping humankind during profound Earth changes is shared with Bear and the other White Spirit Animals.

It's worth reminding ourselves that extraplanetary impacts like

Fig. 3.4. Chauvet-Pont d'Arc Cave painting of lions. Ice Age art from approximately 32,000 BCE.

those that caused such upheaval at the end of the last ice age can happen to us in any century. On July 23, 2012, NASA stated that the Earth had a near miss with a solar flare or coronal mass ejection (CME), causing the most powerful recorded solar storm in the past century and a half. Faced with the possibility of all or most of our technology and civilization being sent back to the Stone Age by eliminating all computers and all energy and electrical systems worldwide, scientists are no longer making jokes about cataclysmic events and off-planet phenomena that can have, and have had, devastating global impacts in the past.

For decades scientists like physicist Paul LaViolette have, as mentioned previously, maintained that such an event as a galactic core explosion was largely responsible for wide-scale destruction. Graham Hancock shows how extraplanetary events caused the end of the last ice age. Such "wild card" events, as John Peterson of the Arlington Institute calls them, are so massive that there is no way to adequately prepare for them (though I am an advocate for underground housing for this and other reasons).[4]

Native legends recount that, after helping the impoverished and stricken humanity overcome their adversities, the White Spirit Lions left, promising only to return when humankind was in danger once again. And so they have returned. First observed in the 1930s and 1940s and later in 1975, the White Lions' reappearance in the twentieth century affirms ancient Zulu prophecy.

ZULU SHAMANISM

The Zulu people recognize a supreme being, Umvelinqangi (One Who Came First) or Unkulunkulu (Very Big One), but it is the spirits of one's deceased ancestors who communicate the needs of their descendants. The ancestors appear in the form of dreams, illness, or snakes, among other animals. Unlike Western culture, which shuns and disposes of its elderly, Zulu elders are sacred. They are taken care of by their families and are regarded as the link between generations. With a traditional belief in evil spirits, their sangomas (healers) and seers are the ones who help rid the people of those things that cause accidents, loss, or grave illness. Using ritual, prayer, chant, and dance, along with herbs, remedying illness is part of one's spiritual journey, not simply seen as some peculiar bodily malfunction. Illness is a journey of returning to health and wholeness that concerns the spiritual life of each person, their family, clan, ancestors, and the community.

In the Western world, illness is most often treated as an enemy and the body a war zone. Rather than crisis being viewed as part of spiritual growth, both the sick person and their maladies are reduced to material abnormalities that, like habitats we have destroyed, become subject to similar strategies. Cut, burn, and poison is not only a warfare strategy, it's an "acceptable risk" philosophy that has been at the heart of the Western world's approach to life in general and in the treatment of illness specifically. Just as the Native traditions elevate the person and their challenges to a shared path with others, their views of the Earth are similarly holistic and mindful of the connected fabric of life. Everything, while differentiated, is part of an inherent unity. Western ideologies, however, have historically focused on utilizing all aspects of life as commodities rather than created partners, be they forests, lions, or other human beings. The death economy can be readily seen in the way we have treated the world and the dire consequences we now witness worldwide as ecological ill health, animal abuse, and dysfunctional human relations. A life economy would instead seek to elevate each situation for the betterment of The All.

Marking the great gateways of birth, puberty, marriage, and death with ceremonial offerings, dances, songs, and stories holds Zulu culture intact. (That said, many Zulu people are also Christianized by missionaries.) Marriages must be consensual between the young female and the male to whom she will be wed. The marital interest is expressed by letter, and the couple kisses for the first time only when the woman's father has agreed to the marriage, which often follows quickly on the heels of the girl's first menses. To what extent these traditions are still honored depends upon one's tribal clan and family.

THE TEACHINGS OF CREDO MUTWA

Vusamazulu Credo Mutwa—a preeminent African *Isanusi* (high ranking shaman) and guardian of *Umlando* (the Great Knowledge)—is also a traditional sangoma (healer). Mutwa broke his sacred oath of secrecy as a Zulu shaman in order, he said, to keep indigenous teachings alive in the world. His visions, which he has had since the age of seven, compelled him to speak out, even though it is forbidden and one is deemed to be cursed for the transgression.[5] He attributes the tragic murder of his son and other hardships to his speaking out, sharing traditional teachings publically. But as he has stated in his books and many interviews over the decades, his own inner heart and the great mother Amaravar who guides his life—the green-haired red woman he met in his visions during three years of illness, hallucinations, and spiritual initiations—encouraged his sharing of the shamanic legacy received by him as an inheritance handed down for many generations. This legacy is one that promotes kinship with all life, which Mutwa insists is his obligation to share with the world.

One of Mutwa's ecological teachings emphasizes the importance of gold as a purifier of our Earth's waters and that its removal from the Earth in his homeland of Africa must be stopped. The well-being of the 4,258-mile Nile River (from the word *Nilus* in Latin, meaning "river valley") is of international concern. Lions keep an ecosystem intact, and the Nile provides the ecosystems of ten nations with life-sustaining, gold-purified waters. Together they show that gold is an inner treasure. This also tells us about the purity of the lion's golden heart, impervious to the acid of hatred, selfishness, and anger, which pollutes lives as poisonous waste does Earth's waters. The Nilotic gold of purity and lion represent both the giver and taker of life, as ancient cultures rightly testify.

It is interesting as well, in looking at the heart of the lion as being the setting for the precious emerald gem of universal love, that in ancient alchemy the image of the green lion eating the sun is symbolic of a process by which a green, liquid sulfate called vitriol purifies matter, leaving gold behind. When vitriol is very pure, it becomes a devouring acid (lion) that eats through practically anything—except gold. Ultimately the lion is guardian of the soul. The green lion of alchemy, as the emerald of the heart, devours the sun or lower ego to become the soul that is golden, pure, incorruptible, and eternal.* (See plate 9 of the alchemical green lion.)

The connection between lions and gold has been known for millennia. It seems there is an inner alchemy we are being asked to recall and put into action whereby, with resolute love of the world and guardianship of it, we will find the pure-hearted way to solve our shared problems. To attain hearts of gold—radiant, and of the greatest value in one's own bodily kingdom of self—is to become the king or queen of one's own incarnation. It means becoming lionhearted humans. As an esoteric initiatory process, it is an overcoming of all fear and instead experiencing harmonic bonding with divine guardianship—the love ray that dissolves all impurities of intention or action into a unifying force of good for the planetary family. It is the quest of every person to elevate his/her consciousness to that of being noble hearted, for then the Tree of Life we each represent is balanced in beauty and truth, qualities that give courage its bright shine.

The traditional Zulu story of the White Lions' origins is well told by Credo Mutwa.

White Lions and Off-Planet Beings

Oral traditions recall the appearance of White Lions over four hundred years ago during the reign of Queen Numbi in the region now known as Timbavati. A shining star was seen to fall to the ground, but when Queen Numbi and her people approached, they found it to be a shining ball of metal, brighter than the sun. Queen Numbi, who was an elderly and infirm woman, was swallowed by its light and received by strange beings. When she emerged again, she had been restored to health and youth. The fallen star remained there for some days and then rose back into the sky.[6]

---

*While writing about the lionhearted alchemy, I had a dream about Shimon Bar Yochai, the great second-century rabbi kabbalist and author of the Zohar. After his death he was affectionately called "the Ari," meaning "the lion" in Hebrew.

Once more we hear of the connection between where White Spirit Animals live and off-planet beings who make contact with humans in need. After this encounter, many animal abnormalities were observed and were attributed to the radiation, which was regarded as the cause of the white skin mutation. As Mutwa recounts, "Cattle with two heads were born repeatedly. Lions, leopards, and even impalas with snow-white fur and green eyes were born. . . . This story is one of the most amazing in Africa. Even to this day, white animals are still being born in Timbavati. Some years ago, a snow white elephant with beautiful blue eyes and long tusks used to roam the area, until white adventurers shot it."[7]

This incident brings up a theme that we see among modern people who feel compelled to kill others. One must ask why is it that certain humans feel justified and triumphant when they murder another living being—human or animal? Answers to this question lie deep in the psychological illness of dissociation that we discussed earlier. For some reason, our species has a built-in "denial mechanism" that allows us to do unconscionable things that corrode our precious hearts and souls.

Today, with over a billion humans on the African continent comprised of more than three thousand different tribes and more than two thousand distinct languages, the land of the White Lion is anything but homogeneous. For thousands of years, African stories, fables, and myths of these myriad traditions were passed down as part of an oral tradition from generation to generation within traditional tribes and clans. In oral traditions, stories and myths take on the character of the teller and sometimes enjoy alteration, adaptation, and addition as time goes by. History is a living, organic, and dynamic medium that connects over the ages. However, at the heart of the diversity are common and unchanging themes.

One of the main themes is the relationship between the Great Spirit Creator and the Earth: all living beings belong to one great unity. This is the "golden mean" of Earth-based societies worldwide. Humans and all of Creation are one consciousness, one life-force expressed in its varied forms. This philosophy informs all shamanic traditions. Indeed, oneness is central to all wisdom traditions as the fundamental reality of existence and nonexistence. Trans-species telepathy is also a common process practiced worldwide. Telepathic communication functions outside the bounds of normal time and space and is a skill utilized throughout many cultures as part of basic human communication. These psycho-navigational skills are not limited to the material world but include the spiritual realms and the animals who join us as allies.

THE PLEIADES

The Dogon people of central Mali say that the *nomos,* who were like mermaids given that they were part aquatic and part human, came from the planet Sirius to elevate mankind after the sinking of Atlantis. The Chokwe people of Zambia believe that their ancestors and teachers came from the Pleiades to instruct their people in the arts of agriculture, astronomy, and medicine. The Pleiades star cluster, also known as the Seven Sisters and Messier 45, appears to us in the constellation Taurus. It contains hundreds of stars, of which only a few can be seen by the naked eye. These stars formed 100 million years ago. They are 1/50th the age of our sun and are estimated to be about 425 light years away, which according to elder lore did not prevent their primeval teachers from coming to Earth.

Many traditional peoples speak of their star ancestors, but not as modern peoples do: as "aliens," which implies "unrelatedness." Traditional cultures regard these visitors as relatives, beloved elders. The Iroquois speak of the first woman who fell from the sky. The Hopi say that their *Katsinas* (Kachina) are also star people. Credo Mutwa says that "The people of Rwanda, the Hutu people, as well as the Watusi people, state, and they are not the only people in Africa who state this, that their very oldest ancestors were a race of beings whom they called the Imanujela, which means 'the Lords who have come.' Some tribes in West Africa, such as a Bambara, say that they came from the sky, many,

many generations ago. It was a race of highly advanced and fearsome creatures, which looked like men, and were called the *Zishwezi*. The word 'Zishwezi' means the dival or the glidal-creatures that can glide down from the sky or glide through water." Mutwa continues with his widely shared explanation: "Throughout South Africa, amongst many tribes, you'll find stories of these amazing creatures that are capable of changing from reptile to human being, and from reptile to any other animal of their choice. And these creatures . . . do really exist. No matter where you go throughout Southern, Eastern, Western, and Central Africa, you'll find that the description of these creatures is the same. Even amongst tribes which never, throughout their long history, had contact with each other at all."[8]

As an elder in the lion shaman tradition, Mutwa is devoted to saving today's lions from extinction. These lions, the shaman insists, represent the spiritual heart of the world upon whom humans and ecosystems depend.

The White Animals that we meet in these ancient traditions are messengers of change. They are wisdomkeepers and chroniclers of Earth events much like human historians are. They speak to the ancient past and the vast, unfolding future. Similar to human prophets who warn of great challenges or pending calamities, they also teach that the impacts of these events can be attenuated by our own individual choices and actions.

As seen with White Bear, whose presence in our lives stems from the last ice age, in the same manner, the connection between Timbavati, Greater Zimbabwe, and the Egyptian Sphinx culture of Egypt relates to the primeval ice age cycle that ended in 12,500 BCE. There are shared commonalities, in addition to the White Spirit Animals' ice age origins. One is the ancestral claims of their relationships to off-planet elders. This is reflected in the belief that the lion kings' elders come from the Pleiades.

In his *New Materials for the History of Man,* R. G. Haliburton discusses a pygmy race in the Atlas Mountains, near Morocco. They were four feet tall, red-skinned, and with bushy hair, which sounds much like the aborigines of Australia. He also advanced a theory based on flood stories worldwide, noting in his 1863 publication that cultures around the world share a common date in the calendric year upon which they honor the dead, their ancestors, and the New Year. This date corresponds to the anniversary of the end of the last ice age and subsequent tsunamis and floods that occurred worldwide. While there are many cycles inside a glacial age period, with a warming and cooling and warming and cooling taking place over a time span lasting from thirty thousand to forty thousand years, some dramatic climate changes have happened much more quickly over a period of only five hundred years. Some researchers attribute such overwhelming change in short time spans to off-planet events such as galactic core explosions, meteorites, or comets striking the Earth and other cosmic events that cause radiation. These events eliminate a high volume of bio-forms, survivors adapting in some fashion to new or hostile environments. In one of my prior books, *The Future of Human Experience,* this is explored at length in several chapters as the cyclic nature of great civilizations rising and falling, and with Earth events such as the Sixth Extinction and inter-glacial period we are in now in our current, twenty-first-century lives.

All of these cultures chose the rising of the Pleiades on the horizon as the New Year. Again, according to Haliburton, "In European calendars, the last day of October and the first and second days of November are the festivals designated as All Halloween, All Saints, and All Souls Days." This often three-day ceremony worldwide has been called "the Festival of the Dead or the Feast of the Ancestors. It is now, or was formerly, observed at or near the beginning of November by the Peruvians, Hindoos, the Pacific Islanders, the Tonga Islands, the Australians, the ancient Persians, the ancient Egyptians, and Romans, and the northern nations of Europe."[9] These ceremonies begin when the Pleiades' seven visible stars shine on the horizon, marking the beginning of the new year and the time when ancestors are honored. Times when the Pleiades are closest to Earth seem to coincide with global and colossal loss of life.

Dates comparable in time to November 17 in the Gregorian calendar are the same time period that many cultures use for reverent gatherings. For example, the Jews and Muslims mark this date in their own calendars as the onset of the deluge during Noah's time.

The Pleiades function as a calendric alignment that guides and regulates agricultural, spiritual, and community life in both the Southern and Northern Hemispheres. The Pleiadean signifier is found on clay, wood, and stone tablets throughout the world. Their origins point to an alignment with our galactic center, which is marked by the three stars in Orion's belt. As Haliburton recounts, "The ancients believed that Alcyone of the Pleiades was the center of the universe—that Paradise, the primal home of humankind and the abode of the Deity and the spirits of the dead, was in the Pleiades."[10]

For Northern Hemisphere viewers, the Pleiades can be seen above and to the right of Orion. It reaches its highest point in the sky midway between rising and setting around 4:00 a.m. in September, at 12:00 midnight in November, and 8:00 p.m. in January. The moment when the Pleiades are first visible at night on the horizon unites all of humankind's stories, calendars, and memories of a worldwide deluge.

Similar to Africa, India is also host to the lion. The month of November in India is called the "Pleiades month." On this Asian subcontinent, Lion takes the form of Narasimha or "man-lion." Narasimha was Lord Vishnu's fourth incarnation. He had a human body and a lion head. As an incarnational god, he was able to kill the demon Hiranyakashipu who cannot be killed by human, god, or animal. But because Narasimha is all of these—human, god, and animal—he was able to kill the demon. This mythology is very similar to the Greek story of Hercules. Lionhearted courage enables us to accomplish enormous tasks that otherwise seem impossible. We hear echoes of this legend in C. S. Lewis's *The Lion, the Witch and the Wardrobe,* the first of his seven novels in The Chronicles of Narnia. Aslan the lion embodies the lionhearted and inspires courageous faith in miracles and group effort. In the tale, these two things are able to thwart the White Witch who has ruled Narnia for a hundred years. The witch is eventually overthrown when the children in the story and the mystical animals under the lion's guidance join forces in their pursuit of freedom, overthrowing tyranny.

THE LIONS OF TODAY

The African lions we know today—of which the White Lion is a member—are thought to have evolved over one million years ago. The lion is part of the genus *Panthera,* which also includes diverse species such as tigers, cougars, leopards, and jaguars. The Northern Hemisphere also hosts large felines but they draw from different genera, for example, there is the mountain lion (*Puma concolor*) and the bobcat (*Lynx rufus*). *Panthera leo* (the African lion) died out in northern Eurasia ten thousand years ago along with many other mammals in the last glaciations.

Today 77 percent of all lions in captivity are of unknown origin but may carry genes of their now-extinct ancestry. Before they were hunted into extinction everywhere except Africa, and a few places in Asia and India, lions were at one time supposedly the most plentiful terrestrial animals, second only to human beings.

Lions live mostly in the south Saharan grasslands and on government and privately owned sanctuary preserves in Africa, Indonesia, and India. Like other apex species, they may also live in zoos and circuses where their lives are filled with abuse, limitation, and emotional depravity. As with the mountain gorilla of Africa, which has been decimated (only one thousand individuals remain), lions are not faring well except on protected ranges where the goal is to prevent the ongoing murderous poaching of them, which is making them nearly extinct. Asiatic lions (*Panthera leo persica*) are close relatives of African lions. Less than six hundred Asiatic lions exist, and most live in India's Gir National Park and Wildlife Sanctuary.

Lions in the wild live ten to fourteen years. Males die earlier than females largely as a result of territorial disputes. Preferring savanna and grassland to other terrains, lion prides are composed of related females and males no older than age two or three. A male lion needs about fifteen pounds of meat a day, a female eleven pounds, making wildebeest a favorite prey. Group hunting increases the likelihood of success. The guarding function of the pride is left to the male lions to whom the pride is familial.

The average gestation period of a female lion is about 110 days, which is much less than most bears who give birth after 182 to 236 days. Lion cubs are birthed in a cave, on a reed bed, or in a stock thicket of grasses that provide some protection to the vulnerable newborn. When giving birth and up until her offspring are at least six or eight weeks old the mother lion lives isolated from the rest of the pride. She hunts for food close to the den, while her cubs rest. Lions generally have one to four cubs in a litter. Depending on the number of cubs and the mother's constitution, each infant lion weighs two to five pounds. Although they are born blind and remain so for a week, the cubs begin crawling in their first few days of life. The lioness moves and makes a new den several times each month, which is thought to prevent predators from tracking their scent. One by one, the mother carries her cubs by the nape of their necks to the new location. If more than one mother in the pride gives birth, they may join up to form a communal nursery.

Young cubs are vulnerable to predation by hyenas, leopards, and jackals but may also be killed by a male lion taking over pride leadership. Although such infanticide has been accepted by most ethologists, recent reexamination of data suggests that it is less common than previously thought and that there may be other underlying motivations for it. Cubs remain with their mother for at least two years under her guardianship and training, just as bear cubs do with mother bear. (See plate 10 of a lioness with her two cubs.) Females rejected by a pride become nomads, traveling alone or in pairs.

Unlike some herd-like animals, lion prides depend almost entirely on the females to hunt for food. Joining forces at night, they prey on zebra, giraffe, hogs, impala, and many smaller animals as well. The hunt choreography is well coordinated and each pride member plays her part in bringing in food for the community. Lions, like bears, while capable of killing other mammals, prefer to scavenge for their food and this practice makes up 50 percent of their diet. Just as bears look for ravens to lead them to dead animals, lions watch for vultures to advertise the way to the remains of hyena kills. But when a lion has its prey, it kills it quickly either by suffocation or strangulation, cutting off air to either the brain or the heart.

Although the male lions will fight for both protection of their prides as well as the takeover of one, it is ultimately the females in the

Fig. 3.5. Portrait of three lions (one female and two males) of a pride, all resting one morning. Taken in the Maasai Mara Reserve in southwest Kenya, January 23, 2012.
By Benh Lieu Song

pride who accept the new male leader by their acquiescence to his mating efforts and his rearrangement of male hierarchy. But the female constellation remains intact for the fifteen to twenty years they live. Elephants, whom we will join later, also share this lifelong matrilineal constellation, making the female in these million-year-old lineages carriers of their history and teachers of their young.

The mother is the center of the wheel about which most of mammalian animal life in the wild revolves. It is telling that so much human predation targets both females of childbearing age and the male leaders of the herd, and in so doing obliterates animal cultures. This accounts for the rash of behavioral abnormalities and psychological disease such as PTSD in our human and animal populations.

Status and role in the pride is dynamic, changing as younger lions mature and older lions age. The younger males are removed from a pride and sent on their own by the age of three. Not as practiced in hunting, and having been fed by their mothers, sisters, and aunts, hunting school is cooperative. Young males sometimes search out older males who are no longer attached to a female pride, with whom they may range and hunt. Pride members will care for an elder, often toothless lioness as long as she can keep up with the pride. However, a male lion in the same situation, if he does not have male companions, is usually left to fend on his own. A lone impaired lion usually ends up being preyed upon or dying from battle wounds from horned aggressors.

Pride males live both among their communities and at their fringes, guarding and protecting pride members who can number as many as thirty lions. In exchange, they partake of the females' kills, though the male lion rarely shares his own catches with others. Lions are affectionate, nurturing, and highly playful. When at rest, they rub heads and lick and groom each other, with cubs relentlessly playing with each other and their elders. (See plate 11 of a pride of lions at rest.)

Similar to Bear, and as we will see with Elephant and Buffalo, the lioness is the preserver and teacher of tradition. This was the way with humans before the patriarchy uprooted maternal goddess traditions and caused the erosion of mother-centered cultures and ethos. The processes used for creating a truly shared society, consent of the governed, was exchanged instead for hierarchical structures of domination. Collective consensuality is the essence of matriarchy. In its place was installed the rule of power by men primarily, or patriarchy.

Matrilineal lion culture is led by the strongest male lion, which is responsible for the pride of females and young cubs. The term *King of the Jungle* has been popularized in children's plays and songs, while the theme of motherly love resonates across time within humanity's imagination. The lion is a recurring theme in Western culture. The 1966 film *Born Free* tells the story of an orphaned lion cub named Elsa who was raised in captivity and returned to the wild. The film was based on the work and lives of George and Joy Adamson. It has become an endearing movie for all ages. At the same time (1965–1967), highlighting this lion interest, the Japanese Mushi Production studio released the cartoon series featuring Kimba, a rare White Lion released into the wild after living as a cub with humans. His vision was to bring people and animals into peaceful coexistence. Obviously, someone at Mushi did their research! The goal of the cartoon White Lion echoes those in other traditions of White Lions who come to aid all sentient species and bring peace on Earth.

L. Frank Baum's 1900 epic novel *The Wonderful Wizard of Oz* was another story with a lion as its central character. It was also turned into a film, the 1939 Metro-Goldwyn-Mayer (MGM) production, whose Cowardly Lion proves to be quite the reverse and earns a heart from the Wizard in recognition of his courage. More recently, Walt Disney's 1994 animated *Lion King* celebrated the species around the world.

Using roars and scent marking as communication, male lions demarcate their territory and the associated pride. They communicate using a variety of tones and voices—the snarl, hiss, cough, meow, woof, and the roar made famous by MGM. (Every MGM film since 1917 opens with a snarling, roaring lion, performed by a number of trained lions over the decades.) Wild lions' nocturnal roars can be heard as far as five miles away, although a shaman can hear the roar that is inaudible to the ears of other humans.

Lions live near water sources as often as possible to optimize hunting and drinking. In terms of the threat of extinction, as with other species, the feline species' loss of habit and human hunting poses its most serious risk. Human encroachment on wild lands has put sizeable prides in danger of extermination. As an endangered species, since the 1950s the lion population in Africa has been reduced by 50 percent, leaving only approximately twenty to thirty thousand lions alive in the wild today.[11]

Unfortunately, the lions are not the only species in radical decline.

SPECIES DECLINE ACCELERATING

According to the World Wildlife Fund's (WWF) 2014 Living Planet Report, Earth's wild vertebrate population—all mammals, birds, reptiles, amphibians, and fish—declined by 52 percent between 1970 and 2010.[12] In the span of a single human lifetime, wild vertebrates have had their populations cut in half as a result of human hunting and land appropriation. Rampant human population increases, unsustainable land use, and poaching are lead causes. The report also states that "The No. 1 cause of wildlife declines is habitat loss and change, which is reducing 45 percent of the animals studied. Hunting and fishing, both intentionally and via 'by catch' is next at 37 percent." Population sizes of vertebrate species—mammals, birds, reptiles, amphibians, and fish—have declined by 52 percent over the past forty years. In other words, those populations around the globe have dropped by more than half in fewer than two human generations.

Some of the most severe, recent losses have occurred in South America, where multinational corporations have been destroying the rain forests for decades to raise cattle for beef production and palm oil production. Per the same report, "Vertebrate species fell 83 percent from

1970 to 2010 in the neo-tropics, a bioregion that includes most of South America, Central America and the Caribbean as well as parts of lowland Mexico and South Florida." Unsurprisingly, the poorest countries are hardest hit. "Low-income countries have seen a 58 percent decrease of vertebrate wildlife since 1970, compared with an 18 percent drop in middle-income countries. The wealthiest nations have seen a 10 percent increase, although their rising resource use correlates with the global trend of biodiversity loss." In effect, says WWF's Keya Chatterjee, "Wealthy nations are outsourcing resource depletion."

One has to wonder why this isn't what we talk about in public, during presidential campaigns, in our offices, in our homes, and at our religious and spiritual gatherings. I have joked that if one sports league a week were eliminated, a football league, then a soccer league, then a basketball league for instance, the entire world would be in an uproar! Why is there so little public sentiment or intelligence about something as serious as species' extinction? These statistics do not presage a minor wake-up call. They are a red alert telling us that we have already gone beyond a tipping point. The serious question is: How are we to stave off calamitous collapse of all biological life-forms? One simple solution as part of a larger strategy is to save the apex animals of each ecosystem. This is one sound method for preserving an entire hierarchy of life in each locale. This is the message of the White Spirit Animals: "Save as many of us as you can."

Years ago, Lester Brown, founder of the Worldwatch Institute, told me that the health of a nation could be gauged by the literacy level of the women who live there and the health of the trees. For when the tree canopy is decimated, an ecosystem begins to collapse. It was determined that these two factors predicted the size of families, because education generally leads to having smaller families, lessening human impacts on the ecosystem. Literacy also meant that the women in the community were able to care for their children and have small businesses and livelihoods, making them more independent. Species' decline and habitat destruction orchestrated by megacorporations are related to the economic quality of life of a given region. The lower the income, the more devastating the impact on the land, its ecosystems, and wildlife. "We're gradually destroying our planet's ability to support our way of life," stated WWF CEO Carter Roberts in the Living Planet Report cited above. "We have the knowledge and tools to avoid the worst predictions. We know that we all live on a finite planet and it's time that we started acting within those limits."

Conservation means taking responsibility worldwide and enacting practices in each locale that show love and compassion for all life. It was prophesized that the White Lions would return when humanity was on the verge of disaster. Apparently, now is that time.

LION SHAMANISM AND LION KINGS

White Spirit Animals are central to spiritual traditions and their sacred rituals. They are organized in matrilineal orders, and have province over the Earth. This conforms to the hypothesis I intuited after my own encounters with these messengers in the wild. It is essential that we see them each as guardians of the cosmos and the Earth's ecosystems. Like White Bear, who holds a role as guardian over the direction North, from where spirit ushers, and over the planetary space in the northern part of the planet, in the African tradition of lion shamanism the lion is heralded as the guardian of the entire Earth.

The Zulu Lion King

There is a popular legend about a Zulu lion king and priest named King Mageba (1667–1745), who was on the verge of being killed in a battle between the Zulus and the Mangwani. During the fighting, however, a pride of lions intervened and attacked the enemy, thereby freeing the king and saving his life. The lion who led the rescue pride was a grown cub that the king had raised and returned to the wild, but whose left paw, which had been wounded during capture as a young cub, revealed his identity to the king.

To this day the king of the Zulu nation is called "Ingonyama" (lion). The ancient people call Lion the "Queen of Heaven" and in Zulu tradition reincarnating as a lion, and not a chief or king, rewards brave warriors.

Like Bear, Lion has been known to protect entire tribes from harm and it is by touching the animal that lion power is gained. As with Daniel in the Hebrew Bible who was not eaten or harmed after being thrown into a pit full of lions, or a bushman sitting side by side with a lion and coming into rapport with it, harm and aggression are circumvented when one is in telepathic communication with animals.

The power of an animal is not given to its abuser or killer as many hunters mistakenly believe. The power of an animal and its aptitudes are shared with a human through respectful relations. It is through this pacific communiqué that harmony is maintained. Domination is supplanted by a mutual recognition of the sentience and awareness of both species. So it is with all animals at all scales of being. When one has rapport in consciousness, peaceful trans-species exchange is able to take place and forces are joined to achieve a mutual goal. This mutual trust and respect is at the heart of all human-animal collaboration. This type of noble partnership speaks to the purpose of service and how our lives concern more than just our individual selves.

As the White Lions told me when we met in the spring of 2013, if we do not preserve the apex guardian species, our ecosystems and life as we know it will be thrown into chaos.

CANNED CAMPS

Today in South Africa there are animalcide camps called "canned camps" where White Lions are systematically raised and then shot to death for a price. The murdered lion's skin and head bring as much as $65,000 to $120,000 in the marketplace, but the cost to our souls is bankruptcy. Overall, the lion trophy business in Africa is valued at 91 million dollars a year.

The term *canned hunting* was brought to the public's attention in 1997 by the British current affairs television program *The Cook Report,* which uncovered the fact that endangered animals, and especially the sacred White Lions, were being abducted from their prides and put into cages for wealthy foreign "hunters" to pay to murder. As shared by Kevin Richardson, a conservationist and animal behaviorist known as the "Lion Whisperer,"

> Journalist Roger Cook went undercover posing as a hunter, with the intention to film a "canned lion" hunt. Before pulling the trigger he revealed to the people involved who he was and what he was doing. A scuffle ensued but luckily the tv crew and the team managed to get away unscathed. The piece was later aired and footage emerged that was secretly filmed on another farm of a lioness being shot from a vehicle next to a fence whilst her cubs watched from the other side, isolated from getting to her. This naturally caused an uproar and upset even the most hardened non animal lover. It was dubbed a "National Disgrace" and government was implored to do something.[13]

Unfortunately, these death camps continue today and are often part of a lucrative tourist-driven cub-petting industry as well. Young lion cubs, captured from the wild or bred in captivity, are handled and walked by humans until it is no longer safe to do so. Then these same little furry, beautiful, petable lions become the captive victims for the next generation of "kill for fee" industry racketeers.

Like other conservationists in Africa today, the Kevin Richardson Wildlife Sanctuary's "ultimate goal is to minimize the number of large carnivores being kept in captivity and to highlight the direct link between the cub petting industry and the 'canned' hunting industry, by educating the unsuspecting public to the horrors associated with this unscrupulous practice."[14]

Today, even with public awareness increasing about these horrible realities, White Lions are not afforded any legal protection—nor are any of the other 20,000–30,000 remaining lions in Africa. If not imprisoned and later shot for a price, many are stolen and placed in zoos and circuses around the world. In fact, there are supposedly only thirteen free White Lions living in their indigenous heartland of Timbavati today. All the others are in captivity or being guarded in private sanctuaries.

So conscious are these majestic animals, as Richardson shares in films about his life and conservation efforts, one can come into gentle rapport with the great king of the beasts. He, like Charlie Russell and other wildlife "whisperers," makes clear that established relations with these sentient animal beings are nurtured over long periods of time. As Richardson explains, many of the lions he works with in his films, and has saved, he has known since their births.

As mentioned earlier, it is not by brutalizing or overpowering animals that we can enter into peaceful relations with them but through respectful engagement. One can communicate with the lion and the lion with the human, as can all animals and all humans who make the effort to do so. However, as shamans are quick to tell us, our modern technologies that feature computer screens, cell phones, and television can interfere with this natural ability. Even the shaman who has acquired these skills may lose them by spending too much time engaged with these external devices.

LISTENING FOR THE LANGUAGE OF CREATION

A related story about "biotic antenna" is relevant here.

The Power of Uncut Hair

During America's war in Vietnam, Army trackers who had been hand selected from Native American tribes were forced to cut their hair once they entered military service, as were all servicemen. When this happened, they lost some or all of their extrasensory capacities. Having forewarned the army that this could occur and having witnessed that the American Indian soldiers indeed did lose some of their ESP, the army conducted tests of trackers with uncut hair and trackers with cut hair. Thereafter, the army changed its policy so that Indian trackers were able to keep their hair long.

Similar to a spider's web, hair functions as an acoustical receiving and sounding instrument. Native Americans state that hair is an extension of our nervous system, making it part of our personal receiving tower's wiring. While not all trans-species communicators need to have long hair, among many indigenous peoples the tradition continues.

All shamans of the world stress that the material, spiritual, human, and animal worlds are interconnected and always will be. Being able to shift one's attention and consciousness into rapport with another life-form allows for communication and leads to wise and sustainable choices. The Zulu believe that trees, like lions, also have destiny and purpose bound up in the human journey on Earth. The Zulu's ancient off-planet elders are said to be half human, half animal. Credo Mutwa explains that we and the animal kingdom are interrelated and our obligation is to take care of the animal kingdom as we would our family members. Some families, such as Mutwa's, are ancestrally bound to the lion as their sacred totem, obliging them to protect any female—human or animal. The lion shaman, like the lion itself, is a protector of life.

In the Chassidic tradition, deity takes no form but is in all life-forms. So while this human-animal relationship would be stated differently than it is in the Zulu tradition, there is similarity. The animal soul presides over our needs, our bodily functions, our desires for food, for movement, for procreation, and for pleasure as well as bodily survival. The divine soul imparts the wisdom needed to fulfill one's purpose while incarnate, directing the animal soul by the greater mind and loving intentions of one's heart. When we are in silence, the Zulu believe, one can hear the language of Creation. This listening honors everything for its sacred purpose and helps us find our right action in that relationship with all others.

Mutwa asserts that while the prophecy of the former King Shaka speaks of his successor the seventh king being the last king of their people, that prophecy is not written as fate. This is relevant to our current situation. People can change what appears to be the prophecy of extinction. There is no doubt that we live in extraordinary times that are both catastrophic and potentially miraculous.

THE MAASAI LION GUARDIANS

Heart intelligence can help us transform past destructive practices into approaches that sustain and elevate life, as we saw in the case of the British Columbian rain forest. We can shift from a prevalent death economy to a life economy by making an effort to elevate all life in every situation. The Lion Guardians, founded by biologist Leela Hazzah and zoologist Stephanie Dolrenry in 2007, is an important example of this.

The Maasai of East Africa live in present-day Kenya and northern Tanzania. For centuries they have hunted lions as part of their initiation into manhood. The lion's imminent extinction has not stopped these rituals. Those who still hunt as a show of manhood have begun to hunt in groups so that one lion is killed per ten or so young men, rather than ten lions or one per person. Certain Maasai members of the organization known as the Lion Guardians offer an alternative initiation to manhood by emulating another lion quality, that of protector instead of killer.

The Maasai live a mostly pastoral life and depend on their livestock to feed their families. Subsequently, when livestock is killed, it is regarded as a serious loss. Livestock is currency and a status symbol. If the Maasai lose any of their livestock to lions, or they believe that it was lion kill, they retaliate by killing lions. Lion Guardians, seeking to halt this killing of the lions, helps return lost livestock and lost herders, rebuilds animal corral fencing, tracks lions, and notifies herders or others when lions are near. As a conservation program, Lion Guardians states in its literature that it "is based on the integration of social and biological sciences, including traditional and indigenous knowledge."[15]

A decade since its founding, this nonprofit conservation biology effort employs Lion Guardians throughout East Africa, made up of Maasai and other pastoral community members in seven locations who are each paid the equivalent of a hundred dollars a month. Each Lion Guardian is taught to read and write, and each is tasked with tracking, naming, and knowing the whereabouts of the lions they protect. Their ultimate goal is to prevent any conflict with lions and to reduce lion killings, thereby increasing their now dangerously small population. As Lion Guardians inform us, in the past fifty years Africa has lost 50 percent of its lion population.

Once again we see that an ethos of care, instead of an approach of exploitation and destruction, can change what has been historically part of the death economy to a life-elevating economy instead. Enlisting members of local communities to reshape and redefine their relationship to their own environment and its populations, human and animal, has accomplished this.

This is unique to Lion Guardians, as historically animal conservation has focused on the animals but not the local communities in which the animals reside. In this case Maasai elders helped the founders of Lion Guardians create a program that is beneficial to the community, its economy, its members, the ecosystem, and the animals they live among in the wild. In Amboseli, Kenya, the Lion Guardians have documented a near tripling of the lion population since beginning their work there.

All of the apex species are essential to their corners of the world. Preserving these vital species is a good insurance plan for the biosphere, because without them, ecosystems where they now live will be dismantled. Where the animals are cared for and nurtured, local economies are supported.

SYMBOLOGIZING

Humans and other life-forms possess a consciousness that operates like a switchboard, taking in calls and connecting them where the messages need to go: signals received, signals sent. Symbologists and indigenous people speak of these signs as the vital information we have called toward us from the universe with our desires, thoughts, and actions. The things we assemble around us in our lives—jewelry, drawings, or other creative forms of expression, places we like to visit, images that show up in prayer or meditation—all reflect our search for patterns of meaningful relationships. Signs, archetypes, symbols, and totems are aspects of the same phenomena and are deeply embedded in spiritual traditions planet wide.

One universal law describes how all things are related in octaves, much like piano notes on the seven octaves of a piano keyboard. What this means, as a practical key to use in our lives, is seen in all shamanic and Native cultures. As an example, the image of a lion is capable of drawing lion wisdom to the person who has focused their attention on that figure. The symbolic representation of something—a charm, a sculpture, a drawing—brings to its user the inner nature of that which is being represented. This is what empowers totems and is what fuels vision quests, when a person discovers what animal or animals are theirs to learn from. Many shamans and medicine healers utilize this form of totemic magic in their work.

In the same way, masters and teachers often communicate with their students through a process whereby the student studies and reflects upon the master's image in a photograph or a painting. What monotheists often call "pagan worship" or "pantheism" is actually a form of functional "low magic." Objects act as symbols of special life-forces and powers that a person, using focused attention, can draw from. A lion shaman therefore may wear a necklace made of lion claws, just as bear healer will wear a necklace made of bear claws.

Because female lions are given province of guardianship and

protection over humanity and are called the Queen of Heaven, it is reasonable to assume that when spiritual elders are joined by the spirit of these animals, these animals lend their powers to their allied humans. Anyone who has ever witnessed true medicine men and women—who may temporarily shape-shift, manifest objects, and accomplish healings—understands that it is not simply a question of faith or belief. The work of these spiritual healers, who improve the health of a person or who make it rain, involves genuine transformation of matter using agents that are invisible or that come seemingly out of nowhere.

Much if not most human communication and that in the natural world happens in the invisible spectrum in the medium of consciousness. It is not necessary to exchange images or words to communicate. The light that makes all potential actual is animated by the living force of Creation, which is filling you and me, the bear, the lion, and the stars.

In fact a phenomenon called presentiment shows that people's bodies "subconsciously sense the future when something important is about to happen, even if the people don't know it."[16] It is as if the universe anticipates our next move before we are even conscious that we will make it. This is often experienced as déjà vu—something one feels one has already seen or experienced in some way. This is also why people may recognize that an event is about to happen seven seconds before it actually does take place.*

The U.S. space agency, NASA, is convinced that traveling at warp speed, faster than the speed of light, indeed is possible and is conducting experiments based on this premise. Those who have experienced UFO contact or who claim to have visited such craft have said they traveled at these accelerated speeds. Inner consciousness is limited by neither time nor space, so it seems reasonable to assume there are similar laws that apply to the material world.

---

*I find it funny that this is the same delay period (seven seconds) for a "dump button" in live radio. The broadcaster runs seven seconds ahead of what the audience hears so that the producer can cut out any words outlawed by the regulatory agency that a host or caller might accidentally utter.

WHITE SPIRIT LION LESSONS

One dream of mine reiterated that we should assist all of the White Spirit Animals and their corresponding species with dedicated urgency. They are part of prophecies that speak of Earth changes, including future snow- and ice-scapes common in a glacial age. They tell us to design and build covered cities of white domes and underground habitats. They council us to enlist the elders of the Earth's Native traditions for guidance in making peace with the animal and plant worlds. Russell Four Eagles, a medicine healer in the Oneida way, recounts his grandmother's words on the issue of Earth changes, "The Creator in his infinite wisdom has made things to work one way when we take care of them and another when we don't. If we take care of Mother Earth, she works for us; if we don't she works against us. Both ways are perfectly right for each situation. Remember the Creator not only gave us free will, he also gave it to his child, Mother Earth."[17]

The animals of the wild teach us a very civil approach to living in a wilder state, calling men to become guardians and protectors, not killers of other men, women, and children. This is not an archaic model but rather an enlightened model of security, sustainability, and longevity. The female lion teaches us, as the Queen of Heaven, that by re-creating matrilineal cultures, we align human society with archetypal order by which all living mammalian species prosper. A pure heart is the source of wisdom and restoration. Nurturing the environments of home and childhood education assures a healthier society and a happier one. The system of governance that matriarchies maintain insists on the consensus of the governed. Down through time, cooperatives where women form businesses and share childcare tasks have been prosperous for individual women, their children, and their communities. The science of happiness, or what is now called positive psychology, measures wellness among humans and shows that this kind of nurturing and shared freedom results in the highest satisfaction in both the life and health of the community. Most, if not all, of the human traditions that the White

Spirit Animals have aligned with were at some time matriarchal or still are. Indeed, most Native American tribes remain so today.

As we near the close of our sojourn with Lion, it is noteworthy to share a particular lion encounter that I had at the beginning and end of writing this book. As a child I owned a most magnificent Steiff male lion, which I had picked out at FAO Schwarz in New York City as an eleventh birthday present from my parents. At the time I was obsessed with lions. I wrote my fifth-grade science report, which I still have, on the lion prides of Africa. (See plate 12.) While writing this chapter I had only one specific intimate dream experience in which I encountered a lion directly, though the lions imparted wisdom teachings to me telepathically during the day.

Laughing at Lion

In this lucid vision, an enormous male lion came and roared at me only inches away from my face. He was so close I could feel the heat of his breath and smell grass on his mane. Surprising even to me, rather than being afraid, I laughed. It was funny to me at the time because I knew in fact it was a lot of bravado and I loved lions anyway, so why would a spirit lion frighten me?

As I wrote the lions' story with their collaboration, it became clear that my laughing in a lion's face was offensive, insulting, as it would be if one laughed in any king's face. Lion let me know that it is no "laughing matter" to laugh at lions. But still he was a big funny lion like the one who used to sleep on my childhood bed, reigning over the entire fourteen-member animal menagerie I tucked in each night according to a very thought-out and egalitarian rotation system.

In my experience with this dream lion, he was like an imitation of himself, character acting, and he knew that I knew it was an act—that he was not angry at all but instead was testing me in some way. But I think it is for this reason that while I dreamt fluidly with all the other mammals—Bear, Elephant, Wolf, Buffalo, and even whales who came

Fig. 3.6. Majestic White Lion
By Stano Novak

along for the stories and have their own to share—I did not dream easily with the lions. After two years of writing, and two days after completion of the manuscript, I woke from sleep, on the edge of conscious and not yet conscious in the luminal place like the edge of a horizon just lit by the rising sun. I finally had a dream-like encounter with Lion.

A Dream of White Lion

There, centered in space, with nothing else around him, stood a gorgeous male lion as majestic as could be—awe-inspiring. His body was lit by the sun making him appear golden. It is not often in dreams that one encounters a being so entirely majestic and powerful as to take one's breath away, but this is how I felt during this dream, experiencing what the ancients tell us about the lion's royal presence. I bowed my head gently toward him and he nodded at me with loving kindness, making clear that all was forgiven and that the lions are grateful for my efforts on their behalf.

The White Spirit Animal species of the world are not less evolved, less conscious, less sentient, or less deserving of autonomy than we are. They are our guardians, our teachers, and a beacon to our shared hearts. With the decimation of their culture through hunting, captivity, and habitat destruction, their ancient culture, like human cultures of Africa and the Amazon, is being lost. Preserving the traditions of all beings is a call from the wild.

For the White Lion to reappear at this time in humanity's awareness signifies the need for great courage and localized leadership. Lions teach us the powerful love and determination needed to do what elevates our communities and ecosystems as a whole. The White Lions of Timbavati, like those cherished in the ancient world, remind us that refining our inner natures, as well as protecting the entire Earth, is our golden-hearted purpose and shared soul destiny.

4
Elephant

Teacher of the Buddhic Way

At all times I think to myself:
How can I cause living beings
to gain entry into the unsurpassed way
and quickly acquire the body of a Buddha?

THE CONCLUDING WORDS OF THE SIXTEENTH
CHAPTER OF THE LOTUS SUTRA

THE WHITE ELEPHANT is portrayed with adoration in the disciplines of mythology, religion, literature, and more generally in art and culture. Elephants have been extant since at least 1600 BCE, participating in numerous human endeavors—land clearing, building, temple parades, entertainment, and war. Similar to the lion, elephants have symbolized royalty and status.

FAMOUS ELEPHANTS IN HISTORY

In 1861 America's sixteenth president, Abraham Lincoln, was offered a sacred White Elephant by King Rama IV of Siam for the president's use in the Civil War. It was a gift that Lincoln kindly refused.

Emperor Charlemagne (742–814 CE), whose empire included most of Western Europe, had a legendary African elephant, Abul-Abbas, who had been given to him by the caliph of Baghdad, Harun al-Rashid. Abul-Abbas was brought from Africa by a courier, Isaac the Jew, via

Fig. 4.1. Asian elephant (*Elephas maximus*)
From *Brehms Tierleben* (*Brehms Life of Animals*) by Alfred Edmund Brehms (1829–1884)

a long voyage that skirted the Egyptian coast up to Tunisia and then into the Mediterranean, where boat and elephant finally docked in a neighboring port city near Genoa, Italy. There are no details on how the gentle giant fared during his sea journey but we do know that he created quite a stir at every port and town along his route. Abul-Abbas was a beloved member of the court, in part because few Europeans had ever seen an elephant. History tells us that he was employed for battle, crossing the Alps to reside with his master and allegedly leading other elephants into war.

Gifting world leaders with White Elephants is an old tradition. The White Elephant that Pope Leo X (1475–1521) received from King Manuel I of Portugal in 1514 was shipped from its native India to Lisbon and on to Rome. Hanno, as he was named, was only a four-year-old toddler. His capture deprived him of being nursed by his mother within the constellation of aunties and siblings that make up a typical elephant natal family. For fifteen more years, he would have lived among his natal family until mature enough to leave and mate. He would have grazed among them in the jungles and wallowed in watering holes, enjoying the pleasurable life of an elephant in the wild.

Hanno arrived in Italy, along with the Portuguese ambassador, in time for the pope's coronation. Hanno's portrait became as famous as that of the pope's. As recorded by the poet Pasquale Malaspina:

> *In the Belvedere before the great Pastor*
> *Was conducted the trained elephant*
> *Dancing with such grace and such love*
> *That hardly better would a man have danced:*
> *And then with its trunk such a great noise*
> *It made, that the entire place was deafened:*
> *And stretching itself on the ground to kneel*
> *It then straightened up in reverence to the Pope,*
> *And to his entourage.*[1]

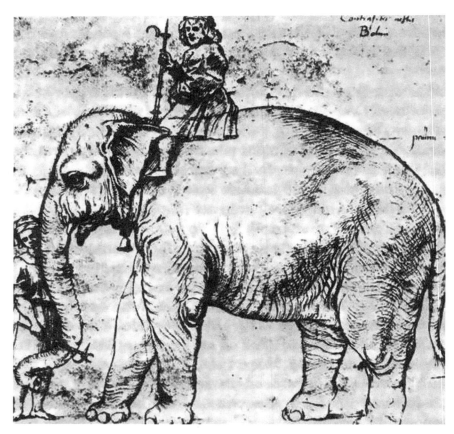

Fig. 4.2. Hanno the baby White Elephant (1510–1516)
gifted to Pope Leo X (1475–1521)
By Raphael (1483–1520) or Giulio Romano (1499–1546)
after a lost drawing by Raphael

Hanno was the best known White Elephant in Europe and continued to be a favorite of the pope. He was a key feature in papal
events for two years before falling ill. After receiving a purgative laced
with gold, Hanno died on June 8, 1516, in the pope's presence. I like
to imagine that the pope was at Hanno's side when he died, and that
the young elephant received a blessing from the holy man just as any
beloved friend or head of state might. Hanno was only seven years
old when he passed on, seventy-three years short of an elephant's life

expectancy. He was buried far from home and family, and though loved, it cannot be ignored that he was terribly exploited, held captive, and that he lived—as his early demise indicates—under conditions of maternal and familial deprivation and emotional hardship. The urban setting of sixteenth-century Italy was hardly like Hanno's birthplace: the jungles of India.

THE ELEPHANT DISPOSITION

When we are around elephants, something magical, elevating, and awe-inspiring occurs. Simply put, elephants make us happy. They elevate our spirits. They bring peace to our hearts. They make us feel joyous. Most people today, however, encounter their first elephant in unnatural settings—in zoos, circuses, entertainment parks, or on elephant rides or other forms of exhibitions and entertainment.

Despite the abuse and violence meted out by humans, elephants seem to tolerate our species well beyond limits that we ourselves deem acceptable. They are forcibly taken from their homelands and families, almost always witnessing the brutal deaths of their mothers and aunties who desperately try to save them. Then they are brought into deplorable conditions that eventually lead to premature death. Yet even though they possess phenomenal strength—the single flick of a trunk can send a full-grown man yards away—they rarely strike out. Elephants seem to be masters of forgiveness in ways that few humans achieve. It is easy to mistake their restraint as an absence of psychological and physical pain. But their seeming tolerance comes from within, a deep and profound respect and embrace of nonviolence.

These qualities of elephants have been recognized since the last ice age when they first began to live among humans. Such is the natural disposition of the elephant, whether white or gray or any other skin tone, and whether small or large. Elephants who have not been subjected to the madness of humans who mistreat them possess a calm mind and loving heart. When we are around them we can experience this through our own heart's rapport with theirs. Elephants embody both beauty and grace and we feel this when we see them.

A CROSS-CULTURAL PERSPECTIVE
OF THE ELEPHANT

The depictions of female elephants caring for their young is endearing to everyone. Elephant maternal dedication is a theme found in cave art and is found in illuminated manuscripts as well. Pliny the Elder (23–79 CE), a naturalist, author, and army commander, wrote that the elephant "in intelligence approaches the nearest to man."[2] I would add to this by saying that elephants possess qualities that we admire yet seldom achieve, and in many respects the elephant is more evolved than many human beings. This is why I believe that the elephant is an ethical exemplar, a teacher of an elevated state of awareness. I have learned this in writing this book, dreaming with them, and listening to their stories.

In Hindu mythology, the deity Ganesh (also Ganesha) has a human body and an elephant's head. He is the deliverer of success and his elephant head represents the soul or Atman, while the elephant's trunk of one thousand muscles represents the sound of Creation: OM. It is the sound ushered in from the cosmos and it brings everything into being.

In Nepal, Ganesha is known as *Hermaba* and has five heads and rides a lion. Southern and northern Indian myths liken Ganesha to an unmarried brahmachari who renounces the world in service to divine enlightenment. He is the patron of the creative process in both the arts and sciences, and the deva who illuminates wisdom. The White Elephant helps birth terrestrial life and divine Creation, and creates and removes obstacles from a person's life to further their spiritual evolution. Elephants are envisioned as being the guardians of all forms of life, and they trumpet their excitement, praising the source of all life. As Hindu tradition teaches, the holy elephant stirs the Milky Way. Different from other creatures, such as Bear who guards the North and the Great Spirit, or Lion who is assigned to protecting the world, Elephant is an agent of Creation from the Milky Way to Earth.

MEETING THE BUDDHIST
WHITE ELEPHANT

When I began searching for the nature, spiritual legacy, and ecological importance of the White Elephant, I was immediately drawn to Buddhism, specifically the Lotus Sutra of Mahayana Buddhism (*Saddharma Puṇḍarīka Sūtra*). I assumed that, as we have found with the White Bear and White Lion, there would be texts, spiritual traditions, and core values associated with Elephant and evidence of its holy place among human societies. The Lotus Sutra was originally translated from Sanskrit into Chinese (265–317 CE). It contains one of the best known, if not the most significant story about the White Elephant and the Buddha, whose teachings are collated in these sutras. I suspected that the Buddha may be the human representation of what elephant consciousness is actually like—*Buddhic.*

While the story of the Buddha's birth is well-known to many, it is worth sharing here because of the elephant in it and the role that it plays in the traditional representation of wisdom.

The Story of Buddha

Siddhartha Gautama Shakyamuni was born into a royal family sometime between 600–400 BCE. His father the king was respected for his love of justice. His mother, Maha Maya (Maya meaning "love" or "beauty" in Sanskrit), was a woman of great valor. Together the two ruled over their kingdom, Shakyas in Lumbini, in what is today's modern Nepal in the Himalayan region near Tibet.

After twenty barren, childless years, Maya dreams that she is taken by four devas to the Himalayan lake Anotatta. There they bathe and perfume her before dressing her in celestial clothes and flowers. After she is purified in this manner, according to one traditional version of the story, a beautiful White Elephant appears, carrying a perfect white lotus in his trunk. After walking around Maya three times, he enters her womb through the right side of her body and disappears inside of her.

When the queen tells her husband of this dream, he calls wise men to interpret it. They conclude that it is an auspicious dream about her having been chosen to give birth to the Purest One, who will become a very great being. But the royal parents are also told that if their son stays in the royal household, he will indeed become a world power as the king was hoping, and yet his behavior might be brutal. On the other hand, if he is raised outside the royal palace where he can see the world, he will become a great spiritual leader.

Near the time of childbirth, the queen ventures toward her hometown, stopping under a sal tree whose wood is used for building lumber, which elephants help harvest and carry. There, under the tree, she gives birth to the Lord Siddhartha, who will later become known as Buddha ("he who achieves his aims" or "he who is awake"). Seven days later, the queen dies, leaving her sister to raise her son in the royal palace. Thirty-five years after that, this same sister will become the first nun in the Buddha's sangha (community of monks). Unlike many other traditions, women were admitted to the sangha. There was no discrimination based on one's class, race, sex, or past history—something that is truly reflective of one of the greatest egalitarian wisdom traditions on Earth.

The years go by and Siddhartha grows up in the palace, protected by the royal household. He is surrounded by wealth, beauty, and security. But eventually, when he finally ventures outside the palace walls, he discovers that the world is very different from what he has experienced. He sees the suffering of others, learns that things die, and that people feel terrible pain and unhappiness.* The stark contrast with the life of luxury he has

---

*"On the first trip, the prince saw an old man. He came to know that everyone had to grow old. On the second trip, the prince saw a sick man. He came to know that everyone could get sick at any time. On the third trip, he saw a dead body. He knew that everyone would have to die one day. On the fourth trip, the prince saw a monk who was happy and calm. He made up his mind to leave home so that he could help people to find peace and happiness."[3]

led leaves him restless, and at the age of twenty-nine he departs from the palace, leaving his wife and son behind, and goes out into the world as an ascetic monk committed to austerity.

After six years of wandering, Siddhartha comes across the bodhi tree. He seats himself under its canopy and vows to sit there until he achieves enlightenment and an understanding of suffering. One by one, his ascetic companions abandon the young monk, leaving him alone on his spiritual quest.*

After forty-nine days in silence, Siddhartha, who has now become Buddha, is shown what he was to call "the Four Noble Truths and Eightfold Path of Enlightenment." The Four Noble Truths are foundational principles: the truth of suffering, the truth of the cause of suffering, the truth of the end of suffering, and the truth of the path that leads to the end of suffering. The Eightfold Path is translated into English as qualities that each person is encouraged to cultivate. They are: right view, right intention, right speech, right action, right livelihood, right effort, right mindfulness, and right concentration. Together they have become the basic precepts of Buddhism. Centuries after the Buddha, these principles guide millions of human beings worldwide.

Buddhism is often called the middle path because it requires neither indulgence nor extreme deprivation, but offers instead a modest and sincere undertaking to free oneself from ignorance, greed, hatred, and other common human challenges that are the source of suffering.

Over the next forty-five years until his death, the Buddha taught the dharma—the basic teachings of Buddhism that instruct on the manifestation of reality and the laws of the universe, including divine realization or nirvana. This state, Buddha maintained, is the birthright of all living beings who practice right thought, right speech, and right action. Liberation from suffering is accessible and achievable by all, no matter his or her station or walk of life.[4]

---

*The great mythologist Joseph Campbell referred to these solo ventures and trials as "the hero's journey." Also called "vision quests," the purpose is for one to go into seclusion in order to find one's true identity and purpose, to find meaning in one's life.

This is the primary reason that I have been attracted to Buddhism since my teens. I find it liberating to encounter a philosophy that does not require intercessory agents to broker our relationship with divinity. The path we walk in each lifetime is truly under our own direction. Each of us is obligated to become self-mastered, and the underlying process for this undertaking is the journey the Buddhist tradition honors and cultivates. We obviously benefit from teachers and guides, community and family, but at some point in every life it is the individual person who comes into rapport with the sacred within and without. This makes us, as the Buddha hoped, conscious participants in the alleviation of the world's suffering and our own. The Buddha insisted up to the last teaching day of his worldly life that his disciples should follow no leader.[5] I have taken this advice to heart and have followed it my entire life.

It's also interesting that in Buddhist meditation the untrained mind is sometimes compared to the gray elephant running wild while the calm mind is represented by the White Elephant. The elephant is associated with the power to make rain, and elephants have been depicted as rain clouds themselves flying in the skies. I wonder if elephant tears aren't the rain of enduring compassion?

After I began dreaming with Elephant I learned that in Buddhism enlightened people are often compared with elephants.[6] I am sure I am not the only modern person with a deep affection for these wonderful creatures. In fact, a white one almost came into my life decades ago.

In the 1970s I was interested in adopting a white pygmy or Asian Borneo elephant in need of a home. At first I thought it would be fantastic to do so. I had rented a barn studio for my sculpture works at the time so it was easy to envision how to transform the stalls into an open space for the elephant. He could graze in the large surrounding fields, which included a spring-fed pond that we skated on as children. Before contacting its owner, who was advertising an available elephant he could no longer care for, I called some experts familiar with captive elephants.

Once I learned about the practical realities of caring for an elephant—they eat a hundred pounds of food a day and drop two hundred pounds of skat (dung), and they need a great amount of space, to say nothing of fencing—I went no further with this notion. I should have taken to heart instead the lessons of Elephant: humility, patience, responsibility, and commitment to family and community—personal qualities that, at twenty-one, I was not focused on cultivating. Also, I was not schooled about the deeper spiritual meaning of the Buddha and the elephant as is found in this teaching: "When Dona encountered the Buddha sitting at the foot of a tree he appeared 'beautiful, faith-inspiring, with calm senses and serene mind, utterly composed and controlled like a tamed, alert, perfectly trained elephant' (A.II, 38)."[7]

As a telepathic communicator and research dreamer, and confirming my own experience of the reality of the elephant as Buddhist way-shower, it was delightful to come across a remarkable poem in the Lotus Sutra scriptures. Buddha's virtues are extolled there in terms of the anatomy and qualities of the noble and majestic Elephant. "Gentleness and harmlessness are his front legs; simplicity and celibacy are the hind legs. Faith is his trunk, equanimity his white tusks, mindfulness his neck, his head is careful consideration, Dharma is his belly and solitude his tail. Meditating, focusing on his breath and utterly composed, this mighty elephant walks, stands and sits with composure, he is perfectly trained and accomplished in all ways (A.III, 346)."[8]

It is said that prior to his incarnation as the Buddha, Siddhartha's soul lived inside the body of an elephant. So great was this affinity that the Buddha never looked over his shoulder if he needed to see what was behind him, but rather turned completely around as elephants do because of their limited eyesight. This is called his "elephant look."[9] But most surprising was the discovery in the opening Sutra of this description of a divinely balanced and awakened human being:

Thus have I heard. Once upon a time the Lord was staying at Râgagriha, on the Gridhrakuta mountain, with a numerous assemblage of monks, twelve hundred monks, all of them Arhats, stainless, free from depravity, self-controlled, thoroughly emancipated in thought and knowledge, of noble breed (like unto) great elephants, having done their task, done their duty, acquitted their charge, reached the goal; in whom the ties which bound them to existence were wholly destroyed, whose minds were thoroughly emancipated by perfect knowledge, who had reached the utmost perfection in subduing all their thoughts; who were possessed of the transcendent faculties . . .[10]

The Lotus Sutra is cherished as the most important teaching of Mahayana Buddhism and expresses the connection I feel with Elephant as a Buddhic way-shower. Learning about these passages in the Sutras also confirmed the authentic nature of my telepathic conversations with White Elephant.*

WHITE ELEPHANTS OF THAILAND

In Thailand, White Elephants are loved because of their relationship to the Buddha's birth, but all White Elephants found belong to the Thai king. The white color of elephants is attributed to recessive genes inherited from their parents. In reality, their skin color is not white but rather pink, and lacks the pigmentation that other elephants possess. The royal White Elephant has been sacred in Thailand for centuries and symbolizes fertility, abundance, and success. Historically, young Thai kings kept several White Elephants in their stables to assure long and prosperous reigns. Treated like a purebred, a "royal White Elephant" must

---

*The Sutra of the Lotus Flower of the Wonderful Law forms the basis of the Tiantai, Tendai, Cheontae, and Nichiren schools of Buddhism. These sutras (or threads) are arranged in ten volumes and twenty-seven chapters, addressing both personal transformation and the betterment of the world through individual practice.

meet certain criteria that the Bureau of the Royal Household oversees in order to assure that the royal White Elephants have the appropriate qualities in appearance and behavior. The White Elephant is also associated with honor, and the Royal Order of the White Elephant is bestowed as the nation's highest official award. As an ongoing symbol of state power, Thailand's late monarch, King Bhumibol Adulyadej, had ten White Elephants, which were housed at his royal palaces throughout the land. (See plate 13 of a holy White Elephant.)

In neighboring Myanmar, White Elephants are exhibited in the capital Nay Pyi Taw. Laitongrian Meepan, owner of the royal elephant Kraal in Ayutthaya Province and the largest Asian elephant breeder, asserts that: "[A royal] White Elephant is an honourable position. Not all 'white' elephants are entitled to such an honour. They have to perform good deeds. . . . (In the past) they died for us in wars. They helped build cities. They fought on foreign soils for us. And they helped generate income for us."[11] As in most countries where they are revered and considered to have godlike status, elephants are nonetheless treated as commodities. Captivity is captivity regardless of the style of imprisonment.

TODAY'S ELEPHANTS

Similar to bears and lions, elephants have a matrilineal culture. The male and female calves are raised primarily by females. On average, they are weaned at four years of age, with male elephant bulls leaving the family between nine and twelve to engage in a second stage of socialization with older bulls. Females remain with the natal family.

The matriarch that is the oldest of the females will be in charge of the family or herd. The male elephants travel with other male elephants and they all interact in an amorphous network. Normally an elephant and its family will walk up to fifty miles daily, or even more depending on the availability of food and water. Watering holes are social gathering places where social etiquette, grooming, playing, and camaraderie are fostered. Groups of varying sizes come together at these watering holes as well as at dense grazing areas where eating and socializing go together.

When bulls mature in their late twenties or early thirties, they experience musth, the period when reproductive hormones levels rise and the bulls seek a mate. Those familiar with the elephant nature know that, like a reckless adolescent, sometimes the bulls act out. Most bulls have been eliminated from today's zoos and circuses because of their power, their independent intolerance of brutality, and often their intolerance of captivity itself. This has had the effect of further destroying the innate culture of elephants in captivity worldwide.

The matriarch plays the role of respected elder who leads the natal family. She is the keeper of wisdom. The beneficial impact of elephants on the ecosystem is what makes Elephant the pinnacle of an entire ecosystem. They are apex herbivores, in counterpoint to lions and bears, which are apex carnivores and apex omnivores, respectively. As apex, or keystone, animals in their ecosystems, elephants are sometimes referred to as bioengineers. They, like farmers, spread native seed in the field wherever they go, through their excrement, or dung. The African forest elephants, which eat berries, fruits, and other seeded plant life, disperse more seeds in their habitat than any other African forest animal. While also spreading seed the greatest distance, their dung is natural fertilizer. An elephant digests only 50 percent of what it eats. Thus, many other species feed on elephant excrement for the rich nutrients it provides.

Elephants can reach into high branches of trees to shake down and obtain fruit, which also feeds warthogs, kudu, and baboons. As competent well diggers, they know the location of underground sources of water. They roll in shallow water holes to cover and protect their delicate skin from the heat of the sun. Needing other dispersers of heat because they do not have sweat glands, their ears act as large fans, releasing heat efficiently from their massive bodies. When elephants widen watering holes and deepen them, they improve that aquatic resource for the entire habitat community.

By pushing over trees, consuming bark, and trampling over areas repeatedly, elephants change forested lands into savannas, thereby creating thriving grazing lands for numerous other species. When elephants leave a forested area they will frequently have opened up the forest canopies in that area, bringing sunlight to the forest floor. This benefits gorillas, bush pigs, buffalo, and others. As we saw with Bear and its impacts, and Lion in its homeland, without the elephants in Asia and Africa massive ecosystems will be decimated and an accelerated die-off of species and plant life will occur.

Elephants (family *Elephantidae*) are the largest land mammals on Earth—herbivores supping on roots, leaves, and grasses. Centuries ago there were 350 different species of elephants. Today, there are only two: the Asian elephant and the African elephant with its two subspecies (though it is debated if they are actually that separate): the African savanna and African forest elephant. There are four subspecies of Asian elephants including the Borneo or pygmy, the Sumatran, the Indian, and the Sri Lankan.

The average baby elephant weighs about two hundred pounds. The fully grown Asian female and male weigh between four thousand and ten thousand pounds. The African male elephant can weigh as much as seventeen thousand pounds. As anyone who works with them knows, elephants are astoundingly gentle. They walk as if on air. Also, the sounds of their calls echo across landscapes wherever they range. They are in general patient with humans but when chronically abused will retaliate. This has happened infrequently in zoos, entrainment lockups, and in villages that encroach on their territories or when their young are stolen for training as workers, which often ends in early death. Herd members will make clear that they are not unconscious beings, but very much aware of transgressions by humans.

If we run our hands across the skin of an African elephant, we find that it is noticeably wrinkled. Our hands will tell us that she has a single hump on her head. The smaller Asian elephant has smooth skin and two distinguishing humps on her head. Yet it is the larger African elephant that has two finger-like appendages on her trunk.

Fig. 4.3. African elephants

These work like our own hand's thumb and opposing index finger. The Asian elephant has only a single appendage at the end of her trunk. In addition to the scale and weight of their bodies, it is their trunks especially that make them unique in making and using tools. Despite outward differences, the various elephant species share traits and natures in common.

Zoologists, when looking at animal behavior, associate all elephants with the primates (apes) and cetaceans (whales, dolphins, manatees). All of them exhibit common characteristics such as self-awareness and the ability to communicate with their own species and others at great distances. Elephants express emotion of all kinds, retain memories over decades of time, and follow specific matrilineal routines, roles, and routes. They learn performance and creative arts as well as how to execute audio mimicry and perform musical accompaniment. Elephants can be taught to do an unnatural headstand, and in the modern era have been engaged in painting pictures using brushes held by their trunks. They can also play musical instruments and sing in their own fashion.

The Thai Elephant Orchestra was founded and is directed by David Sulzer, a neuroscientist at Columbia University. He is also a composer. The Thai Elephant Orchestra has produced three albums of sanctuary elephants playing instruments built for them to use, replicating the sounds of traditional Thai instruments.[12] As sanctuary caregivers point out, this too is an exploitation of elephants and is possible only because they are in captivity—and still they are being used as a commodity by which humans can make an income. One hopes this kind of exploitation will stop so that all elephants can experience natural freedom.

When in close proximity to each other, elephants are very tender, touching and entwining each other's trunks, which, as mentioned earlier, have over one thousand individual muscles, making the trunk a sophisticated sensory and physical tool. They also rub bodies and hold each other's tails for emotional as well as communal protection. Mothers use their trunks to connect with calves walking with them. There is no mistaking the body language of loving, nurturing, and gleeful play, protection, and communication that takes place in the elephant culture.

THE INHUMANE SOCIETY

To appreciate the present story of these gentle mammoth beings who have walked on Earth since their divergence from the wooly mammoth six million years ago, it is critical to know that African elephants numbered in the millions at the turn of the twentieth century. Now they teeter on the brink of extinction. The ivory trade, which has flourished since the first century, and human appropriation of land, has decimated these species. African elephants are killed en masse by guns, poisoned, and hacked to death for their ivory incisors (tusks) that can reach lengths up to eleven feet and can weigh as much as 250 pounds.

Real ivory is still sought after even though polymers have been created to replace it. Ivory is desired for its softness and ease of carving but polymers are adequate in this way as well. Several centuries of colonization in Africa, which has included institutionalized game hunting, is accountable in large measure for the declining elephant population there, as well as the decline of other species. The legacy of patriarchal cruelty and obscene domination of the landscape, the wildlife, and the Native peoples now pervades the African continent in an endless cycle of trauma and violence.

It is my belief that the failure of African nations to protect these great noble elephant teachers and their lion kings destroyed the deeper currents that run between the ecological ethos of all peoples and their spiritual teachings. Africa has been taken over by the culture of AK-47s, brutality to women and children, especially—massacres in the name and symbol of totemic, heroic power. The mass murdering and indenturement of elephants and people of all ages are tied into an underground economy that finances the trafficking of humans, weapons, and drugs. Government sanctioned culling involves the obliteration of entire elephant families, which are being shot from helicopters and jeeps in what is a most savage form of animalcide. It is a barbarism against the sacred.

The elephant civilization now mirrors that of humans. Communities have been literally and figuratively dismembered. Elephants in captivity are enslaved for labor, commerce, entertainment, or zoo-directed breeding programs, like their human counterparts who are made captive for sex entertainment and free labor.

Gay Bradshaw emphasizes that there is only one way out of the destruction taking place worldwide, and that is by undertaking radical personal and cultural change.[13] Her research documents the science demonstrating sentient consciousness in animals that, like ourselves, enjoy family, culture, story, and play, and in parallel, are vulnerable to suffering and trauma. Bradshaw established the field of trans-species psychology to underscore "how the corpus of science has established human-animal comparability in mind, brain, and consciousness, meaning we are very similar to each other in our makeup." Elephants, similar to human victims of war and genocide, are collapsing from the symptoms of post-traumatic stress disorder. The ongoing slaughtering of the African elephants for their tusks and the kidnapping of Asian elephants for use in labor or entertainment have led to an overall destruction of their herds, their matriarchal hierarchies, and their sense of being, belonging, and education. All of this trauma and displacement has had devastating effects on the elephants' psychological and physical well-being.

"Western scholarship," Bradshaw highlights, "has labored under a two-tiered system of difference where concepts, language, and methods are segregated according to categories of human or nonhuman animal. The rationale for such division stems from the assumption that nonhuman animals lack higher-order faculties considered unique to humans. Critically, animals have been denied voice. This has led to ethical and legal standards, which permit the use and abuse of animals in ways prohibited for humans. However, as theory and data accumulated since Darwin demonstrated, all vertebrates share common brain structures and processes that govern cognition, emotions, and consciousness. A trans-species psychology understands nonhuman animals as conscious, sentient beings. This approach moves beyond ethograms (a kind of behavioral inventory) and other ethological methods by conceptualizing animal expressions as *symptoms* rather than signs.

"For example, from a traditional behaviorist standpoint, stereotypes, which in elephants is often repeated swaying or head bobbing, have no goal or function. But, from a psychological standpoint, stereotypes are externalizations of profound internal distress, [outward signs of inner imbalances]. By recognizing symptoms as voice, a psychological lens removes the silencing effects of objectification." Rather than seeing animals as things, when we relate to them as feeling, thinking, self-aware beings like our own species, we enter into an entirely new and reciprocal relationship.

"Trans-species psychology," explains Bradshaw, "integrates data and theory from neuroscience, psychology, and mythology that speaks to the fact that we share pretty much the same things. In other words, you don't need two different ways of looking at human and animal minds. It takes the same theory, the same perspective to really understand what animals are thinking and feeling just as we do with humans." How clever of us to design an entire scientific, academic, and livestock industry that dissociates itself from the trauma and pain it is responsible for.

"We tend to forget that animal cultures like those of the elephants," Bradshaw highlights, "are really a vast civilization. So to really understand the elephant [and any other species] and the elephants' lives, you have to study them in an historical way. We see that elephants used to inspire a feeling of awe in humans but today, because of the trade in ivory, poaching, habitat destruction, culling (which are orchestrated killings), capture for zoos and so on, elephant society has been fractured into psychic fragments. It's been dismembered, Zohara, as you put it. . . . Many of the young elephants are motherless."

Bradshaw makes clear that, as we see in human society, the loss of parenting has tremendous impacts on the elephants' matriarchal system—traditional learning, knowledge, and values that are historically passed on to the calves through the female elephants. This has been truncated and lost. "The science that we use as our epistemic authority," notes Bradshaw, "that talks about animals having feelings and ways of thinking like we do, of having a particular culture and all sorts of experiences like humans have in community, contradicts the rationale used to kill animals. Humans can harm or kill a wolf, a bear, a puma, a shark, and any other animal legally because it is assumed that animals do not possess lives of value in the way that humans are assumed to have. And yet science shows that this is not true. The agencies and scientists in charge of making decisions about wildlife ignore the truth, the science, for the purpose of making money and exercising power."

Bradshaw is not alone in her understanding. Even "neuropsychologists," she clarifies with regard to scientific acknowledgement of animals' awareness, "are making another point—that you can't evaluate human suffering by traumatizing other species and studying them. The modern mind has created a very dramatic ability for dissociation. But trauma does not stop with the victim. It comes back and repeats. The turmoil modern humans have inside is now mirrored in the land, animals, and Earth."

Being able to say one thing and do another, to cause harm to another species and not feel that suffering in oneself through compassion or empathy, makes a statement about human beings, not animals. These are imbalances in the human being that become very clear when we do an honest self-evaluation of our conduct on Earth. "We need to feel connected with other species and ourselves," as Bradshaw puts it. "This is a very profound phenomenon that really marks our culture. We think of ourselves as dis-connected from nature. But we are never disconnected, we only *feel* disconnected, and as many, many scientists and spiritual leaders have pointed out, this misperception has caused the profound destruction we see today. The suffering of the elephant is no different from our own. Their losses are losses to our own souls and lives."

We see the same pattern of abuse across species. Whether it is rats and rabbits in labs, monkeys or mice, cows and their calves, hens and their broods abused on their way to becoming table food or food by-products, all suffer from the institutionalized violence that characterizes our modern era. What trans-species psychology elucidates has been recognized by indigenous peoples for millennia: the understanding of human-animal comparability. We know that animals share with purpose and protect others. Observation of them in their own environments proves this. We know animals have a sense of self and belonging, personality, differences in intellect, styles of play, family, food preferences, and that they experience the loss of their own kind and other kin with grief. "The whole scientific point is that animals share feelings and emotions like we do," Bradshaw rightly claims. "And the difference is almost like the difference in cultures between people."

Scientists and sanctuary leaders like Gay Bradshaw show us there is much less difference between animals and us. "Science is really calling us and saying, 'Well, if that's the case, then we need to have the same kinds of consideration for other species that we have in respect for ourselves.'"

Another woman world renowned for her care and protection of elephants is Dame Daphne Sheldrick, who has worked with elephants for more than fifty years and in 1992 was named as a United Nations Environment Programme Global 500 Laureate. She is an author, conservationist, and expert in animal husbandry, and is especially knowledgeable about the care and rehabilitation of young orphaned elephants. One of her notable accomplishments is having come up with the formula to replicate a mother elephant's milk, allowing her to successfully raise young orphaned elephants whose mothers had been killed by poachers. Devising this formula took twenty-eight years and was a constant process of trial and error. But finally, having determined the crucial, missing element of the formula—coconut oil—she found success.

Dame Sheldrick believes that the reason we humans have empathy for elephants is because we are so similar to them. Among other things, "Elephants share with us humans many traits—the same span of life, (three score years and ten, all being well)," Dame Sheldrick writes, "and they develop at a parallel pace so that at any given age a baby elephant duplicates its human counterpart, reaching adulthood at the age of twenty. Elephants also display many of the attributes of humans as well as some of the failings. They share with us a strong sense of family and death and they feel many of the same emotions. Each one is, of course, like us, a unique individual with its own unique personality." I and many other animal caregivers know this to be true. "They can be happy or sad, volatile or placid," she explains. "They display envy, jealousy, throw tantrums and are fiercely competitive, and they can develop hang-ups, which are reflected in behaviour."[14]

Dame Sheldrick also makes note of the attributes they have that we sometimes lack. They have "incredible long-range infrasound, communicating in voices we never hear, such sophisticated hearing that even a footfall is heard far away, and, of course they have a memory that far surpasses ours and spans a lifetime. They grieve deeply for lost loved ones, even shedding tears and suffering depression. They have a sense of compassion that projects beyond their own kind and sometimes extends to others in distress. They help one another in adversity, miss an absent loved one, and when you know them really well, you can see that they even smile when they are having fun and are happy."[15]

Dame Sheldrick founded the David Sheldrick Wildlife Trust in memory of her late husband, the famous naturalist and founding warden of Tsavo East National Park in Kenya. The trust saves elephants wounded or lost from animalcide. An example is the young elephant Ndotto, born August 5, 2014, and one-and-a-half-year-old Zongoloni, found, like many elephant orphans are, standing guard over her collapsed and dying mother, a victim of human brutality. The Sheldrick wildlife trust makes it possible for anyone to foster an elephant by contributing financial support.* The trust's website is full of amazing rescue stories of elephants, black rhinos, and other wildlife in its care.

---

*According to the David Sheldrick Wildlife Trust's website (www.sheldrickwildlifetrust .org), the aim of the Orphans' Project is to rear the orphaned elephants in such a way that they grow up psychologically sound and in the fullness of time take their place back where they rightly belong, and where they can enjoy a normal wildlife among the wild elephant community of Tsavo National Park. Elephants need space. The Tsavo Conservation Area is over sixty-four thousand square kilometers in extent, and as such can provide the space an elephant needs. No space in captivity is adequate for an elephant, however attractive it may appear to us humans.

TRANS-SPECIES TELEPATHY
IN THE ELEPHANT

The nonlocality of consciousness that humans sometimes experience is clearly demonstrated in the natural use of telepathy by elephants—and by dogs, bears, birds, and between species as well. In 2003, Lawrence Anthony, a noted environmentalist and author, founded a wildlife conservation organization, the Earth Organization, in South Africa. The books he authored include *The Elephant Whisperer: My Life with the Herd in the African Wild* and, with Graham Spence, *Babylon's Ark: The Incredible Wartime Rescue of the Baghdad Zoo,* and his posthumously published book, *The Last Rhinos: My Battle to Save One of the World's Greatest Creatures.* He died in his sleep on March 2, 2012, at his home on the Thula Thula Private Game Reserve in South Africa.

Several days later, more than twenty elephants from two herds arrived over a period of twelve hours, congregating around his home. They lingered there for two days, demonstrating their feelings for a lost friend. Their homage also was testimony to their telepathic capacity, for none had been there in over a year and a half. Each year since then, on the anniversary of his death, they make the same trek to his home to honor their deceased friend.

Lawrence Anthony saved these elephants from certain death when, in 1999, an acquaintance called him and requested that he take them in, explaining that otherwise they would be killed. Having had no experience with elephants, he nevertheless agreed to give it a try. The elephants were introduced to Thula Thula and, over the years, he became their friend. He slept among them at times, as he explains in his writings, and became a trusted member of their community. His leadership, patience, and compassion returned their dignity and freedom after their prior experience of trauma and terror perpetrated by other men. Anthony, like others whose lives are devoted to elephants and the animals, understood the elephants' needs, communicated with them to answer their concerns, and appreciated their deep emotional attachments and delightful sense of loving play.

For his love, generosity, and care, upon his passing, they went to say thank-you and good-bye. They loved him and honored him with their own elephant funeral procession and wake. They knew of his passing because elephants, like all animals, are intimately connected to all humans and to each other, but especially to those who show them kindness—or the inverse, those who are brutal to any of their species. They, like most of us thousands of years ago, have extrasensory perception that is keenly developed.[16]

RITUALS FOR THE DEAD

It has been demonstrated conclusively that the dismembered remains of a dead elephant are visited by living family members. They will even carry the deceased to an appropriate burial area or retrieve bones and return them to the site where the body lays dead or decaying. They will also pick up bones, touch them with their trunk, or raise their foot over the body to take some sort of informational calculation, perhaps identifying what group the deceased body is from or how recently it has died. They will cover the dead with leaves, branches, and grasses and mourn the deceased with visible tears and sounds of loss. People familiar with these sounds of loss say they are akin to a mourners' chorus, which even the birds seem to notice. When a calf dies not only the mother but other matriarchs as well will produce sounds comparable to the way humans cry. They may grieve into the night and often remain several days beside the body of the herd member in obvious and tearful bereavement.

This demonstration of telepathy is well-known in the literature of animal communication. As noted author and parapsychology researcher Rupert Sheldrake, Ph.D., articulated in his book *Dogs That Know When Their Owners Are Coming Home,* animals communicate telepathically at a distance. I have had hundreds of conversations with animals and do so today as part of my own volunteer service in speaking for animal beings that other humans are unable to hear. Whether it's someone's lost cat stuck under a deck or a deceased dog visiting to say thank-you, whether it's a bonobo matriarch telling me about bonobos taking care of discarded human infants during the Ice Age or foxes and deer asking for supplemental food due to scarcity in winter—I hear their messages. Modern Westerners tend to see this as a remarkable gift or something strange, "new age" mumbo jumbo. But, as we have learned, telepathy between species is ancient and real and vital to our collaboration on Earth.

Unlike most modern humans, animals have not lost their trans-species capacities and transdimensional awareness. It is the human population whose talent for this form of universal communication has atrophied. J. Allen Boone (1882–1965), a *Washington Post* correspondent and caregiver of a German shepherd film star named Strongheart, wrote the magnificent pathbreaking work *Kinship with All Life*. In it he tells wonderful, true stories about nonverbal communication between animals, insects, and humans. Such communication is a constant theme in popular culture throughout humankind's history, giving other forms of sentient life position and importance as trusted and loved companions and guides, helpers, and friends, viewed by Native traditions as custodians of Earth and star wisdom.

In addition to the supersensible ability to communicate outside of the constraints of time and space, elephants use audio and seismic communication through vocalizations and stomping their feet. Other animals, such as rabbits, white-tailed deer, and banner-tailed kangaroo rats, to name a few, do this as well. Tusk digging sends signals through the substrata of the Earth to distant relatives, as does percussive foot drumming. This is a common method of location to location communication between species and is why Native peoples use smoke signals as a way of alerting other tribespeople and kin at a distance to tune in psychically for messages. Drumming and dance tell the receiver about the other's status—whether they are in danger or preparing for combat or courtship. Those with their ear to the ground or, in the elephants' case, their foot to the ground, are receiving or sending information for others to hear.

Caitlin O'Connell-Rodwell, Ph.D., a biologist and ecologist at Stanford University, observed while doing research with her colleagues on mitigating conflicts between elephants and farmers "that elephants actively facilitate localization of seismic signals . . . aligning themselves perpendicular to the source, placing their ears the greatest distance apart from the source, presumably serving to maximize the interaural time differences (ITD) used for localization of low-frequency sounds."[17]

MANKIND'S ABUSE OF THE ELEPHANT

I met elephants for the first time as most Westerners do, at the zoo—the Baltimore Zoo in Maryland, to be exact. It is the nation's third oldest zoo and was founded in 1876 by an act of the Maryland General Assembly. In those days, in the 1950s, one could buy peanuts from a vendor, strategically placed by the elephant house, to feed to the elephants. But the elephants' captivity made me sad. Knowing that even my dogs had more freedom than all the animals at the zoo was a devastating realization. The tenacious practice of keeping elephants in zoos, despite it having been openly established that this is detrimental to their health, derives from a strange combination of things. People are told that zoos help elephants because they are protected in captivity and in the wild they are killed. Yes, it is true that they are killed in the wild, but in captivity they suffer the life of a prisoner who has had his or her family taken away, and has to endure brutal "training."

Zoo life is nothing like life in the wild. In the zoo, elephants are frequently housed in concrete structures with little space to move around in. Outside, their surrounding areas are not anything like their homelands, where they may migrate for hundreds of miles a season. Female and male elephants in captivity run the risk of becoming infertile from the stress of imprisonment. They are also masturbated and artificially

Fig. 4.4. Adam Forepaugh's White Elephant—Light of Asia—in New York City,
being transferred from a steamship to a barge for shipment to Philadelphia
Frank Leslie's Illustrated Newspaper, April 1884

inseminated so that they produce baby elephants, a proven moneymaker for zoos and circuses.

The rate of infanticide and early death of captive elephants is astounding and testifies to elephants' deep need to be in control of their fate, emotionally, physically, and biologically. The mean life expectancy of elephants in European zoos is fifteen years for Asian elephants and sixteen years for African elephants, meaning that they are dying fifty years sooner than they would in the wild.[18] I am aware of one particular zoo's elephant exhibit that is sponsored by a children's pediatric hospital, which is obviously devoted to healing children. This is a great irony to me, for it is a telling example of our cultural blindness to animal suffering.

Our desensitization to the inner life and the abject quality of life that wild animals have in captivity is global. We gloss over their loss and celebrate our emotional and sometimes zoological gains at their expense. Zoos claim that they provide education about conservation to the public. But what children and their families learn about in this case is an elephant on the point of total psychological and/or physical collapse. Today, the new and more popular theme of justifying these multimillion-dollar "species' prisons" is done by suggesting that the only way we may preserve certain species is by breeding those already in captivity, and by maintaining them in captivity. Again, this is a story about humans justifying our impacts on wildlife and the Earth. The captivity of wild animals is not due to wildlife's impact on humanity or terrestrial landscapes. People believe they are helping the elephants and other captive wildlife at the zoos. This way of thinking is customary, but it needs to be transformed into a species-centered awareness, making the preservation of the animals' native habitats and their freedom our collective priority. This is authentic conservation and species protection.

According to the UN Refugee Agency, one out of every 122 people on Earth is currently uprooted from their home due to war, persecution, or poverty.[19] It is estimated by the World Economic Forum that climate change may add another 25 million to 1 billion people worldwide who will be forced from their homes over the coming decades.[20] This involuntary separation from one's place of origin, often from a multigenerational homeland, has precipitated a violent, abusive, and dangerous human slave trade. The elephants' story of capture, abuse, and exploitation is a prelude to our own. Their disappearance may become our own story—it's as if we are walking in their gentle, though massive, footsteps to our own demise.

In 2000, between 13,000 and 16,500 elephants were captured with lasso, traps, and tranquilizers in Asia. Kidnapped when young or later in life, they will have long working lives under the care and domination of a mahout who has generally a long family tradition of raising, training, and caring for elephants as a way of life and a means of making a living. In India these partnerships can begin at the birth of both child and calf. But like other cultures that exploit elephants, violent torture and chronic abuse is used to break the elephants' own natural instincts, making them like prisoners of war—captive inmates always alert to any noise, action, or step humans in control may make. They are in constant hyperalert, or the reverse: they are catatonic from years of captivity and oftentimes from abuse.

Carol Buckley, founder and director of Elephant Aid International and founder and former director of the Elephant Sanctuary in Tennessee, "is considered the world's foremost expert on adult elephant trauma recovery and care having worked over forty years in the field, first in the circus then as an elephant rehabilitator and activist."[21] (See plate 14 of Carol Buckley with an elephant friend.) Her work with elephants in captivity in the United States and Canada extended recently to work with elephants in Thailand, India, and Nepal. She conducted a series of interviews entitled "From Agony to Ecstasy" with Gay Bradshaw (referenced earlier), for *Psychology Today*.[22] (All of the following quotations from Buckley in this section derive from this series of articles.)

Buckley describes the process that elephants endure to make them completely submissive to human handlers. *Phajaan* is a practice employed to break an elephant's spirit, which profoundly changes the animal. It is simply animal torture, which is no different from what humans do to each other under the perverse banner of war. War breaks people and engenders post-traumatic stress syndrome in countless individuals the world over.

Buckley explains that in the process of phajaan, "a young elephant is forcibly taken from his/her mother and confined in a wooden pen called a crush that is barely bigger than the baby elephant; the legs are tied down to posts of the pen so they cannot lie or sit down or turn around. Over the next few weeks, the infant elephant is provided limited water and food, is deprived of companionship, given no shelter from the sun and elements, which in itself can be quite harsh and life-threatening. As if that is not enough," she adds, "Then [they are] relentlessly beaten, stabbed, and frightened with fire by the *mahouts* (the men in charge of elephants) with an array of metal and wooden weapons."

"Their mouths and tender trunks and anus," Buckley continues, with words that make any feeling person wince, "are also prodded and made to bleed. The baby is terrified, defecates and urinates from fear and pain. It is a horror. This continues until it is evident that the ritualistic breaking has been successful."

She points out as well that most people meet their first elephants in a zoo, and when we see them rocking, pacing, swaying, head bobbing, and displaying other repetitive behaviors, it is not because this is natural or that they are happy, as visitors are often told. These neurotic habits are the result of trauma and deprivation. Observing this kind of repetitive neurosis in many captive elephants will change your experience of any zoo.

In zoos, no captive elephant enjoys a habitat like the one they had in the wild. They may seem adequate to us, but they can't be compared to the native environments the elephants would inhabit if free, nor the happiness built into any species' self-determination.

Describing the horrendous ordeal of elephants that has been emulated in the West by zoos and circuses, Buckley makes clear that this phajaan breaking developed initially in the tribal communities of India and Asia. Zoos and circuses chain the elephants' legs "to the ground, preventing the baby from moving in any direction. Like their counterparts in Asia and India," she points out that "they too are provided limited water and food, deprived of companionship, and relentlessly harassed with sharp metal bull hooks until they comply with the human 'trainer' consistently. Not only are the practices and intent similar in the West and in India and Asia, but the mindset of the men torturing the elephants is the same. Their approach to training elephants is hauntingly similar. To this day circus elephant trainers think, talk about, and act toward elephants exactly the same way as do the mahouts in Asia."

The impact of these breakings is readily obvious, as is the trauma of captivity in zoos and circuses. One will often note that captive

Fig. 4.5. An elephant and its mahout
From *Diversi capricci* by Stefano della Bella (1610–1664)

elephants have sunken and dull eyes. They may be lame from stand-ing on unnatural floors of concrete, or in many cases suffer from poor care and malnutrition. "But when you see an elephant in the wild who has grown up with his/her family and has been able to live like an elephant should, and was evolved to do," Buckley emphasizes like a mother fawning over her beautiful children, "it is a completely dif-ferent story. They are full of life, they play, and their eyes sparkle. The light inside is shining bright, whereas in many captive-held ele-phants, the light has gone out." The same thing has been observed in other animals, such as buffalo held in corrals versus those still able to migrate in open territories.

Like the transformation of the White Bear Rain Forest's calculated efforts to protect the bears there from being hunted, and the Maasai's protective stance pertaining to lion hunting and killing, Buckley is doing the same thing among the cultures that employ elephants for their livelihoods. To help teach mahouts and others working with elephants, she offers Compassionate Elephant Care trainings, which her organization, Elephant Aid International, teaches. It is "a system of caring for and handling captive-held elephants that is free of dominance, punishment and infliction of pain. It enables a caregiver or mahout to manipulate the elephant's behavior, while maneuvering safely around or atop him/her in a free-contact environment."[23]

Buckley, like others, works tirelessly to see the end of elephant captivity in zoos, circuses, and other unnatural imprisonments. She also plans on opening a new elephant sanctuary in the United States. It will house former circus and zoo elephants that cannot be released to the wild but who need to be cared for properly and given back the autonomy they deserve—to be elephants in a natural setting. Carol Buckley is the quintessential elephant guardian and may be considered to be an elephant shaman, one who enters their lives to help heal them and the world through nonverbal communication.

But clearly, despite the propaganda about our cultural habits, elephants in zoos, circuses, and those used for labor of other sorts are abused and deprived of natural life and freedom from violence. This deprivation and chronic centuries-long abuse of elephants is what makes the sacred White Elephant that much more of an anomaly. Among elephants, only the White Elephant can be assured that humans will provide them with some kindness, protection, and little work, though they too are taken into captivity, depriving them of their beloved families' sacred routes, communities, and natural course of life. Any living being deprived of autonomy, freedom of movement, sustenance, and bonds of kin develops psychological and physical maladies, whether in the human or animal kingdoms. Indeed we are very much alike.

Sad to say, there are only approximately three hundred fifty thousand African elephants and an estimated thirty-five thousand to forty-five thousand wild Asian elephants alive today. Mike Chase, founder of Elephants Without Borders, says that if the current trends continue, "in 10 years' time we could lose 50 percent of Africa's remaining elephants."[24] If the same kind of murder was visited on human beings worldwide, 50 percent of 7.3 billion people would be dead (this equates to more than 3.6 billion people). Every other one of us would be killed. If you have four children, two would be murdered. If you have a spouse or partner, one of you would be attending the other's funeral.

Only some male Asian elephants have tusks, making these creatures less vulnerable to being poached for their ivory but more at risk of being kidnapped and forced into a life of indentured servitude. Most female Asian elephants do not have tusks. In Africa, however, it is a different story. African elephants, both male and female, have tusks, and all of the old male tuskers are targeted by hunters. As well, the poachers continue to go after the matriarchs and the younger elephants, with tusks the size of a ruler. In Kenya on May 30, 2014, a beloved elephant named Satao was shot with a poisoned arrow and then had his tusks removed with a chainsaw. Satao's face was so maimed that he could only be identified by his ear, by mud patches on his body, and by other personal markings that park rangers were familiar with. Kenyans everywhere were bereaved and I too wept when I saw the images on a CNN report. It's sobering to see these great, amazing holy animals reduced to murder victims and to witness their killer's role in humanity's insatiable hunger for their tusks in exchange for weapons, cash, and power.

One of the largest mass elephant slaughters in decades took place in Bouba Ndjidah National Park, Cameroon, in 2012. Armed with grenades and AK-47s, more than three hundred matriarchs, babies, and bulls were slaughtered. During 2011 alone, one out of every twelve African elephants was killed in similar animalcide. Central Africa has already lost 64 percent of its entire elephant community—one hundred thousand elephants were killed in three years. "Revenues from the ivory trade currently benefit criminal gangs, corrupt military units, and terrorist groups such as Al-Shabaab in Kenya and the Lord's Resistance Army in Uganda and Sudan. . . . The price of a dead elephant to a poacher or corrupt official is significantly less than is paid at the other end of the supply chain. . . . But when compared to wage levels in poverty stricken, rural communities, it's a significant amount." One killer said he received $550 for ninety-four pounds of ivory (almost forty-three kilos; he made $12.80 per kilo) yet as one goes up the illegal market chain, the value in China for raw ivory can be as much as $2,100 per kilo.[25]

And in terms of calculated murders and shipments of elephant babies to Chinese and American zoos, the elephants' troubles keep increasing. Costing less to ship when very young, since cost is by the pound, separating elephants from their mothers and family can hardly be called, as zoos claim, a tool in conservation. Marc Bekoff, professor emeritus of ecology and evolutionary biology at the University of Colorado in Boulder, makes clear that "The shameful complicity of the zoos is being sold as 'conservation,' when it's nothing more than a business deal to restock zoos' elephant exhibits."[26] Conservation by its very nature is meant to return wildlife to their natural environments.

COUNTING ELEPHANTS

The largest wildlife census ever undertaken was begun in February 2014 with a goal of surveying the whole of Africa's elephant population. The survey was conducted by air, with more than ninety researchers taking part. The combined distance of this undertaking, as one report explained, "is like flying to the moon and a quarter of the way back—or circling the globe eleven and a half times."[27] There was hope that the news would be positive. It was not.

The International Union for the Conservation of Nature (IUCN) is the organization that determines the conservation status of any given species. The information that they collected on the status of elephants, the Great Elephant Census, in Africa is harrowing. Their report, released in March of 2016 reports a 30 percent overall decrease in the elephant population, primarily due to barbaric poaching. "One of the most shocking discoveries is a 53 percent free fall in elephant numbers in Tanzania—from an estimated 109,000 animals in 2009 to 51,000 in 2015. A recent study published in the journal *Science,* showed that for more than a decade Tanzania has been the main source of illegal elephant ivory shipped out of East Africa."[28]

The Great Elephant Census found increasing numbers of elephants in some areas, stabilization in others, and serious declines elsewhere. In response to earlier declines in Tanzania, the Tanzania Wildlife Authority was established to expand elephant habitat and protection in the Selous Game Reserve in Ruaha-Rungwa. Over twelve hundred square miles were added to the Ruaha National Park for the same reasons.[29] One hopes this report of the elephants' serious demise and the ecosystems they maintain becomes a wake-up call to conservation planners and international law enforcement to protect our planet's elephants.

There are already indications that this is happening, that pressure worldwide is proving to be effective in ending the demand for elephant ivory. The United States, under president Barack Obama, stepped up to the challenge when it established framework protocols in 2016 that severely restrict the commercial trade of African elephant ivory, resulting in a near complete sales ban. Today, ivory may only be bought and sold when accompanied by documentation proving it is of a certain age, and also that it was legally imported. More recently, ivory exports have been restricted, and trophies derived from sport hunting have been further curtailed as well.

The bigger, more exciting news is that China, where 70 percent of the world's ivory products end up, announced in 2016 that it would close its legal trade by the end of 2017. If this does indeed happen, odds are very good the elephant populations will rebound significantly across all of Africa.

There are economic as well as ethical and spiritual reasons for keeping elephants alive. A single elephant that lives out its seventy to eighty years of life is worth seventy-six times more alive than dead, given that it is capable of bringing in an estimated "1.6 million dollars in ecotourism."[30] Once again, the White Spirit Animals and their species contribute to a locale's tourism dollars. It's interesting to contemplate that our economic needs in the locations in which all these species thrive may drive human protection of them all, demonstrating how we can turn the death economy into a life economy where no one is harmed—human or animal—and life is restored to greater balance.

DREAM RESEARCH

While dreaming with elephants I was told by them "to expect the best from people, but not to sugarcoat the brutality of humanity and to be clear that the choices being made now have such vital impacts on the near and far future." I feel I am honoring their request. It is why the spirit animals came to me in the first place—they are fully aware of how dire a predicament we all are in. We are sitting in "the last chance café" at the end of town so to speak. We can see and know precisely what is the best course of action for restoring the Earth, and we should encourage each other to be part of making these changes.

Dreaming has always been an integral part of my creative process, as has paying attention to waking visions. Both have been the impetus for each of the four books I've authored. The Greeks were renowned for their use of dreams as a healing medium. Dreams were also used for foretelling events as many prophets have described and deepening an understanding of our own lives. C. G. Jung considered dreams to be core material for psychological understanding. Today many transpersonal, Jungian, and humanistic psychologists encourage their clients to recall and study their dreams.

Dream research is not much different from going to a library and looking in a card catalogue by topic or author to find sources on the subject being researched. Today the search engines of the Internet make it possible for a dream researcher to verify, very quickly sometimes, what it is that the unconscious or higher mind imparts through particular dreams. Psychologist and dream research pioneer Stanley Krippner was the director of the Dream Laboratory at the Maimonides Medical Center in Brooklyn, New York, from 1964 to 1973. He explains that "All of us dream about five times a night. It doesn't matter that we don't remember them all. It's really a way the individual is able to sort through the impacts of their experience, and sometimes, when we pay attention to them, they can give us healing information, or answer lifelong questions, or help with someone else's troubles."[31]

As mentioned earlier but bears repeating here, dreams are a way humanity has continued to evolve. Dreaming is a vital skill practiced by shamans worldwide—the ability to gather information from the unseeable but knowable realms, to heal, to derive information, to contact the deceased, to carry on conversations with spirits, to read the intention of others, and/or to facilitate healing for an individual or a whole community. Service and humility, as I have found in doing telepathic work with animals, are key to this amazing holy doorway into our natural extrasensory and telepathic talents.

"Courage, Compassion, and Endurance"

Elephants visited me in a dream when I began this book, and blew soft little puffs of air into my almost broadcast-deafened left ear, tickling it and showering me with affection and appreciation for telling their story. There were about eight adults and three young ones who approached me, tiptoeing in their amazingly graceful way (they do actually walk on their toes!). Sometimes in my dreams I would see them flying, an experience portrayed by the Hindu mythologies whose flying elephants and Airavata, the White Elephant, become the vehicle of Indra, appearing from the churning of the milky ocean.

When I dreamt of a flying elephant I was reminded of the flying, animated film character Dumbo of the 1943 Walt Disney film. He first moved my heart on my sixth birthday, which I celebrated with some of my first-grade friends at the movie theatre where we all learned together, amid popcorn and candy, that this being was kind, and that this big creature loved its mother and its mother loved him.

Some of my elephant dreams seemed more mystical, wherein devas trumpeted the glory of Creation in the heavens, the messengers of wisdom, matriarchs of the universe, guardians of the Earth. In one dream, the snake and the spiral of Creation all seemed to come from the orbit of Elephant and it took me many months to actually understand its meaning. But another night there was a large group of older females that screamed in horror. They were running in chaotic circles as if surrounded by enemies, and stampeding with desperation.

Elephant herds usually travel between three and five mph but can as a group run up to fifteen mph in crisis, and a raging bull can run as fast as thirty mph. In this dream, the elephants later showed me their legs, indicating that this was all that was left of them. They kneeled as if in supplication the way a person might get down and pray for their own lives before an enemy or in petition to God to spare them from death. Their heads were disembodied, their flesh hacked with machetes and riddled with bullets, their babies stolen or left in total desperation and isolation. This dark dream disturbed me for weeks and insisted that I, as they directed, tell their real story and not "sugarcoat" human brutality.

Another elephant dream I had was more like a morning

headline. In it I heard a practiced street barker shouting out loud, over and over again, the essential nature of the elephant and its teaching. There were only three words he repeated: "courage, compassion, and endurance."

I have found being among their spirits—in making an effort to hear their inner stories and historic ones, to express their purpose as great spiritual teachers—both wondrous and heartbreaking. For indeed, they are the most gentle among us. Their patience with humans is unsurpassed. They are the most noble examples and instructors of right living. However, our dishonoring of their role and the abuse they have suffered is shameful. Such tragic karma human beings have created.

My very first dream of elephants was actually a dream about snakes. In the dream I was watching three white, almost translucent snakes that were eating (swallowing) each other. It is fairly easy to see that an elephant's trunk might create an unconscious association with snakes. But what I did not know before I had this dream is that the Lotus Sutra, spoken of earlier, has its own close alliance with snakes, as the following narrative describes. Learning about this after my dream was confirmation that I was on the trail of White Elephant, the way a tracker follows a trail in the physical world—by signs, clues, and hints.

Buddhist tradition says that after the Lotus Sutra's great teachings of liberation were scribed in ink, they were hidden away for five hundred years. After that they were presented to the fourth Buddhist council in Kashmir, which gave them over to a generation who could understand them. But during these five hundred years of waiting they were hidden among the *nagas* or "snake gods" who were sent into an underground kingdom (Naga-loka or Patala-loka) full of beautiful palaces and an abundance of treasure and gems. These beings, composed of a human upper half and a lower half that is the body of a snake, are guardians of treasure. But they are also guardians of water, which takes the form of rivers, seas, and wells, guarding the living treasure for life on Earth.*

This was an important clue for uncovering the spiritual purpose of the White Elephants and their kin. When we watch them play in water, their tremendous happiness and sense of well-being is obvious. (See plate 15 of a baby elephant playing in water.) As adults, elephants are excellent swimmers and in a crisis have been known to swim up to five miles with their trunks above water. Sometimes en route to feeding grounds where they need to cross a deep river, some of the baby calves drown. Without the earth beneath her feet, the mother elephant cannot hold up her young for very long.

Dreaming with Elephant was a vigorous experience. Elephants regularly sent me the pieces they wanted me to share and that I needed in order to tell their story, not simply as it pertains to science and history but about their spiritual purpose as well. Just as we have seen with the White Bear and White Lion, spiritual communities include these special messengers of the wild, and they honor them in their lexicon of consciousness, transformation, and collaboration. They all play a role in some aspect of creation and guardianship, as do the White Wolves and White Buffalo whose stories lie ahead.

There is one more elephant-related dream series I would like to share. For two nights I dreamt of two men whose faces were familiar but I could not identify. After the third night of seeing their faces only as remnants of a dreamscape, it dawned on me who they were when I woke up. They were the television host Charlie Rose and former senator of Virginia John Warner. I wondered why these two men had shown up in my dreams. As explained at the start of this book, each chapter of this

---

*These snake guardians represent prominent beings in Hinduism, and the birth of the serpents is celebrated on *Naga-panchami* in the month of Shravana (July–August) each year. The female *naga*s (*nagini*s or *nagi*s) are serpent princesses of striking beauty. Brahma instructed them only to bite evil people or those who would die early. These beings are said to be of a strong, handsome species that can assume either wholly human or wholly serpentine form; they are potentially dangerous but often beneficial to humans.

work, because it is the animal's point of view profiled, engages humanity through telepathy and dreams—and these dreams offer more evidence of this process. When we ask an animal for their help, if we are sincere, humble, and helpful, they will answer back. Each of the spirit beings and, for that matter, each of the human prophets I have written about in my other books, were my teachers during the creation of each manuscript. By associating with the writing of any deceased teacher or living one, the student comes into rapport with them. By studying the nature and oral teachings of the cultures that revere each of these wise animal messengers, we can come into rapport with their consciousness as well. Through a sincere desire to serve others of any life kingdom—of the mineral, plant, animal, human, and spiritual realms—we are able to have empathy with them, to feel their feelings, and to hear their thoughts.

In this instance, my curiosity was bubbling over trying to figure out what Charlie Rose or John Warner might have to do with elephants. I also wondered if this dream series had another connection to my life, given my history in radio and television broadcasting and covering politics for over three decades. I asked the magic Google by typing in *Charlie Rose* and *elephant* and was quickly shown an important exposé that Rose had hosted on his television program on July 28, 2014, with African Wildlife Foundation's Patrick Bergin and others. It exposed the hideous, illicit, and barbaric ivory trade in elephant tusks.

I then conducted the same kind of minimal search about the five-term Republican senator from Virginia, John William Warner, former secretary of the navy (1972–1974), and chairman of the Senate Armed Services Committee (although the general population may know him as Elizabeth Taylor's sixth husband). I learned that in 1980, during the mock political convention of the Republican Party, while visiting his alma mater—Washington and Lee University—Warner interacted with the party's elephant visitor, Jewel. This may have been a female elephant, Jewell, who Ringling Bros. and Barnum & Bailey Circus bought in 1954 and donated to the Arkansas Zoo in 2011, fifty-seven years later. Their names are the same, despite the slight variation in spelling, and my hunch is that it is the same elephant. On September 8, 2013, Jewell was euthanized at the Arkansas Zoo when she could no longer get up on her own. Whether it was the circus's Jewell or another elephant named Jewel that was befriended by Warner, Elephant was talking to me in my dreams and insisted that I pay attention to the repeated images I saw over several nights.

The day after this dream I happened to watch a 1984 BBC miniseries called *The Jewel in the Crown,* which featured India's elephant worship and that country's use of elephants, especially White Spirit Elephants, in ceremonial parades. I turned on another BBC series

Fig. 4.6. Jewel the elephant with Senator John Warner at
Washington and Lee University in Lexington, Virginia
Reported by Tom Harrison for Washington and Lee University in
the *Lima News,* February 4, 1980

whose main character's name was Jewel, confirming for me that Jewel(1) the elephant had something of import to share. Was she asking me to tell about the well-known Feld company's and other circus's abuse of elephants? Was she pointing to Feld Entertainment's sanctuary for elephants, which the company says is dedicated to the conservation of elephants but is where, in reality, formerly captive animals live out the rest of their very difficult lives?

Was it not significant that, while writing this very chapter, on March 5, 2015, Feld Entertainment's Ringling Bros. announced their plans to discontinue the use of elephants in all of their shows by 2018, thus ending a practice that was one hundred forty-five years long? On May 1, 2016, the last of its thirteen traveling elephants performed their final curtain call in a Rhode Island show. Ending their use of elephants in the circus earlier than planned, Feld Entertainment stated that "When they are moved, 42 Asian elephants will call the [two hundred-acre] Conservation Center home."[32]

The cessation of exploiting and cruelly "breaking elephants" in order to keep them captive and obedient is an answer to a prayer to alleviate the suffering and oppression of these great beings. It has been the goal of activists for decades. In hearing Feld Entertainment's original announcement and news of the early retirement of their elephants, I felt that a jewel in the animal kingdom's crown—the elephant—was shining on us all.

This dream story is a very telling example of the power of dream research. During waking time, one follows the clues acquired in dreamtime. One can also cultivate the dreamscape by asking specific questions before going to sleep, thereby incubating the dreams to come.

I pray that innumerable elephants will be born in freedom to replace the hundreds of thousands of them who have died in shackles and who have met their demise because of human greed. May we revere their natures, emulate their love of children and community, and learn from them the benefit of compassionate action in the world.

WHITE SPIRIT ELEPHANT LESSONS

I would like to close our journey in the Buddhic way, with the White Elephant and its kin, and encourage everyone to learn more from and to be inspired and educated by their dreams. Simply ask, before going to sleep, to resolve some issue or learn how to do something or to get information about a person you are out of contact with. When our body rests, our soul and mind have an opportunity to collaboratively access the subtler realms of existence where all potential stirs around and within us.

Dreams help us access the collective unconscious, our own histories, and much older ancestral ties, as well as all of life everywhere and *everywhen*. The dream process detailed in writing this book is the same dream practice of shamans, medicine men and women, and other intuitives who use dreams as a part of their own spiritual search. I did not invent these stories; they are simply a record of my process of using dreams to listen to other forms of life.

I asked Elephant for guidance, as I have each species written about in this book. It is each animal's consciousness and voice that I want to give volume to. So I trust that when I dream of a certain animal while writing about them, each is in fact communicating what is meaningful to them or what they feel might be meaningful to others, from their collective experience. Of course, there are other explanations as to the source of these dream stepping-stones, yet wherever they come from, they indeed are part of the elephant story. The elephants are telling us, as they did by pointing me to Charlie Rose and Senator John Warner, to appreciate that our good deeds toward any species are recognized by them in their collective memory, not just our own.

In these instances, with Rose's efforts to protect elephants through his exposé and Warner's fond greeting of Jewel, I suspect there was gentleness and an exchange of feelings that was genuine and the elephants are paying homage by sharing these moments of human-to-elephant kindness. Had they not shared this in my dreams, I would not know about these great elephant acts of gratitude.

Elephants teach us compassion in the profoundest of ways. They enlighten us and awaken our heart's wisdom. They are the quintessential nurturers and caregivers of the planet and its ecosystems. They can arouse our souls to loving action. They show us that when any of us perform a kind deed, have a pure and loving thought, or speak and act well toward others, we illicit a change in deep space, somewhere in the Milky Way where these great cosmic mothers stir the cosmos and help give birth to a more compassionate, manifest world.

5
Wolf

Escort on the Threshold

If you talk to the animals, they will talk with you and you will know each other. If you do not talk to them, you will not know them, and what you do not know you will fear. What one fears, one destroys.

CHIEF DAN GEORGE (1899–1981) OF THE
TSLEIL-WAUTUTH (A COASTAL SALISH BAND,
BRITISH COLUMBIA)

WOLVES AND HUMANS have been deeply intertwined for millennia. Biologists regard the gray wolf (*Canis lupus*) as the species that, second only to humans, have been the most widely distributed on the planet. Historically, the gray or timber wolf and its color variants, multicolored or pure black and white wolves, roamed throughout Eurasia and North America and were plentiful in most of Africa and in the arctic tundra.

THE CLOSE RELATIONSHIP
BETWEEN WOLVES
AND HUMANS

The wolf's distinctive howl has been a part of the night soundscape since time immemorial, as have their morning calls that let loose as the night imperceptibly turns to dawn. Wolf calls are used to keep the pack connected and also function as sonic boundaries for any animal or human in the vicinity. At one time, wolf howls were a familiar sound that were almost everywhere in the woodlands and wilds of the United States, as common as a rooster's crow on farms and homesteads. Because they are also masters of stealth, camouflaged among the trees or their silhouette blended into the mountain crest, wolves often go undetected by the human eye. Sometimes the only way one knows if Wolf is present is if a bird or some other creature lets on. Throughout human history, Wolf has been near.

Tamarack Song, author of *Entering the Mind of the Tracker* and *Becoming Nature,* suggests that wolves and humans have such an instinctual and deep bond today because wolves taught humans to hunt. Wolves always show the way to deer, elk, moose, and caribou, and a good hunt means nutritious meat for the tribe. Song shared in an interview how "We gradually became hunters in our own right, so that we could stand beside wolves and hunt along as equals to wolves, and we started to scavenge each other's kills, and we had this respect for each other. We learned from each other about the hunt and oftentimes cooperated in hunts, with the wolves scaring up a herd of antelope or caribou, the human hunters getting into position to take advantage of that."[1]

Ancestral wolves of modern-day domesticated dogs who stayed near to human camps and caves benefited from the food offered by their human associates and in return protected the human's camp from predators. Through this central interdependence, we are connected to wolves in ways that are unique. "Dogs," Song points out, "have been bred by humans to have the traits we like, replacing the pack with the human companion," reflecting dogs' undying love for their primary people and rescuers.

Despite their genetic relatedness, dogs, wolves, and coyotes are very different from one another, which is why Song is creating a sanctuary for captive-bred wolves and wolf-dog hybrids. Such interbreeding between domestic dogs and captured wild wolves does not erase the

Fig. 5.1. Wolf
By Stéfan, ca. 1641

essential wild wolf nature. They remain wired to hunt and roam freely in packs, immune to human control. Failing to live up to human expectations of domestication, hybrids are frequently abandoned, captured, and killed in shelters, or shot out of fear of their unpredictability and hyperalert nature.

Many North American tribes have wolf themes in their cultures. In the East, the Lenape of Delaware and the Shawnee, a migratory Algonquin tribe, have a wolf dance. Other Algonquin such as the Iroquois and the southeast Cherokee, Ojibwa, and Creek all have well established wolf clans. In the plains, the Skidi tribesmen (one of four distinct bands of the American Plains Indian nation, the Pawnee, whose name means wolf) historically would don wolf pelts by throwing them across their backs. Then, crouching down on all fours like a wolf, they would quietly steal close to camps in order to capture the horses belonging to soldiers, settlers, or other tribes. The hand signal for Wolf among the Skidi or Wolf Pawnee, representing the two ears of a wolf, interestingly enough is shaped like the peace sign made popular in United States in the 1960s.

Some tribal traditions teach that Wolf and other star beasts are responsible for co-creating the seasons and hence the trees and plants upon which animals and humans depend. Similar to Bear, Wolf is revered as a guardian animal. While Lion is regarded as the guardian of the world and is symbolic of the nobility of the human heart, Elephant is reflective of Buddhic consciousness and mother love. Wolf gives psychic vision into hyperspace. Almost every American tribe has Wolf as part of its totem lexicon. Those who are deemed wolf-like are endowed with Wolf's known qualities: intelligence, intuition, a deep bonding nature, and telepathic powers, as well as a love of play. Wolf's cosmic territory is the Milky Way road, which in certain traditions is called "the wolf road" or "path of spirit."

Wolf is a visionary, a spiritual messenger who can see into the invisible realms, but one who also heals and is resourceful in identifying what is needed. The Shoshone people who, before European occupation, originally lived both east and west of the Rocky Mountains describe Wolf as a noble creator god. While some traditions associate Wolf with the East and the color white, others such as Pawnee see Wolf representing the southeast direction. Despite localized variants of meaning, all share an overriding archetypal universality of an alert and powerful guardian, an escort of the threshold.

Wolf also signifies good health. The giving of wolf fetishes is a customary practice, bringing protection for well-being to the carrier of the fetish. I experienced Wolf's healing when, for instance, Wolf told me to walk in the woods more. Wolf can confer on its human partners the qualities of courage, loyalty, endurance, cooperation, and strength. Wolf is the national animal of the Chechen Republic, Russia, admired for her nobility as a caring mother and for the strength that pack members show in battle and the hunt. This identification is a reflection of the spirit of the family unit and the safety and company the pack offers. It also represents the wild and boundless spirit that an individual feels in his or her own body. But it is the White Wolf that is regarded as the great prophet of all wolves and the embodiment of Wolf's spiritual powers.

The White Wolf Dream

Each White Spirit Animal and its species are associated with a specific cosmic purpose and ecological role. All of these beautiful creatures of the wild have always been our sisters and brothers in sentient life. As they said to me when they first appeared in a waking vision, "Here we are, your brothers and sisters, and we have an urgent story to tell about our shared Earth and spirit." Humans have always been regarded as partners for the preservation and sustainability of the Earth.

White Wolf explained this to me in a series of dreams. I was shown a cargo truck with an African American man sitting in it. The truck was empty, but the man made clear he was going to fill it up with produce and go on the road to sell it, but was debating whether to name the truck Restoration, Conservation, or Preservation.

It took me two days to understand the message of this simple dream. Finally I realized that by reordering the three words, their first letters taken together stand for CPR (cardio-pulmonary resuscitation). Wolf made it very clear to me that if humans remain predatory toward the animals—for the lion heart is nearing a heart attack, elephant mother is near extinction, the bear den is empty of bears, the remaining buffalo will become table food— then the only one left will be the elusive White Spirit Wolf. The animal kingdom is alerting us to our perilous conduct, greed, and destruction, and the consequences of this unnatural abandonment of our internal guidance system for balanced and reverent living on Earth. After centuries of abusive and shortsighted industrial and technological practices, the animal kingdom is calling us to their Elder Council Circle as if to declare, "Heed our words," the entire Earth needs CPR.

SIRIUS AND THE NIGHT SKY

Just as Bear, Lion, and Elephant are signatories in our heavens, Wolf too reigns above us. The star Sirius, often referred to as the Dog Star, is the brightest star in the sky. It is a binary star system located in Canis Major, Latin for "big dog," whose English name humorously reminds me of the popular song, "Who Let the Dogs Out?" recorded by the Bahamian group Baha Men and released as a single on July 26, 2000.

Sirius has an illustrious history with Babylonian, Sumerian, and Egyptian civilizations, and with other ancient civilizations worldwide. The Egyptians based their agricultural cycles on the star's helical rising, or the day on which Sirius is visible just before sunrise. The star's rising is connected to the flooding of the Nile, and it first appears near the summer solstice. Sirius was also thought to cause certain symptoms in humans including the seasonal weakening of men and the arousal of women. In Homer's *Iliad,* Sirius rises with the sun and is the attributed cause of sultry summer days, hence the reference to the "dog days of summer." Sirius is called "a sorcerer" or described as "glowing" in Greek. When Wolf's visage is seen in fires by people gathered around to cook or for warmth, it appears as a magical helper, a mysterious shape-shifter who comes to humans when we need guidance.

Wolf is a traveling protector of the Great Spirit working with, as legend has it, brother/sister Bear as guardians of the North and

Fig. 5.2. The star Sirius (1600)
By Hugo Grotius (1583–1645)

protectors of the Milky Way road. Together, they partner to protect the Great Spirit of Creation. The Pawnee believe that Tirawa, the Great Spirit, placed Wolf Spirit in the sky to guard the evening star and that Wolf's brothers—black bear, mountain lion, and wildcat—stand as protectors of the moon. The North American Plains tribe, the Blackfoot, call Sirius "dog face" and the Cherokee associate the star with the super-red giant Antares, which is the brightest star in the Scorpius constellation. This makes the two stars, Sirius and Polaris/Ursa Minor, the guardians of the "path of the souls." This is another name for the Milky Way road, returning us to our elephant matriarchs who stir the Milky Way, engendering all life. Here we see the astronomical and spiritual partnership between Bear, Wolf, and Elephant. Indeed, they are our cosmic guardians.

There are similar naming practices and associations outside of North America regarding Sirius. The ancient Chinese astrologers gave Sirius the name of Wolf Star (as opposed to Dog Star) and refer to the actual southern sky wolf constellation, Lupus, as "the azure dragon of the East." The Dogon tribe of Mali believes that their ancestors come from the star system Sirius. The Wolf Star Sirius is considered to be the place from which elder wisdom for the Earth is derived. Sirius is twice the size of our sun and twenty times brighter. Some say that its name comes from the fact that it is in the constellation of Canis Major, which in ancient Egypt is called Sothis and is associated with Isis, the female mother goddess. Osiris as Isis's partner is associated with Orion, the very star system with which White Spirit Lion is associated.

Some Egyptologists note that while the Orion star system filters its light into the King's Chamber of the Great Pyramid at Giza on the summer solstice, it is the star system Sirius whose light illuminates the south shaft of the Queen's Chamber. I like the notion that White Lion is the male guardian and Wolf is the female guardian, comprising a spiritual, cosmic "alpha pair." They both function as earthly timekeeping signatories in the sky.

It is also intriguing that a similar, Giza-like pyramid that holds

the King's Chamber mentioned above has been found on the
of the planet Mars. There is as well an intelligently crafted lan‹
face in the Cydonian region of Mars, which NASA's Viking 1 flyby
identified on May 24, 2001. I researched this in-depth in discussions
with "whistleblowers" who revealed that government contractors, using
high pass filters on the images, deliberately tried to obscure details
and hide the fact that there may be artifacts on Mars that are a product of intelligent design. The late Thomas Van Flandern (1940–2009)
did a phenomenal job of uncovering the existence of other unusual
surface features such as glass tubes and animal effigies. He and others
showed that precise mathematics were used to create a face with two
eyes, a nose, and a mouth on Mars. Before becoming a well-known
advocate for revealing the real images taken of the Cydonian region
of Mars, Van Flandern was chief of the celestial mechanics branch
of the Nautical Almanac Office. In his *Meta Research Bulletin,*
he promoted numerous theories that went against mainstream
dogma.[2]

Speaking out against the government is dangerous and the sup-
pression of information, for personal, political, economic, or societal
reasons, is big business. The majority of the people I have interviewed
over three decades are decidedly out-of-the-box thinkers no matter
what field they may hail from. Most have at some point been ridiculed for their insights and knowledge and for the questions they ask.
Some have lost jobs, while more often than not they are proven correct twenty-five to fifty years later about the very issue they were
ostracized for. Freethinking mavericks, like wolves, function both in
packs and alone. Although not an enemy of humans naturally, Wolf
has been one of the most despised and aggressively killed species on
the planet. The killers of wolves fail to recognize that Wolf is humanity's guardian and spiritual companion and, as some suggest, key to
our survival. Once we collectively decide to stop killing wolves, we
will stop killing other animal kin and reinstate Wolf's status as a capstone species in our planetary evolution.

UNHOOKING
HUMANITY FROM
CELESTIAL MARKERS

Scholars Robert Bauval and Adrian Gilbert suggest that the three pyramids at Giza are an earthly representation of the belt stars in the Orion star system: Delta Orionis (Mintaka), Epsilon (Alnilam), and Zeta (Alnitak).[3] This makes the Great Pyramid at Giza a stellar clock of the circumpolar stars, which never sink below the horizon. For this reason, they represent what the Egyptians called "undying stars." Until the British adopted the Greenwich meridian in England as the "meantime" for calculating longitudes on Earth, which then became a global standard, the Orion star system or the Giza pyramids were used by sacred societies for this purpose.

This change began in 1675 when the British Royal Observatory was built to aide mariners in determining their longitude at sea. Prior to this time, each city in England (and the world) kept a different local time. Since 1851, the Greenwich meridian has been used worldwide for calculating longitudinal measurements on Earth. The change of locations is meaningful for calculating relationships between places throughout time, planet wide, and resulted in a change of more than 31 degrees, 8 minutes, and 0.8 seconds. Not only was this meridian marker change a major factor in the procession of empires, it removed Earth consciousness from the cosmos. Before this historic change took place, all sacred sites were arrayed in harmonized fashion making the galactic center— which Alnitak, a belt star of Orion, points to—the central orientation of all calculations for establishing locations to build, live, and worship on Earth.

To the Egyptians, the meridian was the most important marker in the sky and symbolic of the splitting of the heavens between life (East) and death (West). Sacred societies everywhere knew of this alignment system, making, for example, a sacred stone circle in one country in direct geometric relationship to another half the world away.

Plate 1. The author and her goat, Maria, 1965

The Bonobo Family

Maisha   TEKO   Kanzi

Elykia   Matata   Nyota

Plate 2. Matata, the bonobo matriarch, and her family
By Liz Pugh

Plate 3. The renowned American psychologist and parapsychologist Stanley Krippner at the Whitney Museum, 2015
By Stuart Fischer

Plate 4. *Medicine Man Performing His Mysteries over a Dying Man*, by George Catlin (1796–1872). Oil on canvas, 1832.
....
Smithsonian American Art Museum. Gift of Mrs. Joseph Harrison, Jr.

Plate 5. Ecologist/psychologist Gay Bradshaw with her dog Pir
....
Courtesy of the Kerulos Center

Plate 6. White Spirit
Bear fishing
....
By Charlie Russell

Plate 7. White Spirit Bear
in the Great Bear Rain
Forest in British Columbia
....
By Charlie Russell

Plate 8. Naturalist Charlie Russell with Biscuit,
a Kamchatka (Russia) grizzly bear that befriended him

Courtesy of Charlie Russell

Spernitur à stultis, (LEO VIRIDIS) sed amatur plus ab edoctis.

Radix Artis est sapo sapientum. Æa est MINERA omnium Salium & dicitur Sal amara. Nullo tamen modo poteris Lapidem præparare, absq, DVENECH Viridi, & Liquido, quod Videtur in mineris nostris nasci: O benedicta ergo Viriditas, quæ cunctas res generas, Crescere & germinare facis, Vnde noscas, quod nullum etiam Vegetabile atque fructus nullus apparet germinandos, quin sit ibi Viridis Color.

Plate 9. Alchemical green lion from *"Viridarium chymicum"*:
The Chemical Pleasure Garden (The Encyclopedia of Alchemy), 1624,
by Daniel Stoltzius Von Stoltzenbert, 1600–1660

Plate 10. Lioness with her two cubs

5th grade project

17. AFRICAN LION IN REPOSE SEEMS ONLY A BIG, FRIENDLY CAT

THE LION + THE LIONESS + HER CUBS

THE LION
THE LIONESS +
HER CUBS

1.   THE BLACK-MANED AFRICAN LION USES HIS CLAWS AND TEETH

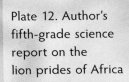

Plate 13. A holy White Elephant outside Yangon, Burma, in March of 2013
By Lars Sjöland

Plate 14. Carol Buckley and Tarra, now forty-three years old, whom Buckley raised from the age of one and credits with being her "mentor and reason for knowing anything I know . . . and do."
Courtesy of Carol Buckley

Plate 15. Baby elephant playing in the water
Photo by Tambako the Jaguar

Plate 16. White Wolf alpha female, Yellowstone National Park
Courtesy of National Park Service

Plate 17. A pack of wolves in Yellowstone's Lamar Valley
Courtesy of National Park Service

Plate 18. Tamarack Song with a wolf pup
Courtesy of Tamarack Song

Plate 19. Buffalo protector Cynthia Hart with an eagle feather given to her by her father, Uriah White Buffalo

Courtesy of White Bison Association

Plate 20. Miracle Moon and her calf Silver Shield Spirit

Courtesy of White Bison Association

Plate 21. Buffalo in the winter river, Yellowstone National Park

Courtesy of National Park Service/Gwen Gerber

Plate 22. Illustration of White Dragon
....
By Ciruelo

Plate 23. Dust bowl, Gregory, South Dakota, 1934

By Rosebud Photo, courtesy of Library of Congress

Plate 24. The author, Zohara Hieronimus, with a few of her dogs: Bailey, Oxford, and Bella

This unhinging of the human psyche from a unifying orientation, which had provided an ancient matrix, diminished our telepathic connections to each other and has obscured our understanding of the relationships between ancient archaeological sites both on and off of planet Earth.

The second great fracturing of humanity's relationship with nature and the universe occurred when the Gregorian solar calendar was introduced by Pope Gregory XIII in 1582 and the lunar calendar was eliminated. This divorced us from an awareness of our biorhythms, which similarly to rivers are bound up in tidal cycles governed by the moon. By pulling the world away from the primordial axis that had been used at least since the last ice age, and by separating Western civilization from the natural lunar cycle that controls all life on Earth, the British naval empire and the Roman Catholic Church, respectively, were responsible for the two most significant changes in humanity's connection to and awareness of our place and purpose in the universe. These two acts of institutional domination have affected humanity worldwide in the past one thousand years by disconnecting us from the galactic "code" and the key to our biological code by which we are partially governed. This is not only true of Western civilization but all living systems on Earth including our DNA, which we now know responds to consciousness. If we cannot see our basic connections, we miss the more subtle ones.

It is fitting that Sirius and its associated guardian of the ongoing journey of the soul, as it passes from material life to immaterial life, is regarded as "undying." The changing of the Pole Star and the exchange of the northern Pole Star of the bear for another star called Thuban reflect the consistent collaboration between human and canid, for what we see in the skies above is mirrored in our lives on Earth. (Thuban was the Pole Star at the time of the pyramids' construction. It depicts a dog and its master, or, alternatively, a shepherd and his herd.) During the next sixty thousand years, Sirius will come closer to our solar system. It is thought that afterward the star will begin to slowly move away from Earth. However, it will remain the brightest star in our solar system for the next 210,000 years.

The expression "As above, so below; as within, so without" pervades all of humanity's spiritual traditions throughout time. This is the basic operating system within every human being through which consciousness utilizes experience and follows an unfolding trail of universal clues, in order to achieve the best outcome in any given situation. Humanity has long expressed a close affinity to the wolf and dog as way-showers and protectors. But after becoming separated from our celestial markers and lunar connection, we lost this basic understanding of our relationship to the universe. It is not just outside of us but inside of us too.

THE GREAT COSMIC NAME GAME

At first, while conducting preliminary research on Native stories about wolves, I did not pay particular attention to differences between cultural assignations of Dog or Wolf to the Sirius star system. However, it became evident from Wolf that for wolves, this was an issue needing clarification, so they sent me clues to this ancient mystery in my dreams.

There was one very important dream that occurred at the start of my dialogue with Wolf. The dream featured numerous underground passageways and room-like caverns. They were quite vast, very clean, and attached to one another by tunnels. The passageways were easy to follow with my six or seven wolf guides, three of whom were white but well hidden. All of the walls of the passageways were painted white and crafted by human hands, similar to plastered walls.

Several weeks passed during which the wolves showed me, in my dreams, many qualities about their lives, about the push and pull tension between packs and how this keeps the fittest members strong so that the best genes of the group are passed down in their litters. They also spoke about their communal tasks, which include hunting, nurturing, and playing. Their descriptions of skilled group hunting remind me very much of the historic Indian game lacrosse, and I suspect the

Indians may have created this game while watching wolves hunt and play. This was the game from which the most competent players were chosen to be tribal leaders and warriors.*

Wolf insisted that there is a vital distinction between Wolf, Coyote, and Fox. Wolves delivered this message in dreams when I first began writing about them. They prevailed with a humorous kind of insistence. "If you understand nothing else about Wolf, this is the primary lesson to share with others," they seemed to be saying to me. My wolf instructor acted very "schoolteacher-like," shaking a paw for emphasis. During the first dream, Wolf claimed superiority to both Coyote and Fox, but then later went on to show me that Wolf and Coyote have relations they don't have with Fox. The wolves said there are members in the pack with various alliances, some with Coyote but not with Fox.

Weeks later, while conducting further research, I learned that Wolf, Coyote, and Dog share the same genetics, but not Fox. As simple as it was, Wolf's explanation was accurate. In talking with Tamarack Song at his Teaching Drum School in Wisconsin, he later confirmed what Wolf had said and shared how it works in the wild. "All wolves and coyotes in Eastern North America are hybrids and they will hunt together when they need to bring down larger game to feed themselves," Song

---

*I grew up playing lacrosse and excelled at it in my youth, even to the point of turning down an opportunity with a Dutch touring team to go professional after high school. I always played attack, in a position called "second home." I was a consistent scorer and invented one shot that I called "the fox shot." I was much smaller than most other varsity players. In fact, whenever I initially walked out onto the field before a match, there was always some laughter because of my small (though athletic!) build. However, I made up for my size with speed, fearlessness, and cleverness. I would run toward the goal purposefully drawing on me up to three defense women, freeing up my running teammates to receive passes. If none were free, or not in the proper position, I would then pivot abruptly and run away from the goal, which caused the opponents following me to scatter in all directions. Still running away from the goal, I was then able to perform an underhand shot behind me to score. Usually, this left the goalie shocked that the ball had entered the upper or lower left side corner of her goal. These were the most vulnerable spots in her territory and in need of careful guarding for a right-handed goalie. It was easiest for me to score with a right underhand shot across the goal. The fox shot seldom failed.

explained.⁴ So the fact that some tribes refer to Sirius as a wolf while others call it a jackal or coyote makes sense because both belong to the canid genus, and this is connected to the issue of the star system Sirius in a primary way.

ANUBIS AND THE STAR SYSTEM SIRIUS

Like millions of others, I have simply gone along with the notion that the star Sirius is the "Dog Star." When I visited Egypt three times with my husband in the 1980s, we were involved in the establishment of the Baltimore-Luxor sister city relationship and met with Anwar and Jehan Sadat. We also helped raise funds for the rebuilding of the Akhenaten Temple in Luxor. As guests of the Egyptian embassy's cultural attaché, we were permitted to enter tombs in the Valley of the Kings and at other locales and to visit the Cairo Museum to film and photograph. We did so with only a single antiquity's guide or none at all. All of the photographing and filming that we did was later stolen from us by the Israeli government.

We had stopped in Israel before returning home, for the purpose of raising funds for the "Shrine of the Book," which houses the Dead Sea Scrolls. At that time travelers could only fly from Egypt into Israel but not from Israel to Egypt. Even though we had a number of world-renowned military and lay psychics attempting to ascertain the particulars of the theft of our film, all but one agreed that we would never see the footage again, and they were right, we didn't. This saddened me, not so much for the images of the antiquities that we had filmed and photographed, but because we had filmed in Alexandria, Egypt, where under the Ptolemaic Rule the Jewish people had flourished culturally. This was of personal interest to me, feeling that I lived in Egypt during that particular time period. Furthermore, by using dowsing, I identified where archaeologists might be able to salvage scrolls from the great Alexandrian library. Some were buried, apparently, in the ancient Jewish district's graveyard.

Unfortunately, we never had the time to follow up because when we turned around several weeks later to return to Egypt to refilm and photograph, sadly Anwar el-Sadat had just been assassinated. Subsequently, we were on our own. Thus we were unsuccessful when we went back to recapture some of what had been taken from us. We were even trailed throughout our ten-day stay in Egypt, as we had been in Israel. The authorities made it clear that we were not trusted due to our U.S. and Israel affiliations. In fact, the situation was so tense that my husband had to remove the Israeli flag from his photographer's vest, which he had placed and sewn on between an American and an Egyptian flag as a symbol of the peace accords that Sadat was killed for and which our activities in all three nations was an effort to support.*

On numerous occasions in dreams, the wolves insisted that they wanted me to understand how the hunting bond and the hunt define their society (as it has in many human cultures along with "gathering"). They also showed me their superb skills at preparing underground dens, staying well hidden, and protecting their pups. They were as well highlighting that they are guardians of the "under world" where human bodies are buried. Later, I wondered if the white painted chambers and tunnels that I had visited in my dreams with my wolf escorts were unpainted ritual kivas of the southwest Indians, or perhaps unpainted tombs of the ancient Egyptians.

---

*We chose cultural high points in each nation's history: the Dead Sea Scrolls in Israel, the Akhenaten Temple in Egypt, and the Great Seal of the United States at home. All three of these represent teachings of unity consciousness. We lobbied the United States Congress to cut a die of the reverse seal of our coat of arms (the pyramid with an eye in the triangle) as companion to the obverse seal (eagle with arrows and olive branch in its talons). Together, when both seals are used, the obverse and reverse seals represent our nation's full identity. To date, no die has been cut of our enigmatic reverse seal. We promoted the use of both seals when signing foreign treaties, which use paper seals to authenticate the president's signature. (See Robert Hieronimus, *Founding Fathers, Secret Societies* for more on this topic.)

Immediately this question brought naturally to mind the Egyptian deity known as Anubis who, after a person dies, weighs the soul and assesses the human deeds that were accomplished during life against the feather of truth. Egyptologists in general say that, yes, the black-painted canid is the dog god, Anubis. Most archaeological literature ascribes the dog god label to Sirius. Some have thought that with its highly pointed ear tips and jet-black coat Anubis is more akin to the jackals who scavenged the ancient Egyptian graveyards. Anubis is almost always referred to as a dog-headed or jackal-headed deity who presides over humans as we shift from the material embodied state to that of a less dense being.

As a dog lover and human companion of many dogs, it seems unlikely to me that a dog, at least those that we know today, would guard the dead unless their primary person or kin family died or they were protecting dead prey. On the other hand, it seems much more likely that they would gladly guard the newborn of any species. It was

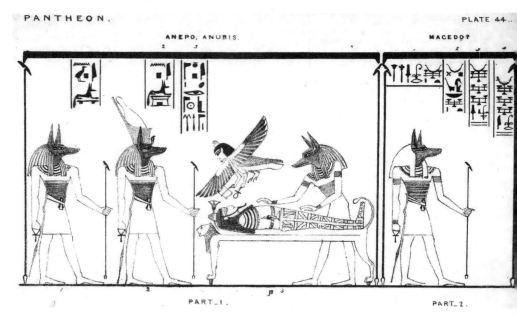

Fig. 5.3. Anubis
From *Manners and Customs of the Ancient Egyptians* by Sir John Gardner Wilkinson
(1797–1875), courtesy of the British Library

during this train of thought that I experienced one of those exhilarating, literally life-changing "aha" moments. I realized exactly what the wolves had been trying to tell me in the dreams of the unpainted tombs. They were clarifying ancient history.

Anubis is a not a dog. Anubis is not even a jackal. Anubis is a wolf and it is Wolf that is the universal guardian of the soul's journey. The wolves wanted me to know that *they* are the ones who protect and guide the spirit of the deceased through the seamless ebb and flow of Spirit in and out of the various forms that we experience. We call these forms "life" and "death," but they are really a "continuum of experience." Anubis the wolf does indeed guard the spirit as it shape-shifts in and out of living forms.

WOLF FAMILIES—WOLF PACKS

A wolf's gestation period is sixty-three days and they will live to at least thirteen if not killed by human predators or dying from injuries as a result of hunting. However, the wolves tell me their life span is beyond that, and can be up to twenty-five years long, the same life span that dogs used to have. Breeding generally takes place between February and March and the breeding alpha female's pups are born in the late spring or early summer, weighing only one pound. The female offspring will eventually weigh between sixty and eighty pounds. The males are slightly larger at seventy to one hundred and ten pounds. (See plate 16 of an alpha female White Wolf.)

Born blind and with eyes closed, pups are nursed by the mother for the first three weeks of life. At two weeks of age, when they open their eyes, their vision falls upon the world and they are able to begin their lifelong journey as a member of the pack. By the third week they can eat regurgitated food fed to them by other wolves, and thereafter they start crawling about outside the den on their own, within the protective watch of the pack.

As the largest member of the dog or canid family, wolves are considered mature by the age of two. Wolf pups will grow up in a pack family consisting of its parents and other siblings of related males and females. Unlike all of the matrilineal mammals we have been joined by so far, wolves are pack animals whose male and female populations are always intermingled. Only two wolves, however, actually lead and organize the pack into the social hierarchy that enables its functioning, especially for breeding, the hunt, and the pack's protection. The packs themselves vary in size from four to ten members, although packs as large as thirty wolves have been observed in the wild. Wolf packs like coyote packs will come together to hunt larger prey and will stay together for several days eating and sharing food, before disbanding to their own territories once again.

Wolf, like Bear, Lion, and Elephant, does not pair up exclusively for life, despite the myth that the breeding lead wolves do. Wolves will have other bonded relations within the pack outside their mating partners, whom they generally find by the age of two. When a wolf's mating partner dies, new relations will be formed, often through visible competition. Wolves are very social, intelligent, courageous, and communicative in numerous ways and benefit by partnerships inside the pack; they are aware of themselves as sentient beings.

The Civility of Wolves

In a dream I had, the wolves presented me with the most beautiful cages that were ironworks in refined filigree, with scrolls and decorative handiwork on them. All of them were empty, however, and the doors were open, making it clear that no matter the beauty, the size, or the quality of a captive environment, cage, or sanctuary, animals become prisoners in them. The wolves made certain that I understood the meaning of imprisonment by going over this in several dreams in a row, underscoring that keeping a wolf in captivity is not a humane thing to do. Wolves would never do such a thing to any animal. Freedom to range is a necessity for them, as they made clear is also the case for Deer, Caribou, Buffalo, Goat, and all their relations.

Fig. 5.4. Captive White Arctic Wolves at Zoo de la Flèche, France
By Chandres

TRACKING ANUBIS

As Tamarack Song points out in *Entering the Mind of the Tracker,* no matter what track we are following, we have to become what we are tracking.[5] Tracking is a type of inner shape-shifting, of aligning one's consciousness and intention with that which one tracks. In my case, back in the days when I was a full-time broadcaster and whistleblower, I had a history of tracking the news and primary eye witnesses. I am a professional news tracker who spent decades covering local, national, and foreign affairs as an investigative broadcaster. My sources of information were not only journals, newspapers, and interviews I conducted both on- and off-air but were my dreams and meditations as well. They provided me with information about foreign and national affairs that I had never read or heard about elsewhere. So for me, tracking and Wolf are familiars.

Author Rick Lamplugh, who writes about wildlife in an effort to preserve wild lands, tells a wonderful story of his own experiences in Yellowstone National Park's Lamar Valley.[6] He describes in his book *In the Temple of Wolves* how he and his wife, Mary, are winter volunteers there, taking visitors out in buses to watch and photograph the wolves. He explained during our conversation, "I wanted to wake up and see this amazing natural beauty and balance and the only way to do that in the winter was to work there. Wolves," he said, "often cover large areas and, to do so, travel as far as thirty miles in a day. Although they usually trot along at five mph, wolves can attain speeds as high as forty-five mph." (See plate 17 of a wolf pack in the Lamar Valley of Yellowstone.)

Lois Tulleners, who owns and operates the White Wolf Sanctuary in Oregon for wolves no longer able to live in the wild, shares "they can smell scents from as far as six miles away, as long as there is no carbon monoxide from cars interfering."[7] That wolves have over 240 million scent molecules compared to humans who have 50 million explains why humans tracking other animals often follow wolves.

Tracking from the spirit world to the material world is a little different from the reverse. Spirit tracking involves a special partnership formed with those at either ends of the connection because it is a subtler rather than a visibly material connection. Retrieving information from dreams is one form this rapport can take, which I practiced as part of writing this book. A perfect example of this was awakening to what Wolf was telling me in my dreams about wolves' role as guardians of the spirit, I wanted to shout out to the world, "Anubis is a wolf!" I had to be satisfied with running through our house at 9:00 p.m. instead, declaring this epiphany, "Anubis is a wolf!" This revelation was thrilling, as if some galactic puzzle had been solved. After my discovery it was hard for me to settle down. I got up from writing and went outside to admire the near full moon. As I stood there looking up, I imagined I saw a White Wolf shadowed on its surface.

The following day, I Googled "Anubis as wolf" and was shocked in that "jaw-dropping" kind of way to find a scientific paper published in 2011 announcing that, based on mitochondrial DNA evidence, the "Cryptic African wolf, *Canis aureus lupaster,* is not a golden jackal . . . [rather it] shows closer resemblance to wolves than to jackals."*[8] In more direct language, as the *Los Angeles Times* put, it "DNA proves it. African 'golden jackal' is really a golden wolf."[9] The article went on to say that the wolf originated in North Africa. New DNA evidence shows that the Egyptian jackal, which had been thought to be a subspecies of the golden jackal, is actually related to the gray wolf.[10] This would have been the animal depicted by the Egyptians as Anubis. In other words, Anubis is "a wolf in jackal's clothing." Science had agreed with what I had learned from Wolf in my dreams. This is a

---

*Note that the animal known as the Egyptian jackal (*Canis aureus lupaster*), as identified by naturalists Wilhelm Hemprich (1796–1825) and Christian Gottfried Ehrenberg (1795–1876) in 1833, is not a "large, rare subspecies of the golden jackal (*C. aureus*)." Researchers came to this conclusion by analyzing 2,055 base pairs of mitochondrial DNA from jackals in Ethiopia. They found that "*C. a. lupaster* is not a golden jackal and should be placed within the grey wolf species complex."

magnificent demonstration of the power of dreaming with another species—a viable research tool.

When this kind of validation takes place, a researcher can know with pretty good certainty that they are on the trail of what they are seeking. Furthermore, using dreams to specifically communicate with the spirit of a species has given me a sense of what our ancestors did and what shamans and medicine healers do around the world to retrieve information about their environment, our shared Earth, and each being's purpose. Dreaming is a majestic inheritance and a shamanic practice that can be used in many ways and contexts as a therapeutic tool, as well as a problem-solving one, for the world's well-being.

As the aborigines and other shamanic cultures teach us, dreamtime, which refers to waking visions in many cases, enables us to redream our world into being with deeper understanding. We can use what we experience in both day visions, as I have, and also in meditation and nighttime dreaming, to gather what is needed to participate more fully in life. For me, working with the spirit of an animal that is not in my physical presence, and not having had personal experience with these species in the wild or in captivity, dream encounters are highly important. They bring truth of some insight that I experience, not just simply repeating what others have said. This has been my life's mantra: "I have to decide for myself what is true." It is also what makes for an excellent and indefatigable tracker, expressing as independence or even stubbornness in childhood, and as tenacity and confidence when an adult.

HISTORY OF WOLVES IN NORTH AMERICA

Most Western children born after World War II first meet Wolf in a fairy tale in much the same way that we saw in the case of Elephant as the animated film character Dumbo, or Bear as Yogi. The legends of

Wolf as dominator originally came from Europe. The French author Charles Perrault (1628–1703) was responsible for seeding images of Wolf the devourer when he wrote *Le petit chaperon rouge*, or *Little Red Riding Hood*. This tells the story of a little girl with whom almost every child identifies empathically as an enduring symbol of fear and danger. It is the story of being eaten by a Wolf.

A later version by the Brothers Grimm toned down the story line a bit. In their later version, Little Red Riding Hood is devoured (as in the original) but is eventually rescued when a woodsman cuts open the wolf's stomach and releases her. Such propaganda reflected earlier beliefs and spawned other fictitious fears and abusive practices toward wolves, which still exist today. In this case it was only by killing the wolf and cutting it open that the child's life was saved.

Demonizing Wolf has also been the province of the ecclesiastical institutions, government-paid wildlife services, and local hunters and their political allies. Wolves are falsely accused of killing millions of cattle a year. However, based on statistics from 2001, less than 1 percent of cattle losses and 0.4 percent of sheep losses caused by predators were from wolf predation.[11] Coyotes, dogs, disease, and accidents cause the majority of unexpected cattle deaths. But this has not stopped cattle ranchers, sheepherders, and others who are just as uninformed from pointing to Wolf as the culprit and making Wolf the target of ongoing extermination. The real truth of the matter is that without Wolf the ecosystems that all of these herds depend on will collapse.

By the 1930s, wolves had been almost entirely eliminated from North America. In addition to being commodified by humans trafficking in endangered animals and their body parts, wolves have been hunted, poisoned, trapped, and shot with great cruelty and vengeance— more so than any other species excluding the cougar and coyote. Literature describing frontier horse and carriage days portrays the wolf as an animal terrorist from whom people had to protect themselves. As a consequence, as we have seen in the instances of other White Spirit Animals, wolf numbers and habitat have been greatly reduced. The gray

Fig. 5.5. *Red Riding Hood Meets Old Father Wolf*
By Gustave Doré (1832–1883)

wolf has been formally listed as a threatened and endangered species.

The extent to which wolves were persecuted is reflected in the litany of superstitions that surround the species.

During the Middle Ages, wolves were ascribed magical powers and wolf parts became an important product in many early pharmacies. Powdered wolf liver was used to ease birth pains. A wolf's right paw, tied around one's throat, was believed to ease the swelling caused by throat infections.

- It was widely believed that a horse that stepped in a wolf print would be crippled.
- The gaze of a wolf was once thought to cause blindness.
- Others believed that the breath of the wolf could cook meat.
- Naturalists of the day believed wolves sharpened their teeth before hunting.
- Dead wolves were buried at a village entrance to keep out other wolves (a bizarre belief echoed today by farmers who continue to shoot predators and hang them on fence posts to repel other predators).
- Travelers were warned about the perils of walking through lonely stretches of woods, and stone shelters were built to protect the travelers from attacks. Our modern word *loophole* is derived from the European term *loup hole,* or wolf hole—a spy hole in shelters through which travelers could watch for wolves.[12]

Hunters and hunted live in a kind of restrained balance and provide for those who scavenge, including their close genetic relatives Cougar and occasionally Fox, but also Raven and Magpie. Even as what biologists refer to as an apex predator, however, Wolf suffers like Lion and Bear from human predators who see these animal kin as better dead than alive, more appropriate as a stuffed trophy or as a character in a bar story of the hunt. But in reality, these skilled apex predators rarely if ever hunt humans or kill or harm them in any way. As Charlie Russell pointed out about bears, if a human and bear encounter each other, it is usually by accident and if the bear does attack a human it is for some specific reason, such as the bear is starving or has been traumatized by humans previously or is protecting its cubs or its den.

The 2015 film release *Medicine of the Wolf* directed by Julia Huffman summarized Wolf's current status in the United States in this way:

> After 40 years of protection, grey wolves were recently de-listed from the Endangered Species Act (ESA), and their fate handed over to state legislatures. What ensued has been a "push to hunt" in Minnesota and wolf country across the U.S. In Minnesota a survey of the wolf's population conducted after the inaugural hunt [in 2012] showed a drop of more than 700 animals—one in four wolves were reported killed, 298 by farmers/property owners and another 413 by hunting and trapping season. The total population declined by 25 percent. Of the nearly 1,700 wolves in the Rockies, 1,100 (65%) were killed in the last two years. Now, after the 2013 and 2014 wolf hunt, we have lost over *one-third of the total population in wolf states across the country. Currently, there are said to be 3,000 wolves in the lower 48 states.*[13]

While currently protected in several states, in most of them wolves are left to the mercy of men and boys who like to shoot, trap, and kill them. Yet wolves, whose family packs teach us about community and nurturing and rearing our young, who walk about eight hours a day as part of daily life, are closer to us than any other capstone species. They have spent time with humanity as its companion in a way no other apex animal has. Why is it that humanity fears and kills the very brother and sister who are responsible for teaching us how to hunt, how to raise our young, and how to steward an ecosystem?

Although it is argued that Wolf is an impediment to hunters who want to have larger deer and elk for sport killing, the science says otherwise. When wolves were reintroduced to Yellowstone National Park, where they are protected until within a foot of the park's boundary line (where hunters simply wait to kill the wolves, not much different from a shooting gallery), the entire ecosystem was improved. When reintroduced, these beautiful animals elevated the health of the whole environment. As described by the cascade trophic china model—which shows that when an apex animal is reintroduced or eliminated from its natural habitat, nothing is left unaffected by it—all of our planet's apex predators like the wolf play a vital role in maintaining healthy ecosystems.

In the case of Yellowstone, wolf reintroduction not only acted to increase numbers and the health of other animals but also positively affected the health of grasses and trees. Even the river's course was changed by Wolf's presence. As Mission: Wolf, a Colorado nonprofit dedicated to the wolf's survival, explains:

Since wild wolves have returned to Yellowstone, the elk and deer are stronger, the aspens and willows are healthier and the grasses taller. For example, when wolves chase elk during the hunt, the elk are forced to run faster and farther. As the elk run, their hooves aerate the soil, allowing more grasses to grow. Since the elk cannot remain stationary for too long, aspens and willows in one area are not heavily grazed, and therefore can fully recover between migrations. As with the rest of the country, coyote populations were nearly out of control in Yellowstone before the wolves returned. Now, the coyotes have been out-competed and essentially reduced by 80 percent in areas occupied by wolves. The coyotes that do remain are more skittish and wary. With fewer coyotes hunting small rodents, raptors like the eagle and osprey have more prey and are making a comeback. The endangered grizzly bears successfully steal wolf kills more often than not, thus having more food to feed their cubs. In essence, we have learned that by starting recovery at the top with predators like wolves, the whole system benefits. A wild wolf population actually makes for a stronger, healthier, and more balanced ecosystem. From plant, to insect, to people, we all stand to benefit from the wolves.[14]

These scientific observations show that capstone species are in fact master shape-shifters of nature, and their presence and purpose is to maintain the health of countless other species as well. Keeping Wolf healthy—as well as Bear, Lion, Elephant, and Buffalo, and their aquatic mammalian relatives as well—is a sacred key to Earth's adaptability in the coming decades. If protection is not offered immediately as sane, scientifically balanced, and morally compelled action dictates, then these creatures will likely go extinct as currently predicted, and as the story of the Japanese wolf illustrates.

THE END OF THE JAPANESE WOLF

Rick Lamplugh describes how "Japan really crystallizes the whole human drive to annihilate wolves, steal their territory, and create wolf haters. Wolves in Japan were revered for centuries—people actually left gifts at wolf dens," believing, as the Shinto peoples do, that Wolf (Okami) is the messenger of the spirit. They also believe in a nighttime escort wolf who mysteriously appears and walks a person through the woods until they safely reach home. But this kind of generational reverence was quickly changed. "Within a short period of time, one human life span," Lamplugh laments, "it went from being a revered animal to a despised one. The reason why is that the Japanese government wanted to bring in what was called modern agriculture, modern ranching, and that meant ranching as it is done in America." An American rancher was brought in, Lamplugh explains, "and he knew how to get rid of wolves. [By 1905] . . . the wolves were gone from Japan and they still are."[15]

Within a few short years, all of Japan's wolves were killed in an aggressive act of animalcide. This was done by the use of government and media propaganda that demonized the wolf as the great danger lurking in every corner, behind every tree and every shadow in the night. Wolf, the public was repeatedly told, would eat children and household pets and livestock of all kinds.

Lamplugh wanted to share the lesson that he believes this story reveals. "I really think that the wolf's survival is a cultural issue rather than a biological issue. Wolves left to their own will breed, reproduce, hunt, and expand their territory and monitor and control their own numbers. That's scientific fact. But with human intervention there is a strong hatred against the wolf that is not reflected in our feelings about cougars that kill livestock. There's something really different about wolves and it goes back hundreds of years. By the 1700s wolves were almost completely eradicated in Europe. There had not been a wolf in three hundred years, when Little Red Riding Hood from the Brothers Grimm was popular, as described earlier. We can teach our next generation to remember things, and that's where literature comes in," he continued, pointing out "that literature can change this taught hatred to learned appreciation."

The sole reason for their extinction is modern humanity's commitment to decimate their numbers and appropriation of habitat. There is only 5 percent of wilderness still intact in the United States. Not only is the wolf's inheritance to live on the Earth with regard for their own species' needs and autonomy important, but also, without these animals, our own survival is put in greater jeopardy and the ecosystems wolves preside over with purpose decline. In the natural world the animals and the ecosystems we depend on for life are all interwoven—physically and spiritually. As Gay Bradshaw advocates, we must stop denying animals their inherent right to be regarded with the same legal and ethical protections that we offer humans. As she opined during my on-air radio interview with her, "They too have the right to coexist without interference. They too deserve autonomy and territory to have families and live."[16]

THE PAWNEE CREATION LEGEND

As we have discovered, each of the White Spirit Animal species has some place in the cosmic Creation process: Bear, Lion, and Elephant, and Buffalo and Wolf as well. The Creation legend of the Pawnee from *Of Wolves and Men* by Barry Holstun Lopez reveals Wolf's secret history:

The Great Council of the Pawnee

It is told in the Creation legend of the Pawnee that "a great council" was held to which all the animals were invited. For a reason no one remembers, the brightest star in the southern sky, the Wolf Star, was not invited. So begins a story of isolation for the wolf, from Creation. He watched from a distance, silent and angry, while everyone else decided how to make the Earth. In the time after the great council the Wolf Star directed his resentment over this bad treatment at the Storm that Comes out of the West, who had been charged by the others with going around the Earth, seeing to it that things went well. Storm carried a whirlwind bag with him as he traveled, inside of which were the first people. When he stopped to rest in the evening he would let the people out and they would set up camp and hunt buffalo.

One time the Wolf Star sent a gray wolf down to follow Storm around. Storm fell asleep and the wolf stole his whirlwind bag, thinking there might be something good to eat inside. He ran far away with it. When he opened it, all the people ran out. They set up camp but, suddenly, looking around, they saw there were no buffalo to hunt. When they realized it was a wolf and not Storm that had let them out of the bag they were very angry. They ran the wolf down and killed him.

When the Storm that Comes out of the West located the first people and saw what they had done he was very sad. He told them that by killing the wolf they had brought death into the world. That had not been the plan, but now it was this way. The Storm that Comes out of the West told them to skin the wolf and make a sacred bundle with the pelt, enclosing in it the things that would always bring back the memory of what had happened. Thereafter, he told them, they would be known as "the wolf people, the Skidi Pawnee." The Wolf Star watched all this from the southern sky. The Pawnee call this star "Fools the Wolves," because it rises just before the morning star and tricks the wolves into howling before the first light. In this way the Wolf Star continues to remind people that when it came time to build the Earth, he was forgotten.[17]

This Pawnee legend reiterates in so many ways the vital significance of gray wolf in the ecosystem, in our spiritual experience of spirit animals, and in our appreciation of natural relations between humans and animals—indeed, between all of us and nature. The Ojibwa say it this way, "As goes the fate and fortune of Wolf, so goes the fate and fortune of Man."

As our Native ancestors show in their stories, and is now shown more recently by Western science, by killing the wolves we bring down the ecosystem and then other species follow in this accelerated extinction. When apex animals are eliminated, the other animal herds and environs they live in also suffer. The inverse is true as well. Where these sacred animals are reintroduced and protected, the ecosystems are brought into balance.

SHAMANISM AND THE WHITE WOLF

The White Wolf has a long association with shamanic cultures worldwide. Much like the star system Sirius A, the brightest star seen from Earth that Wolf is represented by in the heavens, the White Wolf remains a guide for human beings. Like the other White Spirit Animals, Wolf's white coat is often said to be a reminder of the last glacial age. White Wolf is known as shape-shifter and telepath of excellence. Researching Native people's stories, it is fascinating to find how few are actually about White Wolf but how White Wolf is held in such high regard worldwide when she appears. Tamarack Song, who lived with wolves whom he raised from pups, and who has relations with wolves today in the wilder woods of Wisconsin, explains why this is so.[18] "Well, there are a couple of reasons for that," he began. "One is that White Wolf is a phantom wolf, a spirit wolf. In traditional culture this is not mentioned, this is not given voice. So you might hear or read a story or legend about wolves and White Wolf is not going to be mentioned. But," he emphasizes, "White Wolf is always there in the story because White Wolf is the prophet of the wolves, the prophet *of* all of us, *for* all of us. White Wolf," Song summarizes so beautifully, "is the symbol for inspiration, for us to see beyond the apparent, to see beyond the visible, and encouragement for us to envision and go beyond the self, and that is why the White Wolf is a phantom in the background."

His explanation prompted me to recall that the Tsimshian tribal peoples of the British Columbian rain forest never spoke to outsiders of the White Bear. They never even admitted to seeing White Bears or knowing where they were, nor was their existence focused on in much of the Native lore.

Bear Man Charlie Russell brought up his concern when we spoke.[19] He wondered if his own more public relationship with Spirit Bears was an error on his part. He fears that such publicity could lead to hunting them. From a dream I had with Bear, I shared the same fear. Indeed, Russell said that one White Spirit Bear was killed and his skin given to a chief by a person thinking this gesture would be seen as a great tribute. It was instead considered a shameful act of disrespect for life.

However, the overall effect of publicity about the great White Spirit Bear, in films and books over the past few decades, has been very positive. Native people and modern folk have joined together to protect White Bears and their ecosystems. Public exposure thankfully has resulted in increased awareness and appreciation of them, which in turn has led to a collaboration to prevent the extinction of this wildlife species. To save them is to save ourselves.

Getting back to our discussion of Wolf, there have been numerous stories of Wolf's shape-shifting presence and close association with humans. In one of my dreams, a mixed-color wolf stood up before me in front of a tipi. Smoke was rising from an early morning fire and one could see frosted breath in the chill of the season. Wolf was standing among other Native people, though clearly he was a wolf wearing blue pants, a yellow shirt, and black suspenders. Slowly, carefully, he began to fill his animal-skin medicine pouch and showed me the items he carries with him. He placed pine needles, sage, a flint, and a string of shiny metal beads in the pouch. He indicated that the beads were to attract both birds and fish. Wolf carried bear claws on a string as well.

Dreams have so many levels of meaning but it would not be unreasonable to wonder if this was a dream about a wolf-allied shaman. Or perhaps I was being shown the prevalence with which human and wolf have exchanged identities over the millennium and the reputation, as Wolf has, of being a medicine healer, an ally of Bear. The way I heard it in telepathic conversation with the spirit of the White Wolf was that "wolves do human," meaning that they understand us. They speak our language.

Consistent with other Native White Spirit stories, Creation usually involves one or more animals. The Quileute peoples of western Washington and the British Columbian Kwakiutl teach that their ancestors were actually wolves who became men. Shape-shifting myths are sometimes called "therianthropy," which is the capacity of a human being to be transformed into an animal. Having found this among shamanic cultures involving Bear, Lion, Buffalo, and Elephant when it pertains to humans becoming wolves, it is called lycanthropy. In this case, a person turns into a wolf and then may or may not return to human form again.

Pliny the Elder (23–79 CE) notes two examples of lycanthropy. "He mentions a man who hung his clothes on an ash tree and swam across an Arcadian lake, transforming himself into a wolf. On the condition that he attack no human being for nine years, he would be free to swim back across the lake to resume human form." Pliny also notes "a tale of a man who was turned into a wolf after tasting the entrails of a human child, but was restored to human form 10 years later."[20]

WOLF MAGIC

While I cannot say for certain how the interplay of physical vessels between human and animal takes place in shape-shifting, it does seem that animals are perfected emotional beings. The astral body, our emotional body, is animated by a vital force that streams through the flesh and blood of our physical bodies. It is the astral body that seems to intermingle and conjoin between animals and humans through our shared feelings and through a natural or elevated empathic response between both. Using animal pelts and bones, performing songs and dances, paying close attention, and incubating dreams regarding each animal stimulates the subconscious and elevates it to a kind of super-consciousness. In this state, in the mental or causal body, ideas are pulled down into the astral or feeling body where they then manifest afterward in the physical world of form and action. This process is similar to the way an architect's drawing begins as a vision or an idea and is then rendered into drawing form whereupon builders take it and create a physical building.

Shared earlier when walking with Bear, this is how talismanic magic and what is also referred to as "low magic" work to shape and animate matter. Wearing a wolf charm on a necklace symbolizes Wolf and reminds the person wearing it to think about Wolf. Our identification with this particular life-form becomes stronger. When a human being performs any ritual, gives meaning and place to any symbolic object, our emotional attachment, our astral body, and our mental impregnation of the meaning we attach to each "thing" calls to the universe, saying in this case, "Wolf is important to me, I honor Wolf, bring me Wolf!"

We are drawing down from the invisible but knowable realms all things that are Wolf-related. This is why in esoteric teachings one learns that all forms are related in octaves of similars. The same processes are at work in human consciousness. Our intention, awareness, and emotional investment in the symbols themselves enlivens them, because *we* are paying attention to *them,* attributing meaning to *them.* Animate and inanimate totems in Native societies function similarly and, for this reason, ritual tools in all religions are actually able to facilitate a shift in human consciousness.

The focusing of attention in this way, as quantum physics shows, is what enables the mind to observe how the immaterial realm comes into form in certain patterns. When we glimpse a photo of a loved one who has passed away, or we think of them, we are literally calling them up in the universe. Our attention makes the "other" accessible. It also allows for our intentional love to connect with them outside the bounds of either time or space.

Afterlife communication, which I have experienced since childhood with the deceased, may function in this manner. Sometimes I have heard from people I do not know but who ask me to bring a message to someone I have met, even in some chance place like a grocery store line. While it seems wishful thinking to say that love is the field of all potential, and that love is the field of life through which all languages flow—be it of the lion, the elephant, or the wolf, the tree, or the river—it is this field, this divine spirit of love, that permeates everything. It arouses in us, when we open our hearts to it, a profound feeling of connection that makes telepathy operate in people naturally. Telepathy understood in this way as a practice can become a life-enhancing skill.

This kind of shared acceptance and reverence is highlighted in numerous teachings. The aboriginal peoples of Australia preserve "dreamtime" as a function of daily waking life. They, it is known, communicate primarily through telepathy.[21]

Tamarack Song tells a wonderful North American tribal story I especially like.[22] It is about White Wolf's constant presence as the great holder of story, tradition, and prophecy, and as guardian of the Great Spirit who oversees the welfare of human beings.

The Spirit of the Wolf Lives On

When Wolf became extinct or had almost become extinct, in some areas of the world, humans took on the spirit of the wolf, in order to keep Wolf alive—until he could come back and hunt with humans again. The story begins with the beginning of time. In the beginning of time there was the Earth and the only two animals on the Earth were wolves and humans, and they hunted together, they hunted together as one pack. In ceremony they would come together and humans would have the drum and wolves would have the chant. And humans would drum and the wolves would howl. This is how they would honor life, and this is how they would honor the hunt after a successful hunt, by drumming and chanting together. And then the other animals came along and there was confusion, because nobody knew who should be in relation with whom. There were so many other animals, there were so many winged and herd animals, legged animals and scaled animals.

Bumblebee had a vision, and Bumblebee came and talked with Wolf and human and said, "I've been told it is your time to part, for each to go your own way because you have things to teach and things to learn from all the other animals now. It's not just the two of you. We are now a circle, we are a circle of relations." So Wolf and human parted until one day, Wolf was walking down the trail and bumped into a woman. And the woman said, "Oh, I am honored to see you, Wolf, we haven't seen any wolves for a long time." And Wolf said, "Yes, that's because I am the last of our kind. It's my time to go; this is my last day here on Mother Earth." And the woman protested. She said, "Why, we used to hunt together, we have legends, we have stories." And Wolf said, "The Earth is being destroyed, the forests are all cut down, all of my kind have been killed. I am the last. It's my time to go, there's no more room for us anymore."

The woman said, "This can't be, because we were born together, we are like the right hand and the left hand together, how can we exist without each other? We always drummed and chanted together." And then she had an inspiration. She realized why she and Wolf had come together. And she brought out her drum and she asked Wolf if they could drum and chant one last time together. And they did and it was beautiful. The woman listened and when Wolf was howling, she howled along with him—and in this way, she took on the chant of the wolf.

When their ceremony was done, the woman said to Wolf, "You will not die. Your body may go but you are going to live on within me because you have just given me your chant. The chant of Wolf we'll honor within the chant of the humans. When we drum, we chant at the same time, just as when we were together. And when the time comes that you come back in the flesh and be with us, and hunt with us, we will cease your chant and you'll have your chant again and we will have the drum."

"And here in this story," Song concludes, "the White Wolf is in the background, always there but not mentioned. The White Wolf is maintaining the prophecy. It was White Wolf that gave the vision of the prophecy to the woman so that she knew and understood in a greater sense what this relationship was to be. And how closely related they were. So here you see the shape-shifting. You see Wolf becoming human, Wolf becoming woman, and the two existing simultaneously within the same body."

There is another synchronicity about this magical story that is worth sharing for the reason that this happens to every one of us when we pay attention to related things that are happening all around us. During the off-air conversation with Song when he shared this story, I was wearing a White Wolf lariat my husband had given me years ago. With it, I was wearing a bumblebee necklace he had given me only recently, to honor my love and advocacy in protecting the bees. It was synchronous that the bumblebee, human, and the wolf were the pre-existing components of a symbolic journey that was unfolding around me and to me and then described in Song's story.

Wolf's Eternal Companion

In a dream two weeks prior to hearing Song tell this story, I was out in the wild with a pack of wolves. It was snowing. There were six wolves whose coats were of different colors: two brindle, two black, and two white wolves. These six wolves, like those who showed me through the tombs and dens of the underground spiritual realms, were walking in two semi-arranged staggered columns with a path down their middle. This made their walk look like an arrow pointing forward or what is called "wedge walking." Walking in their footprints but behind them was a very tall, strong, and noble Indian woman. As I walked right behind her, watching how she stepped so quietly like the wolves' stealth presence in the woods, I followed them, admiring the beautiful long black hair that fell below her waist in a thick braid. In the dream this woman was an eternal companion of Wolf, much like the story Song shared weeks after I had had this dream. Is this how Native shamans and medicine people knew she was Wolf's eternal companion too, through their dreams?

A few days later, I found the middle tail feather of a red-tailed hawk on the ground at the entrance to the driver's side door of my truck. It was not hidden in the woods, not somewhere I had to search for it, but literally sitting outside of my truck door when I stopped down the driveway by the stream to check something I'd seen. Getting back into the truck I found the feather sitting there in the driveway. I knew it was unusual as soon as I picked it up. They are rare to find, and it is said one receives a red-tailed hawk feather as a sign. Also, they are bestowed only when one has acquired experience and maturity in one's relationship to nature and her spirit, but also to Wolf in particular.

When I first saw the feather, I felt that it was a gift to me from Wolf through red hawk, laying it exactly at my truck door. As Song told me when I sent him a picture to help me identify it, it was "the same kind of red-tailed hawk feather that I was given by the White

Wolf elder," when he had entered the lifelong relationship with wolves. In Tamarack Song's case, this love has led to his plan of creating a sanctuary for captive-bred wolves and wolf dogs who cannot survive in the wild after being housed with humans. Yet neither should they live in people's homes, as they are not dogs and not totally wolves either. (See plate 18 of Tamarack Song and a wolf pup.)

Nancy Red Star, author and Cherokee medicine woman, adopted a wolf dog that was 75 percent wolf and 25 percent domesticated dog. The shelter did not mention his wolf heritage. She was told by the shelter simply that he was a shy dog. It took her three weeks of daily visits just to secure his trust enough that she could pet and befriend him and move him out of his caged enclosure. It was only much later that she found out he was a wolf dog. She discovered this when she took the animal to a veterinarian, who then explained why he was so skittish, afraid of people, and not at all like a domestic dog.[23] As I have learned from interviews with people who live and work with wolf dogs, they are not dogs but neither are they totally Wolf. People buy them from puppy mills thinking it's a great status symbol to own one. In fact, it's injurious to the spirit of Wolf, Dog, and human. It is an unnatural breeding and would not happen without human domination.

WHITE SPIRIT WOLF LESSONS

Wolf, I have come to know, is a genuine way-shower, protector, and important ally of humankind. She teaches us community balance, giving the weak and strong and the young and old a role to play. She and her mate show us partnership and enduring commitment to our young and larger family. Her magical ability to appear and disappear, to guide humans and other species on the trail of spirit, is mysterious—playful and serious at the same time. St. Francis of Assisi is said to have befriended a wolf in the city of Gubbio. After talking to the wolf about devouring livestock and frightening the people, St. Francis told the wolf he must stop his rampage. But then the wolf told St. Francis that he had only hunted out of hunger. At this, St. Francis walked with the wolf throughout the town, whose residents agreed thereafter to feed the wolf regularly, and all troubles ceased.

Wolf's intimacy with us is apparent by the millions of humans who to this day feel closely affiliated with Wolf, as they do with Dog. This bond may be hardwired into our limbic system as Tamarack Song suggests, from the millennia in which we hunted together and learned together in order to stay alive. Like a lost branch of a family reunited with its clan, Wolf's vibrant effort to be present in our lives, to keep the ecosystems wolves inhabit rich and the various species' herds healthy, is something Wolf wishes for humans also. Wolves encourage humans to be of service in the world, and to perform CPR (conservation, preservation, and restoration). Whether as leaders or managers, nurturers or guardians, Wolf teaches humans how to work together. Wolf also teaches us to use insight and patience to assure the well-being of the Great Spirit, which takes part in everything that happens on the entire Earth. White Wolf may not be seen everywhere, but she *is* everywhere and calls us to her, howling across the world drum.

6
Buffalo Rising

Earth Guardians

All creatures exist for a purpose. Even an ant knows what that purpose is—not with its brain, but somehow it knows. Only human beings have come to a point where they no longer know why they exist.

JOHN FIRE LAME DEER
(LAKOTA, 1903–1976)

AFTER LEARNING about the various Native medicine men, women, and shamanic traditions that pivot around spirit animals, one notices that many animals in these traditions can become winged creatures. For some reason the buffalo, besides being the mightiest land mammals native to the North American continent, seem to have a legacy in the spiritual visions of people. In their alliance with medicine men and women, buffalo also seem to be associated with a great capacity for flight. To properly introduce this species there is really no better story I can share than my own experience with the White Buffalo, or bison—the actual genus that distinguishes them from the African water buffalo. (Throughout this chapter I refer to these mammals as Buffalo, as do Native people historically. Many who care for them or breed them today as food commodities refer to them by their scientific name of bison, so as not to confuse them with water buffalo. The two names, buffalo and bison, are often used interchangeably.)

FINDING A MISSING HORSE

The story I am about to tell involves Buffalo and a runaway horse. One recent winter, my niece Lyn called me. She was very upset about a horse that was boarding at her friend's equestrian training farm. He had jumped his pasture fence and was missing. That's all she told me other than the horse's name (changed herein to Copper Top). It is my practice not to ask questions of an animal's human before a reading, other than the name and sex of the animal, if known. I told her I would do what I could to make contact with him, which I was quickly able to do.

There is the possibility that an animal will not answer their phone when a telepath calls, as I learned from my dear friend and teacher the late Terry Edward Ross II (1921–2000). His book on the subject of dowsing, *The Divining Mind,* co-authored with Richard Wright, and his posthumously published book *The Healing Mind* reminds each person to ask the following three questions before getting involved with any requested action. "May I? Can I? Should I?" This gives each of us an intentional frame of reference, of humility, in asking for divine counsel before beginning one's exchange with another life-form. This also protects us from interfering with the destiny of an individual person, animal, or place, or with the desires of that person, animal, or place, to the best of our ability.

Copper Top answered my call immediately in a voice tinged by an emotion like that of a foreigner who is lost and who finally, after many attempts, finds someone who speaks his or her own native language. He answered me in a state of panic, but with relief as well. His first words were "Where am I?" His next question was, "Why am I here?" referring to his strange new place we call Maryland. "Where are my horses?" he asked next.

It was clear that this was a recently relocated horse who had not been told he was leaving sunny Florida, as I later learned, for a place where the weather was below freezing. Fortunately, he did have a blanket on at the start of his runaway journey in sixteen-degree weather.

In fact, he demonstrated what most animals with their senses are still hardwired do, which is to find water as soon as they can.

I called my niece to ask, "Has Copper Top recently moved here?"

"Yes, two days ago," Lyn told me.

I explained that he was not properly prepared for the move to Maryland for training. The horse spoke of missing a dark-skinned groom whom he loved and who loved him and that they did not have a chance to "say good-bye," which had also affected the feelings of the groom, who had a real love for Copper Top. When speaking about the purpose of his arrival in Maryland for training, the horse made clear he had no interest in being trained for dressage work or what he called "the footwork stuff." He also called it "stupid human stuff," which was "not natural for a horse to do at all." In fact he made clear "it hurt his brain," or as we would say, "gives us headaches and causes anxiety."

This was a free-running runner of a horse who still had wildness intact in his nature and did not like inside ring training of any sort, but loved to "run the cross-country type of running." But what he liked most, he said, was "being with a person in the woods and fields, or a light person on my back" when he could prove he was "the fastest of them all." Again I called Lyn, this time to ask her if his nature was a bit wild. Was he up here for dressage training and was he indeed as "fast" as he claimed to be? The answer to all of my questions was yes. For a telepath, getting confirmation is as important as learning of one's mistakes.

Given that Copper Top was missing, the local media had been called and his picture was all over the local news for several days. I did not know this at the time. Since leaving the news-making profession I seldom watch the news on television, though I do keep up to date via online media resources. While I remained sequestered from public attention, an international horse organization that deals in fine stolen horses was called. Soon there were helicopters and people on horses out looking for him.

I was called on the evening of the second day. With any kind of tracking, it is best to alert a tracker, telepath, or animal or psychic communicator as soon as possible that an animal, or human, is missing. All life is vibration and the currents are audible and visible psychically, leading to their point of origin. When the target is lost, stolen, or is a runaway, there is greater interference. But as remote viewers and dowsers demonstrate, we do have the uncultivated aptitude to find *anything, anywhere,* and *anywhen.* We have an internal GPS (global positioning system) that shamans and intuitive humans access.

I tracked Copper Top to one of our reservoirs, but whenever he came to clear fields near the woods he would shy away from coming out where he would be visible to others. He did see other horses while he was hiding, but knew they were not "his horses"—horses he had boarded with in Florida. As it turns out, when a new horse is brought into a barn or corral situation they are most often put in isolation for several days to be sure the rest of the herd will accept them and to ensure that they won't fight with their new herd mates. This is a practice I was not aware of.

In other words, Copper Top was brought almost one thousand miles north by trailer, without explanation, put in a new field that was seventy degrees colder than where he had been, and then left alone during the daylight hours. This might strike some horse lovers as a pointless question, but what horse, what animal, what person would not feel confused, alone, and scared? So he jumped his fence, maybe as a result of hearing a car or truck horn, or the backfire of a passing automobile, as people have reasoned. But that is not what he told me. He was, he thought, going to go easily "find *his* horses in the pasture next door" and instead he found himself utterly lost. As he put it "it was a really big surprise." By the end of the first day, he knew deep in his heart that he had made a serious mistake. He thought he could jump the fence and go right back to his barn and the groom whom he had known in Florida. He also thought that he was a mere pasture or so away from his real home. I did not ask at the time if he thought his Maryland residency was a dream or if he also went pasture-jumping at home.

He complained a lot about looking for the barn. He also kept asking, "Where is my green bucket?" referring to his grain bucket back at the barn. As the days wore on and he got hungrier, he became more insistent. "Where is my green bucket, it should be right here!" he would say as if shocked by its disappearance, insinuating that someone was not doing *their* job. As it was subzero weather and there was little left in the fields to eat, he was hungry, cold, and disoriented.

When I asked a horse expert about this subfreezing temperature, she said, "Oh, he'll be frisky, this cold weather really makes them really active." All I heard him say was "What has happened to my warm spots?"—meaning places where he used to stand in the sun.

Beyond wishing to be out of the immediate crisis of being lost, and not wanting to be trained to do the "human footwork" or be in a new barn with a different color roof than his own back home, what *did* he want? He wanted to be back home near the adjacent barn with a filly he liked. And, he made clear, to be like he was before, loved by the groom and to be a real "helper" in the barn, sort of like a "teacher's pet." He prided himself on his running speed and spirit. He wanted to be allowed to run fast. He was, he made clear, "a champion" winner. However, he had no interest in races per se, another human thing, but preferred to simply run or cross-country ride for the pleasure of running. In other words, this horse had been too restrained by an owner's desire for him to do things that were incompatible with his natural individual makeup—emotionally, psychologically, and spiritually.

There are horses that like to be in shows and competitions and enjoy the routine, the attention and excitement of it all, but there are others who do not. These horses are not pets, even though they are loved. They are commodities that can cost hundreds of thousands of dollars or more a year to purchase and maintain. They are bought, bred, and raised to perform certain skills for their owners. Some horses like it, some do not. Copper Top fell decidedly into the latter category. Essentially almost any animal will do anything for its human providers, even give up its own life, but only if its human companion is loyal, loving, and responsible as well, and only if the goals of the human are in keeping with that animal's own destiny.

By the fourth day of Copper Top's absence, the primary players said that they would stop looking for him. They believed that he had been either stolen or utterly lost in another county somewhere. But I knew this was not the case even though he had been spotted the day before in an adjacent county. I knew that he had not been stolen and was not more than several miles, if not less, from where he began. I encouraged him for two days to follow his tracks home, to go back to the barn, and told him that there would be a human to help him find his new home. He had just met the owner of the equestrian center, who obviously cared about him and his welfare. I referred to her as "his new person," and told him that this new person would help him. This kind of emergency situation brings out the bonds between humans and animals sometimes more quickly than years together can, as often happens among humans in emergency situations.

At this point I was paying attention to Copper Top for hours each day. It was much like the mother of a newborn who will often check that the baby in its crib is still breathing. This experience did not lack emotional swings of hope and concerns of loss, but I was in constant conversation with this wonderful horse. I told him that he needed to find the horses that together with humans were out looking for him, or to go by the barns of other horses he showed me he had seen. He showed me a church that he had run past and then some woods. I told him to move out into the pasture fields he could find, and out of the woods so someone could see him. As I watched him consider this advice, it became clear he was not going to do this by himself. I had a feeling right then that I had to find a human who would see him.

I had dowsed how many days he would be missing and was told he'd be found before the morning of the fifth day. I did what I could to encourage my niece to tell the primary players, with whom I did not speak during this search, this information. I have learned that the more emotionally charged a human is, the more interference they add to psychic reception. Between my niece and me, we had enough charge to power the entire state of Maryland! Love for animals is broadscale. It takes in all sentient life. It sweeps through the heart like a tidal wave of love and when it washes out, only the mistrust or fear goes out to the sea and loving regard comes back in again, over and over and over again. So I told her to tell the searchers not to give up, that the horse would be found on the morning of the fifth day.

Were it not for the buffalo I do not know if this would have been so. Let me explain. A herd of White Buffalo befriended me years ago as spirit allies. There are six of them, a small herd of radiating light, warm and enormous and kind, but also boldly defiant. Knowing I had done everything I could on my own first, I then asked the White Buffalo herd to help me find Copper Top. I summoned the herd by focusing my attention on them and explained the situation, then I asked them to scout for me. I have been taught that in working with spirit allies, human or animal, we should ask for help from them only when there is something we cannot do without their aid. These kinds of telepathic communications happen instantaneously. They take no elaborate preparation other than, honestly, decades of practice, which most people do to refine their psi skills.

I could see them when they found Copper Top, who at that moment was sitting down. They nosed around him to encourage him to stand up, which he was reluctant to do. The buffalo knew that there were humans on horses nearby. I could see them in my mind's eye walking along some trails that Copper Top had also sniffed out and followed up and down, up and down, near water by the stream under frozen edges. This was something he had not seen before and he remarked that he "crunched the water," meaning he had stepped on the icy edges of the stream.

However, Copper Top seemed unmovable. But then I realized he was simply resting, he was not injured. Domesticated horses are not like wild horses in practiced skills of survival, and the temperature was the coldest it had been in years. It was simply not warming up.

Domesticated horses are used to being groomed, fed, pampered, stabled in heated barns, and called by name. The buffalo reported, as in any good reconnaissance mission, that he would not budge from the little slice of sun he was illuminated by.

I then asked the herd of buffalo to do something so unusual that even I was surprised by the request. I asked them "to get a human's attention, to catch a human's eye" at which point the six literally put their heads together as if in a huddle. Then several of them left the huddle and, to my greatest amazement, left the ground with gorgeous wings and made the light reflect off of them as if to get a refracted light ray into a human's eye, just as a piece of glass or metal held to the sunlight will do. I had asked them specifically "to get a human's eye." They did, and literally one minute later, I received a text from my niece. "They just found him," it read.

As far as I was concerned, the flying buffalos had helped humans find this horse. After days of tracking and communicating with Copper Top, the impeccable timing was wondrous. A person can evaluate this synchronicity however they choose.

While it is typical of medicine people and shamans to have helper animals who help them treat humans, souls, and ecosystems, I had seldom asked a spirit animal to do any human work. But when Buffalo came so lovingly to offer help, I knew a relationship existed in a way I had not experienced outside of dogs and cats and other domesticated animals I had known throughout my life. Flying buffalo? Buffalo were not just my allies, they were able scouts and helped to find a missing thoroughbred that had jumped his fence looking for his home, which was 950 miles away.

This is how I got to know Buffalo in the way, I suppose, that Native Americans know Buffalo: as generous of heart, gracious of spirit, civil in conduct. Of all the animals who once roamed the Americas, they are aware of their purpose as stewards of human survival and guardians of the soil's spirit as it blesses the Earth with all things that grow.

BUFFALO HISTORY

The spirit of Buffalo and the spirit of the northern continent's Native peoples are stories of endurance. Buffalo are designed to roam far and wide and so they did with me over the vast lands of their near and distant pasts. They told me many things—of their losses, their triumphs, their fears, and their hopes for the future. Buffalo spoke of the time when human and animal lives were intertwined with gratitude and respect. The lives of Native peoples centered around the buffalo, which they prayed over and honored.

When I think of Buffalo I see their massive herds stretched across the prairies and plains of America. They are joined in their migrations by humans, together crossing the territories with the seasons. I see buffalo-hide tipis standing against the expanse of open blue skies. I smile watching young calves playing around their mothers, romping in the sweet tall grasses of August. I smell the thousands of buffalo who have wallowed in the dirt, enjoying the winds that come up suddenly and then die down to stillness. I am awed by their formidable blockades around anything or anyone they choose to protect. Their massive bodies array in a circle with their heads pointed outward. But, above all, I think about the herd's extraordinary devotion and their overwhelming purpose, which is to protect their young from predators, invigorate the Earth and the spirit of Earth, and bring Earth people to peace and prayer.

Buffalo are willing to give up their lives for the right reasons. They have deep respect for life, so sacrifice for another is a profound act. They prosper well when left to the wild and improve every ecosystem that they attend to, to the extent that their disappearance from any landscape has a hugely negative impact. Traditional healing plants and native grasses vanish when Buffalo leaves. The importance of Buffalo to ecosystem health has been self-evident to Native peoples familiar with centuries of herbal wisdom passed down through family lineages, and has begun to be recognized by scientists who now

Fig. 6.1. American bison (buffalo)
From *The Extermination of the American Bison* (1887)
by William T. Hornaday

appreciate the profound influence of Buffalo on the health of the land.

According to Professor Johan du Toit at Utah State University's Department of Wild Land Resources, "In areas where bison can be introduced . . . bison are probably very important in terms of maintaining ecosystem function."[1] The bison that inhabit the Henry Mountains of Utah roam freely in an area south of Hanksville where domestic ranch cattle also graze under permits issued by the Bureau of Land Management. In spite of that close proximity, it appears, based on genetic sampling, that there has been no interbreeding in the seven decades the bison have been there.

"The disease-free, genetically pure Utah herd could become valuable if other states use it to launch their own herds. . . . Some experts have argued that restoring bison herds in some places would be good for the environment due to the 'tilling' effect of bison hooves and the fertilizing properties of their dung and urine. . . . The DNA testing is part of a larger study commissioned by the Utah Division of Wildlife Resources. The agency is exploring the best methods of managing cattle and bison together in the same area."[2]

South Dakota ranch managers now realize that broad migrations can help solve critical water management problems because Buffalo's sharp hooves break up the soil and improve its ability to hold moisture. Diverse scientists—geologists, botanists, ecologists—as well as government agencies, are now speaking out about the role these apex guardians play in the ecosystems in which they evolved. Once there were millions of buffalo. There are less than half a million now, scattered about in restricted reserves, parks, and on private lands.

By the end of the nineteenth century, the estimated 60 million buffalo had precipitously dropped to barely one thousand. Numbers have increased with conservation but still only a fraction of their original population remains. A mere thirty-five hundred of them are free-living and the majority are not purebred buffalo. Johan du Toit maintains that "Most of the bison that are around today, particularly those on private land, are hybrids."[3]

There are about half a million bison-cattle hybrids that are bred as commodities on private ranches and public lands. They are a modern genetic hybrid engineered by humans. *Engineer* is an accurate term because buffalo and cows do not breed naturally, that is, on their own. As mentioned earlier, there is an intact, genetically "pure" buffalo herd in the Henry Mountain region of south central Utah, where cattle and buffalo have ranged side by side for seven generations and there is no interbreeding. "It confirms that you can have bison and cattle, free ranging, together," du Toit said. "The other really good thing for Utah is that we have here an extremely valuable source of biodiversity."[4]

In contrast to the beef cattle industry assertion to the contrary, the only time the two species crossbreed is when they are held in herd lots together. Recent genetic tests show that the Utah herd is one of the

Fig. 6.2. Historic image of a buffalo herd grazing. Montana, 1909.
Library of Congress

few surviving populations of pure American plains buffalo. These two hundred fifty to four hundred disease-free, genetically pure buffalo will perhaps "seed" other herds in states that decide to host grazing buffalo on public lands.

There are other pure buffalo herds. For example, there are herds in Yellowstone Park, established in 1903, in the Wind Cave National Park in South Dakota (two hundred fifty to four hundred bison), Alberta Canada's Elk Island National Park (numbering four hundred fifty), the Wood Buffalo National Park herd, which was established in 1922, and its subsidiary herds that number over five thousand. In addition, there are numerous private ranches and smaller herds like that of the White Bison Association. It hosts a herd of almost all white, genetically pure bison (buffalo) under the care of Cynthia Hart, whom we will meet later in this chapter. There are buffalo all across the United States of America. Most are treated as domesticated livestock, which is antithetical to their purpose and spirit, and most are not purebred buffalo but bison-cattle mixes.*

Preserving and restoring the wild buffalo is a vital recipe for restoration, preservation, and conservation, or CPR, which is what Wolf said is needed for the Earth. Buffalo who are returned to range ancestral routes will invigorate more than the soil. They will revitalize the soul of the nation as well. This is what Buffalo taught me. Rebuilding natural purebred herds is an ongoing process. A cross-cultural consultant with NASA and ambassador of the Lakota to the United Nations, Joseph Chasing Horse, says much more must be done to protect the buffalo and their North American habitat: "I would like to see something put into place where [the buffalo] would be able to regenerate their herds and be given more of their aboriginal migrating territory," he says. "Since the disappearance of the buffalo migration, we have felt the ecological impact that it is having upon the land. With the disappearance of the buffalo, there are certain medicines that no longer grow, and the Great Plains are being turned back into a desert."[5]

When a survey conducted in 1889 found that just over one thousand buffalo remained in the United Sates, President Theodore Roosevelt (1858–1919) and American zoologist, taxidermist, conservationist, and author William Temple Hornaday (1854–1937) created the American Bison Society (ABS) to save the buffalo from extinction and raise awareness and appreciation for the American icon. In 1907, the New York Zoological Society—of which Hornaday was president and which was to become the Wildlife Conservation Society (WCS) and the Bronx Zoo—sent fifteen buffalo from the zoo to a game

---

*One organization, the National Bison Association (NBA), represents over one thousand members who raise over two hundred fifty thousand head of bison, but this is for the most part mimicking the cattle industry slaughterhouse economy. The NBA has members in all fifty states and ten countries. It is a nonprofit association, which promotes the preservation, production, and marketing of bison.

reserve and refuge in Oklahoma. This was the first formal wildlife reintroduction in the United States. Years later, in 2005, seventy years after it had been disbanded, WCS resurrected the ABS to promote the ecological importance of Buffalo. The ABS bison coordinator, Keith Aune, states that it is their mission to "restore bison ecologically, not just animals in pens but actual functioning animals in the larger landscape."[6]

Despite how violently and dishonorably the U.S. government and non-Native people of the United States have treated them down through time, Buffalo and peace have always gone hand in hand. While Bear guards the North and the healing spirit, Elephant our compassionate capacities, Lion our intrastellar golden hearts, Wolf our ability to take part in the life continuum awake and aware, and Buffalo brings us thundering into the Earth's center with a great stampede of enthusiasm declaring, "We are of the Earth, we are Earth beings!"

WHITE BUFFALO, EUROPA, TAURUS, AND HATHOR

The White Buffalo bull entered Western consciousness through its association with mythology in the Roman story of Zeus, the king of the gods. Zeus turned himself into a white bull in order to abduct and then rape Europa. We recognize the name Europa as the continent that was named after her and the sixth-closest moon of Jupiter (the Roman name for Zeus) and the sixth largest moon of the solar system. Some astronomers believe that complex life can be supported there because it has twice as much water as all the Earth's oceans. It is said that, in Europa's honor, Zeus re-created the white bull as the zodiacal sign Taurus, in which the moon is astrologically exalted. Europa and the naming of a celestial object is similar in province and power to the story of the great bear mother and cubs who were, as described by the Romans, exiled.

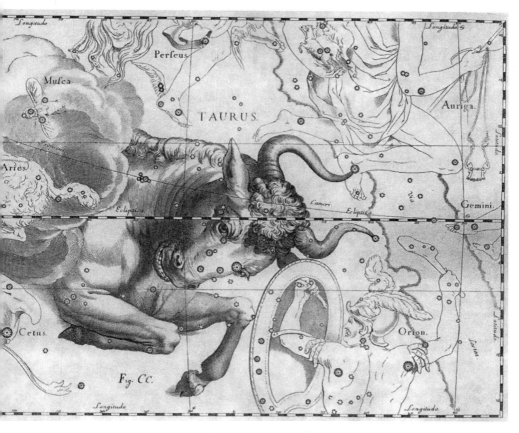

Fig. 6.3. The Taurus constellation
Uranographia by astronomer Johannes Hevelius (1611–1687),
published posthumously in 1690

Europa is often attributed to the wide-faced Egyptian deity Hathor, the sacred female cow whom the Greeks identified as the sky mother, Aphrodite, the sacred mother goddess. Europa also appears as the earlier Phoenician Astarte, of the moon goddess tradition. The cow is still held sacred in many parts of the world and is regarded as the great holy mother of the moon who brings fertility and blessings. Thus, White Buffalo females, also called "cows," are considered to be the holy mothers of the land's spirit.

While Europa herself became the first queen of Crete after her abduction and rape, much like the captive Queen Esther as Queen of Persia (478 BCE) who lived in captivity under the rule of King Ahasuerus, she remained captive. The story of Europa has repeated itself worldwide where girls and women are forced into servitude to abusive husbands, tribes, or terrorists. The lives of many women and the buffalo are similar to that of Europa.

As Europeans expanded their occupation across the North American continent, the mystical White Animals became commodities of power to be owned by the apex predator: men of power. It is Zeus, the European male deity, who foreshadows our modern society's sense of entitlement to exploitation, domination, and ruination as choices one has inherited as the self-proclaimed dominating species. Subsequently, when Zeus takes the form of a white bull, he does so not as a bringer of bounty to the people, nor out of personal reverence and respect, but rather out of lust and the desire for ownership and domination.

Much like Europa, buffalo were victims of the European invasion. The Native peoples who had comingled with Buffalo for thousands of years as one community were also victim of European rape and plundering that led to the near obliteration of both indigenous animals and indigenous humans. This truth has made my writing the story of Buffalo and their human kin so very difficult. Their histories and experiences comprise such a vast subject about which I am unqualified to write, but I feel called upon and compelled to address it in some fashion. So for these reasons I have turned to the holders of their legends for guidance.

THE GREAT AMERICAN BUFFALO

Ten thousand years ago, after many evolutionary derivations from the ice age bison, North America's magnificent American bison, more commonly called for generations "buffalo," came into existence. In comparison with its ancestors, this species is scaled down to half its original size. The buffalo's formal name is *Bison bison* and it's also referred to as "the American or Plains bison." *Bison bison athabascae*, or Canadian Wood Bison, is a subspecies whose original habitat spanned across Alberta, the Yukon, and the Northern Territories. Even its scientific names conjure up the sound of hooves beating, beating, and beating against the soil as the animals run together in the thousands. Whatever their size or their names, all buffalo are the offspring of the great woolly mammoth. As DNA tests in 2015 confirmed, American buffalo are related to our beautiful Asian elephants who are the closest living relatives of the ancestral wooly mammoth.[7] And it is Asia that is the home of the White Spirit Elephants.

Buffalo were the focal animal for the North American Native peoples for thousands of years. They were considered kin, a first brother. Buffalo and humans lived side-by-side as codependent blood relations. Mineconju-Lakota medicine man John Fire Lame Deer (1903–1976) explains how the buffalo provided a complete resource for Native humans.

> The buffalo gave us everything we needed, without it we were nothing. Our tipis were made of his skin. His hide was our bed, our blanket, and our winter coat. It was our drum, throbbing through the night, alive, holy. Out of his skin we made our water bags. His flesh strengthened us, became flesh of our flesh. Not the smallest part of it was wasted. His stomach, a red-hot stone dropped into it, became our soup kettle. His horns were our spoons, the bones our knives, our women's awls and needles. Out of his sinews we made our bowstrings and thread. His ribs were fashioned into sleds for our children, his hoofs became rattles. His mighty skull, with the pipe leaning against it, was our sacred altar. The name of the greatest of all Sioux was Tatanka Iyotake—Sitting Bull. When you killed off the buffalo, you also killed the Indian—the real, natural, "wild" Indian.[8]

Similar to the elephant, the Great American Buffalo is a grazer. They spend their morning hours chewing grasses and sedges, then afterward spend the rest of their day walking or resting, digesting and wallowing in the dirt. Like elephants, buffalo are responsible for turning over the soil, spreading seeds with their scratching hooves and horns, and fertilizing with their dung. The buffalo's way of life encourages new undergrowth and grass that reseeds the plains and valleys where they roam. Unlike cattle corralled by the meat industry and whose overuse of land destroys topsoil, depletes and contaminates water sources, buffalo invigorate the land and the spirit of the land, increasing its fertility and abundant flora and fauna in the Northern Hemisphere.

At two years of age, the female buffalo is ready to mate yet her male brothers do not mate until the age of six. Buffalo usually live twenty to twenty-five years in the wild but are killed at the young of age of four in the modern era, as they have been commodified for the meat production industry. The cow (female buffalo) may bear a calf almost every year of her life. After a gestation period of nine and a half months, she gives birth sometime between mid-April and June. At birth, calves weigh on average forty pounds. Unless it is a White Buffalo, every buffalo is reddish brown when born and will be up and about with its mother within a few hours of birth. At two months, a calf begins to develop horns and the distinctive shoulder hump. The young are weaned at about seven months at which time they weigh approximately four hundred pounds. A full-grown male buffalo will weigh two thousand pounds and the female almost 50 percent less, weighing eleven hundred pounds. The modern buffalo stands about seven feet tall from shoulder to hoof.

Groups of females and their offspring often live in small groups of twenty or less and male buffalo, similar to male elephants, aggregate in smaller groups or roam alone. July marks the beginning of the "head butting" season, which runs through September, when male buffalo start to attend to their chosen cows. Female herds accept the males who may stay around their female from a few minutes after mating to a few days or even an entire season. Once mature, the two sexes live separate from one another on a daily basis, but merge during mating season and around watering holes or during times of danger. Also, as with other animals we have met, each of the female and male communities have an elder leader.

Buffalo reminds us that grasses are the foundation of the ecosystems of the plains and the prairie. Grasses breed life into the soil and protect it from too much rain or wind. Grasses enable the microorganisms upon which healthy soil is based and on which all life depends to flourish. Healthy grasses prevent the Earth from becoming a desert. The millions of acres upon which buffalo graze are regenerated by their presence. They create vibrant wallows, or indentations in the ground made by their massive bodies rolling in the dirt, which fill to make pools when it rains. By the simple movements of Buffalo every day, other animals benefit. The soil and buffalo are literally the ground that has supported the plant and animal kingdoms of North America since the last ice age ended more than ten thousand years ago.

Before the colonization of North America, the buffalo empire was greater than any human civilization on the continent, connecting us directly to our glacial age history, human and beast alike. Like the other prophets of the wild that we have now met, Buffalo know their purpose, which for thousands of years was to manage the soils and inculcate *Homo sapiens* with gratitude. They provided for humans, Earth, and other animals in a reciprocal relationship of mutual service and elevation. However, invading Europeans had little appreciation for these spiritual realities. Instead they were more familiar with expanding their control, which included invasion, plunder, murder, and war against the Indians, animals, and the ecosystems of the entire continent. Today ecocide is institutionalized.

THE OFFICIAL MEETING OF WHITE MAN AND BUFFALO

The first encounter between a white man and the buffalo's massive herds was recorded in 1679 by an adventuring theologian, forty-three-year-old Franciscan priest Father Louis Hennepin, a brave and daring man. While in the Netherlands during the war between the French and Spanish, he almost died of spotted fever while caring for two wounded soldiers. Later, he escaped pirates at sea as well as the Lakota who had captured him. In 1673, Hennepin was sent by King Louis XIV to join the expedition of Rene Robert Cavelier, Sieur de La Salle. He crossed the Atlantic and landed in Quebec where he remained an ascetic monk in the Order of St. Augustine for four years. After this period, he rejoined La Salle and traveled up the St. Lawrence River to the wilderness of the Great Lakes. Here Father Hennepin first saw the massive number of buffalo on the northern boundary of their range. The total number of buffalo at the time was estimated at 60 million. They extended throughout most of North America.

In what is now considered a classic, William Hornaday's *The Extermination of the American Bison* describes how

The range of the American bison extended over about one-third of the entire continent of North America. Starting almost at Tidewater on the Atlantic coast, it extended westward through a vast tract of dense forest, across the Alleghany Mountain system to the prairies along the Mississippi, and southward to the Delta of that great stream. Although the great plains country of the West was the natural home of the species, where it flourished most abundantly, it also wandered south across Texas to the burning plains of northeastern Mexico, westward across the Rocky Mountains into New Mexico, Utah, and Idaho, and northward across a vast treeless wasteland to the bleak and inhospitable shores of the Great Slave Lake itself. It is more than probable that had the bison remained unmolested by man and uninfluenced by him, he would eventually have crossed the Sierra Nevada's and the Coast Range and taken up his abode in the fertile valleys of the Pacific slope.[9]

As roaming herbivores, the buffalo follow seasonal migratory and ancestral paths and trails made over centuries. Without these buffalo trails, neither pioneer nor the government soldier would have known how to cross the territories safely through the maze of water, forests, mountains, and valleys. It is tragic irony that the buffalo paths were the very same trails their exterminators followed and the ones the railroads used to map their course through the territories. Government soldiers and private citizens would ride the rails and shoot down thousands of buffalo a day. It is difficult for any living human to imagine the scale of what the buffalo herd looked like. In a private letter, from September 21, 1887, Colonel Dodge wrote to Hornaday about seeing the last of the great herds, two hundred years after the first recorded sighting by Hennepin, described earlier.

> The great herd on the Arkansas through which I passed could not have averaged, at rest, over fifteen or twenty individuals to the acre, but was, from my own observation, not less than 25 miles wide, and from reports of hunters and others it was about five days in passing a given point, or not less than 50 miles deep. From the top of Pawnee Rock I could see from 6 to 10 miles in almost every direction. This whole vast space was covered with buffalo, looking at a distance like one compact mass, the visual angle not permitting the ground to be seen. I have seen such a sight a great number of times, but never on so large a scale. That was the last of the great herds.[10]

Hornaday calculated what the scale of the remnant herd would have been.

> If the advancing multitude had been at all points 50 miles in length (as it was known to have been in some places at least) by 25 miles in width, and still averaged fifteen head to the acre of ground, it would have contained the enormous number of 12,000,000 head.

Fig. 6.4. Men shooting buffalo on the Kansas-Pacific Railway line
From *Frank Leslie's Illustrated Newspaper*
volume 32, no. 818, June 3, 1871
(Library of Congress)

But, judging from the general principles governing such migrations, it is almost certain that the moving mass advanced in the shape of a wedge, which would make it necessary to deduct about two-third from the grand total, which would leave 4,000,000 as our estimate of the actual number of Buffalos in this great herd, which I believe is more likely to be below the truth than above it.[11]

WILLIAM TEMPLE HORNADAY

William T. Hornaday had many interests and talents; they included zoology, hunting, and taxidermy. He is often cited as the person who founded the American conservation movement. His biography illustrates how hunting and wildlife collections for zoos have been linked to conservation. This confusion and misrepresentation continues today. The Wildlife Conservation Society and its Bronx Zoo claim to support conservation, but their actions and roots derive from wildlife capture and killing, a paradox that is a good example of how dissociation affects all of us. This does not diminish the good that they and other organizations like them do, but it is important to appreciate how even our decisions to help animals are often tainted by our own agendas.

Hornaday was a taxidermist at both Iowa State Agricultural College and Ward's Natural Science Establishment in Rochester, New York. He expanded his interests to travel around the world. "Hornaday undertook a series of scientific expeditions to Florida, Cuba, the Bahamas, South America, India, Sri Lanka, the Malay Peninsula, and Borneo in the 1870s. He soon became known for his dramatic 'life groups' of animals in natural settings for museum displays."[12]

In 1882, he was appointed chief taxidermist of the United States National Museum at the Smithsonian Institution and later founded the Bronx Zoo. He was tasked by the Smithsonian with mounting a buffalo exhibit. When he travelled to Montana, he was stunned by the disappearance of the great herds he had seen only years earlier. His 1886 hunting-acquisition trip to Montana's Musselshell River area was the last time he hunted buffalo. After seeing with his own eyes the mass slaughter of buffalo on his journey, he chose to champion the buffalo instead of killing it. His taxidermy mounts, which have been restored and brought back after years of storage in different museums, are comprised of a great bull and a cow and two calves.

After this expedition west, Hornaday became the buffalo's greatest voice for their preservation and protection. He actively lobbied Congress and the public with, as he would say, "the urgency of the Creator Himself." He saw the impact of ranch-style capture and captivity of the buffalo and the changes that it already had on the species.

Fig. 6.5. William Temple Hornaday with buffalo calf, 1889
Smithsonian Institution Archives, Image #74-12338

Hornaday wrote, "In no feature is the change from natural conditions to captivity more easily noticeable than in the eye. In the wild buffalo the eye is always deeply set, well protected by the edge of the bony orbit, and perfect in form and expression. The lids are firmly drawn around the ball, the opening is so small that the white portion of the eyeball is entirely covered, and the whole form and appearance of the organ is as shapely and as pleasing in expression as the eye of a deer." In contrast, "In the captive, the various muscles which support and control the eyeball seem to relax and thicken, and the ball protrudes far beyond its normal plane, showing a circle of white all around the iris, and bulging out in a most unnatural way."[13]

Hornaday observed another alteration: "an arching of the back in the middle, which has a tendency to make the hump look lower at the shoulders and visibly alters the outline of the back. This tendency to 'hump up' the back is very noticeable in domestic cattle and horses during rainy weather. While a Buffalo on his native heath would seldom assume such an attitude of dejection and misery, in captivity, especially if it be anything like close confinement, it is often to be observed, and I fear will eventually become a permanent habit. Indeed, I think it may be confidently predicted that the time will come when naturalists who have never seen a wild Buffalo will compare the specimens composing the National Museum group with the living representatives to be seen in captivity and assert that the former are exaggerations in both form and size."[14]

Hornaday founded what he called the Department of Living Animals at the Smithsonian and then went on to establish the National Zoological Park in 1889. Hornaday (whose name I like to think of as "horn-a-day," as if counting the buffalo by horns, day-by-day), was responsible for the Permanent Wildlife Protection Fund founded in 1913. He advocated for national parks, wildlife conservation, and international treaties on the subject. The *American Museum Journal* declared in 1915 that Hornaday had "no doubt inaugurated and carried to success more movements for the protection of wild animal life than has any other man in America."[15]

THE EXTERMINATION OF
THE BUFFALO AND THE
INDIGENOUS PEOPLE

Hornaday challenged popular reasoning at the time, which disfavored any expense involved in supporting the buffalo and the Native peoples in their territories. The popular opinion was extermination of both. He argued that it would have been more cost-effective to support the millions of buffalo and manage their overall population and to support the tribes in a logical division of land than it was to make all Indians prisoners of reservation camps and government schools. Land seizure in North America was in actuality an extermination campaign of both the Red Man and the buffalo.

The massive numbers of buffalo and their drop to near-extinction in the 1880s attest to the scale of the slaughter. For years, day after day, an arsenal of weapons was used against them: guns, traps, poison, pits, arrows, and other tools of violent assault. No buffalo was spared. All were killed, young and old, male and female. And the killers were rewarded by the United States government for these atrocities. The horrendous decision by the U.S. Congress to eliminate the buffalo as a means of confiscating land and undermining the Native people who were also killed and imprisoned was the antecedent to brutal factory farming and government-funded experiments on animals and humans, perfected in the industrial age that followed. Buffalo and Indian massacres lay the foundation for the American war economy that has shaped the nation to this day. The war economy is a death economy where "profit" is equated with "progress" even when there is substantial loss of life—ecological, animal, and human. It has become a calculated enterprise crafted and perfected by an oligarchy, which needs to be transformed as well from the "will to power" to "the desire to serve." This is the message from Buffalo. As the Lakota teach, "As the buffalo goes, so goes the Red Man." To that I add, so goes the northern continent and its varied inhabitants of many races.

When President Grover Cleveland (1837–1908), the twenty-second and twenty-fourth president of the United States, enacted a law that made buffalo hunting illegal in 1893, there were only three hundred to one thousand buffalo left. American Indians fared no better. In addition to their being murdered and relocated, they suffered from cultural genocide and millions of Indians died of smallpox, which sometimes claimed 90 percent of a single village. All of these factors contributed to the fractionalization of tribes, traditions, and legacies.

The European conquest of the American lands from "sea to shining sea" demolished all wildlife, not just the Buffalo. Cougars, bears, birds, and the forests and rivers in which they lived were all impacted. The testimony of Secretary of the Interior Columbus Delano to Congress in 1874 reflects that animalcide was deliberately used for the genocide of the American Indians. "The buffalo are disappearing rapidly, but not faster than I desire. I regard the destruction of such game as Indians subsist upon as facilitating the policy of the Government, of destroying their hunting habits, coercing them on reservations, and compelling them to begin to adopt the habits of civilization."[16]

For thousands of years, the Plains Indians lived as nomads, migrating with the great herds of buffalo season to season. These well-worn passages assured humans water and easier open trails for travel. But tragedy upon tragedy befell these great beings that made the westward trails over the continent possible. The price the buffalo paid for leading the way was their lives. Buffalo have a heroic history, a martyred history, which one hopes will rebirth into human gratitude and their reestablished plentitude.

Hornaday estimated that as recently as 1867 approximately 15 million wild buffalo remained in the American West, out of an earlier 60 million. In a letter written to George Brown Goode, the director for whom he worked at the Smithsonian, Hornaday reported that, "In the United States the extermination of all the large herds of buffalo is already an accomplished fact."[17] But as he also highlighted, when the same humans decide to destroy a culture, a habitat, and customs, they had no restraint nor humility, making the new Americans what some have called the "ugly Americans." This shadow is ignored in the schoolroom. The story of the buffalo, and their teachings, reminds us how critical it is to behave with respectful reciprocity as a global community.

Indians and Buffalo were condemned to living on small reserves that were government controlled. Natural freedom is the axis mundi about which all Native Earth-based traditions derive their authority. It is the divine right of an individual to be self-governed by an inner authority, enabling each of us to decide right action. Through a cultivated unity of one's mind and heart, this is accomplished. This interdependence between individuals and the group manifests as collective self-rule, which the Native peoples practice. Historically, among tribes, women were the property holders and had the authority to elect and remove community members from their posts for failing to preside properly. The League of the Iroquois lived the meaning of a bundle of arrows. It is ironic that what our national coat of arms or "great seal" emblazons on its obverse side as symbolic of our outer purpose in the world as a defender of justice and peace was learned from Native Americans, those Congress consigned nationwide to imprisonment and physical and cultural extermination.

The European invasion by migrations westward and their colossal destruction of animal and other humans moved us from a right hemisphere, intuitive way of relating to the Earth, to the left hemisphere, material relationship with the world. A reverence for life and a way of seeing value in all things was supplanted by exploitation and greed, oblivious to the harm it causes. The American use of war as an economic enterprise and to achieve domination is colored by narcissism and self-emulation, very much like Zeus in the Greek tradition. Myths that extol bad role models lead to bad behavior. Stories are not just imaginary ruminations, but provide instructions to the unconscious psyche. Zeus obviously never had a reprimanding nanny or parent to discipline his appetite for domination and guide his heart instead to helping others. He reflects the tradition that indulges bad-tempered young boys who rage, and leads to men who seek power rather than protecting the world. In matrilineal societies, the women's power to correct such behavior is purposeful. In contrast, in patriarchal cultures, the woman has all the obligations of childcare without the societal power as leaders.

Of the apex providers we have studied and discussed, all but the wolf are similar in their matrilineal societal structures. But even the wolf exercises maternal influence. All pups stay with their moms to about the age of two or so, and only then do the young males leave and join older males of their species for further education and protection. This includes schooling to guard and protect the female herds from predators. The entire society is designed to repopulate and protect the females and offspring from harm, which permits the youngest animals to exercise a sense of freedom. Protection and schooling for the good of the society is common to the lives of all White Spirit Animals.

The three years of 1872, 1873, and 1874 witnessed the greatest slaughter of the buffalo. "According to one buffalo hunter, who based his calculations on firsthand accounts and shipping records, 4.5 million buffalo were slaughtered in that three-year period alone."[18] So many were killed, it is said, that one could walk for hundreds of miles on the rotting carcasses as stepping-stones without ever putting one's foot on the ground.

Millions were slaughtered on the plains for two dollars a "robe," as the skinned hide was called. With fewer than a thousand American bison left in the wild, the New York Zoological Society (NYZS) sponsored the founding of the American Bison Society at the Bronx Zoo's Lion House. In 1903 Hornaday brought forty buffalo eastward to live on the allocated ten-acre plot at the Bronx Zoo. Gradually, the herds in the West grew and the buffalo population rebounded. Many of today's buffalo in the western United States are descendants of those original Bronx Zoo animals.

With Hornaday as the "bison group's" president, the organization was instrumental in securing national protection for them as well as rangeland for the establishment of new herds. By 1919, the American Bison Society had introduced nine herds for the preservation of the species. Hornaday claimed that

> Had the bison remained for a few more centuries in undisturbed possession of his range, and with liberty to roam at will over the North American continent, it is almost certain that several distinctly recognizable varieties would have been produced. The buffalo of the hot regions in the extreme south would have become a shorthaired animal like the gaur of India and the African buffalo. The individuals inhabiting the extreme north, in the vicinity of Great Slave Lake, for example, would have developed still longer hair, and taken on more of the dense hairiness of the musk ox. In the "wood" or "mountain buffalo" we already have a distinct foreshadowing of the changes which would have taken place in the individuals which made their permanent residence upon rugged mountains.[19]

William T. Hornaday gave every member of the U.S. Congress a copy of his 1913 book, *Our Vanishing Wildlife: Its Extermination and Preservation*. He was both a visionary and a practical man who regarded conservation as our moral obligation, not just a sensible idea. As Hornaday made clear for the public during his lifetime, the "Birds and mammals now are literally dying for your help."[20] Early on, Hornaday realized the danger that new guns and the automobile industry would pose to wildlife. These technologies would give greater access to wildlife and greater ease by which to kill them. They also distanced other animals from our own species. He wrote, "It is time for the people who don't shoot to call a halt on those who do; 'and if this be treason, then let my enemies make the most of it!'"[21]

Today's cross-species genocide must stop. Human hunting of

wildlife as sport needs to end, as does torturous factory farming and the scientific abuse of all species.

THE MANAGEMENT AND MISMANAGEMENT OF BUFFALO HERDS TODAY

Yellowstone National Park was created in 1872 and the remaining few surviving buffalo became the breeder pool for an almost extinct species. As Hornaday records for our deep reflection, "The business-like, wholesale slaughter, wherein one hunter would openly kill five thousand Buffaloes and market perhaps two thousand hides, could easily have been stopped forever. . . . There is nowhere in this country, nor in any of the waters adjacent to it, a living species of any kind which the United States Government cannot fully and perpetually protect from destruction by human agencies if it chooses to do so."[22] The same remains true today, and it is this reality that everyone involved in the ecological imperative speaks to with shocking alarm—that our leadership and other leaders in the world should be mercenary themselves, failing at the greatest job of all: stewardship of the Earth.

However, although Yellowstone National Park, under National Park Service oversight, is charged with protecting the American buffalo from hunters, it has not always been an exemplary steward. While charged with protecting the buffalo from extinction, the very same park and wildlife officials have facilitated the execution of large numbers of them. Some are also killed by poachers who shoot them when they cross out of the Yellowstone park area. These issues are vital to address.

The park service has put what opponents call an "artificial cap" of three thousand buffalo as what the ecosystem in Yellowstone's four hundred thousand acres can support. When these numbers are reached, there is a systematic culling (selection and slaughtering) of the buffalo. The tragedy lies not just in the intentional destruction of herd life but in the fact that tribes and individuals with congruous open lands

Fig. 6.6. Photograph from the mid-1870s of a pile of American buffalo skulls waiting to be ground for fertilizer

repeatedly ask to take or purchase these buffalo and restore them to native migratory routes for the buffalo's health and that of the ecosystems they could inhabit. Instead, the park service consistently chooses systematic slaughtering of all age and gender of buffalo. As I write these words, the unnecessary killing of Buffalo continues.

To counter the government's violence, an organization called Buffalo Field Campaign (BFC) was founded by Lakota activist Rosalie Little Thunder (1949–2014) and videographer Mike Meese. Rosalie had a command of the Lakota language and cultural traditions as well as having a passionate relationship with and compassion for the Buffalo nation (Pte Oyate). In the winter of 1996–1997, 1,100 buffalo, who, needing forageable foods, followed their "nutrition trail" out of the park and into Montana, were all shot to death by the Montana Department of Wildlife (DOL) and the National Park Service. After that, the Buffalo Field Campaign came into being. It is dedicated to protecting the wild buffalo in the Yellowstone National Park herds and those animals that accidentally wander off property and become targets of hunters waiting in pick-up trucks with long-range scopes. The Buffalo Field Campaign is made up of volunteers who ride out on horses and film or enact civil disobedience when the park service goes into one of its roundups to eliminate and quarantine calves, mothers, and sires, to transfer them to others for slaughter.[23] To date, almost ten thousand buffalo have been killed since 1985 by governmental decree.

BFC is vigilant and ever watchful of the park service. The group patrols the area on horseback and brings lawsuits to the court to stop the government-supported hunting of Yellowstone buffalo. The buffalo in the greater Yellowstone area are some of the few genetically pure historic buffalo remaining in America. Their lineage stretches back to the last ice age. They are like a sacred center, holders of ancient genetics, breeders of resilient offspring for the future.

Stephany Seay, buffalo activist and media coordinator for the Buffalo Field Campaign, explains, "It's all political, arbitrary, and what it comes down to is the power of cattle ranchers in Montana. They don't want to share any grazing land, claiming that the buffalo give the cattle brucellosis."[24] But, as she makes clear, "there is not a single documented case of this, though the wild elk they leave untouched do carry this disease to the cattle." Giving preference to the millions of cattle bred for meat consumption is a sorry excuse for annihilating a wild species.

When the park service rounds up buffalo on horses, they separate the calves from their mothers and the bulls from the rest of the herd, doing what elephant hunters have done in Africa: destroy the matrilineal culture's memory and society of the animals in toto from which they do not recover. "There is enough contiguous land," Seay declares, "from state to state on public lands, private lands with eager participants, to accommodate wild-ranging buffalo, just as we do elk, deer, and wolf or any other animal of the wild. Buffalo are not cattle; they do not destroy the topsoil, water sources, or grazing lands as cattle production does."

These days, the Lakota and other Indian nations have established their own herds in South Dakota and elsewhere through the Intertribal Bison Association (ITBC), and many hope to rebuild the herds to a total count of one million buffalo. Founded formally in 1992, the ITBC has a membership of fifty-six tribes in nineteen states with a collective herd of over fifteen thousand buffalo on one million acres of tribal land. Membership of ITBC remains open and there is continued interest by nonmember tribes in the organization. "ITBC is committed to reestablishing buffalo herds on Indian lands in a manner that promotes cultural enhancement, spiritual revitalization, ecological restoration, and economic development."[25]

The ITBC states that "the reintroduction of the buffalo to tribal lands will help heal the spirit of both the Indian people and the buffalo," though the majority of buffalo are raised for meat production. It is estimated that less than 4 percent of plains buffalo today (twenty thousand) are in herds managed for conservation and less than 2 percent (seventy-five hundred) can be considered pure breeds. Subsequently, most are mixed breeds with cattle. Because of this, most buffalo are pasture-kept and are no longer the ecosystem capstone on the historic scale they once were. They are therefore unable to do their traditional job, which is so vital for ecosystem health and our own. Buffalo's freedom is a spiritual and physical necessity that Native tribes remain aware of and engaged in restoring.

THE MYSTERY OF BLACK DIAMOND

One buffalo story in particular exemplifies the historic exploitation of the buffalo. Black Diamond was the patriarch bull of the New York

Central Park buffalo herd that Hornaday and other members of the American Bison Society used as a poster boy for their cause. He was considered the best of his kind, the biggest of bulls, and a great exemplar of his species and is perhaps the best-known buffalo in American history. Black Diamond is thought to have been the model used for the 1913 Indian head American buffalo nickel as well as for the 1901 ten-dollar note.

However, despite his fame and stature in the eyes of the ABS, the "great bull" was put up for auction on June 28, 1915. On November 10, 1915, a *New York Times* headline read, "Zoo's Big Buffalo Sold to a Butcher. . . ." The article stated that "Black Diamond, the largest buffalo in captivity, will be led out of his inclosure at the Central Park Menagerie and taken to the shambles a week from today. It was learned only yesterday that this finest specimen of Western plains wildlife was going to be disposed of in a slaughterhouse." Black Diamond's fate exemplifies a human's ability to dissociate from life and eliminate a life of one who has served us so well.

At death, Black Diamond was at least five to six years short of his life expectancy. He weighed more than a ton at age twenty-two. Reports

Fig. 6.7. Indian head buffalo nickel (1913)
Designed by James Earle Fraser (1876–1953), National Numismatic Collection,
National Museum of American History

Fig. 6.8. United States $10 banknote, legal tender, series of 1901. The central portrait is a depiction of an American buffalo that may be modeled after Black Diamond (1893–1915), the Great Bull of the Central Park Zoo.
National Numismatic Collection, National Museum of American History

say he was ill, but the fact remains that the park tried to sell him for a profit and to replace him with a younger bull—this was their motivation. Preventing a natural contest between bulls for domination, they decided simply to auction him off as meat. He was judged to be infirm, then transferred by truck to a livestock lot for auction where no one offered to buy him. I would like to think this restraint was initially out of respect for who he was, though later his flesh was sold and made into steaks and his head mounted.

His caretakers stood by him in tears, having no place to put him even if they could have raised the $300 for which he was later sold in a private deal with a big game hunter and taxidermist named "the turkey king." A. Silz, Inc., a dealer in poultry and game, bought the rights to Black Diamond's body and his hide. On November 17, 1915, Black Diamond was slaughtered. His "robe" of thirteen feet was later used to cover Silz's personal Cadillac. Reports of the incident say that Black Diamond "stared directly" at his executioner who shot him to death with a bullet to his head from which he did not flinch.

When I read or hear anyone say buffalo are stupid, or buffalo are cowards, I want to say to them, "The buffalo enabled the survival of the indigenous peoples. What greater sacrifice is there than this? Buffalo know what it is to sacrifice their lives in service. They are not stupid, but loyal, nor are they cowardly. They are fiercely protective of their herds and those who show stewardship to them. Like any human-animal relationship that is built on love and trust, one experiences love and trust from them in return."

WHITE BUFFALO CALF WOMAN

In stark contrast to the European plunder of nature, the Indian nations respect the Earth and all animal kin. The buffalo, especially White Buffalo, is the epicenter of the Lakota nation. So sacred is the female prophet in the story that she, as in other indigenous shape-shifting stories, is both woman and buffalo simultaneously. This is a story, claimed to date back at least two thousand years, that concerns a holy woman who, like the White Lions, some say fell from the stars, bringing with her the White Buffalo and prayer pipe among her other gifts to the people. There are many ways to tell this story. Here is the version of the White Buffalo Calf Woman story, told by Chief Arvol Looking Horse, 19th Carrier of the White Buffalo Calf Pipe.[26]

Buffalo Calf Woman as Told by Chief Arvol Looking Horse

There was a time when all of the animals disappeared. During that time there were no buffalo. All the buffalo and all the animals disappeared. The people said that a great teaching has come among the people when they disrespect the way of life. The Creator Wakan Tanka said to the people, "You are to live a (respectful) way of life and follow the buffalo and respect their way of life." Because they were human beings, the people abused that life. That's when all the animals and the buffalo disappeared.

There were two scouts and they were looking for buffalo. From where they were sitting on the top of the hill, they saw from a far distance, a person coming. The person that came upon them was a woman with long black hair and a buckskin dress carrying a bundle and a buffalo robe. She came to them and said, "I know what both of you are thinking. One has good thoughts and the other bad thoughts." She told the one with the bad thoughts, "Come with me." When he approached her, a cloud enveloped him and when the cloud left him, he was a skeleton. His friend was looking at him and he was in shock to see that. The woman said, "Tomorrow I will bring this bundle to the people. Go, prepare."

So, the scout went back and told the people what happened and the next day the woman brought the bundle with the sacred pipe (inside it). She was singing as she came to the people and she laid the bundle down and she opened the buffalo robe. There was a red stone (bowl) and a stem. She put it together and she started singing the Four Directions Song to the West, to the Grandfathers of the North, East, South and to the Great Spirit (of the sky) and the Mother Earth. Then she put tobacco in the pipe every time. She left the pipe (parts) together and said, "Chanupa." "Cha" is wood and "Upa" is smoke. She gave the pipe to the first Keeper. He put it to his lips and said "Upa," smoke. (The woman continued) "With this Chanupa there are seven ceremonies" (The Sacred Pipe Ceremony, the Sweat Lodge, the Vision Quest, the Sun Dance, the Making of Relatives, The Keeping of the Soul, Preparing a Girl for Womanhood.)

The White Buffalo Calf Woman told them more about the Chanupa and then she left. When she left she went to the West. She went so far and she rolled over and then stood up. She became a young black buffalo. Then a red one, then a yellow one, and the fourth one was a white one. She went over the hill as a white buffalo calf. So, the people were watching her. They said that they would call her the White Buffalo Calf Woman. And the story is that she told the people that next time she would return, she would stand on the Earth as a white buffalo calf.

The sacred bundle brought by the White Buffalo Calf Woman protected the holy prayer pipe within it. Along with another ancient pipe, it is kept in a sacred place (Green Grass) on the Cheyenne River Indian Reservation in South Dakota by the Looking Horse family. Chief Arvol Looking Horse is the nineteenth-generation keeper of the White Buffalo Calf Pipe brought to the people by White Buffalo Calf Woman.

FULFILLMENT OF THE WHITE BUFFALO PROPHECY

Another elder spokesman of the Lakota, Chief Joseph Chasing Horse, says that, "When White Buffalo Calf Woman promised to return again, she made some prophecies at that time. One of those prophecies was that the birth of a White Buffalo Calf would be a sign that it would be near the time when she would return again to purify the world. What she meant by that was that she would bring back harmony again and balance, spiritually."[27]

A number of White Buffalo have been born in modern times, but one called Miracle was the first to receive national publicity. Miracle (August 20, 1994–September 19, 2004) was born and lived for ten years on the farm of Dave, Valerie, and Corey Heider near Janesville, Wisconsin. Joseph Chasing Horse said the birth was a sign from the Great Spirit and that the ensuing age of harmony and balance that Miracle represents cannot be revoked. However, this does not mean, as he put it, that the severe trials Native Americans have endured are over. Indeed, the Lakota nation mounted the longest court case in U.S. history in an unsuccessful effort to regain control of the Black Hills, the sacred land on which the White Buffalo Calf Woman appeared two thousand years ago.

It interests me that just as Lion teaches cooperative heart awareness, and Elephant endows the planet with the energy of Buddhic consciousness, Buffalo reveals a group consciousness of its own that is entirely humble and magnificently powerful, protecting its young collaboratively and giving of its body freely for the well-being of humankind. The relationship of the Lakota people to the buffalo and their holy female prophetess guardian, Buffalo Calf Woman, which also means "falling star" or "meteor," reminds me of the Zulu sky guardians, the White Lions.

In the Lakota case, the White Buffalo Calf Woman also fell from the stars. Her presence impacts most Indian nations of the continent. White Buffalo Calf Woman is found as the central carrier of the great Creator's plan for the people of the plains. She brought them the seven gifts of living and instructed them each in their roles as children, women, and men. The Iroquois have their own legends of a sky woman and the Lakota have a version of White Buffalo Calf Woman as one of the seven stars of the Pleiades. But so vital is her teaching presence for the people that Lakota medicine man and spiritual leader Leonard Crow Dog says that "This holy woman brought the sacred buffalo calf pipe to the Sioux. There could be no Indians without it. Before she came, people did not know how to live. They knew nothing. The Buffalo Woman put her sacred mind into their minds."[28]

All of the Lakota tellings of White Buffalo Calf Woman share the same core elements whether in a short or long story form.

First, the holy woman shape-shifts into a buffalo and then back again into a woman. Second, she brings with her instructions for living that teach ritual and community laws. In addition, as with the other White Spirit Animal tales, the White Buffalo Calf Woman is a holy woman who gives the people tools for physical and spiritual well-being. She is revered to this day and is considered an agent of the recent births of the rare and beautiful White Buffalo. As with other White Spirit Animals whose history involves coming to help humanity during the Ice Age and times of famine, the White Buffalo promise to return when humanity is in need, or as the Iroquois suggest, when the Earth cleans herself.

John Fire Lame Deer (Lakota) (1903–1976) was born on the Rosebud Reservation in South Dakota. In his autobiography, *Lame Deer, Seeker of Visions,* he shares a lovely version of the story about White Buffalo Calf Woman and the gifts she brought to humankind by way of the Lakota. Lame Deer reveals the importance of the heart of the buffalo and prayer pipe journey, whose commitment to peace is something all humans must strive for together—red man, white man, yellow man, black man, all of us together. Excerpted here are the essential points regarding Buffalo's nature, purpose, and destiny with us.

The White Buffalo Woman showed the people the right way to pray, the right words and the right gestures. She taught them how to sing the pipe-filling song and how to lift the pipe up to the sky, toward Grandfather, and down toward Grandmother Earth, to *Unci,* and then to the four directions of the universe. "With this holy pipe," she said, "You will walk like a living prayer. With your feet resting upon the earth and the pipe stem reaching into the sky, your body forms a living bridge between the Sacred Beneath and the Sacred Above. Wakan Tanka smiles upon us, because now we are as one: earth, sky, all living things, the two-legged, the four-legged, the winged ones, the trees, and the grasses. Together with the people, they are all related, one family. The pipe holds them all together."[29]

With these understandings, one better appreciates the prophetic depth of Chief Arvol Looking Horse's wise words of council to us all, as he concludes the story of the White Buffalo Calf Woman and the meaning of the White Spirit Animals.

Making History In The New Millenium

"These prophecies are there about the White Buffalo and the White Animal," shares Chief Arvol Looking Horse," like the [prophecy of the] Eagle and the Condor. There are so many prophecies that are about this time right now, even in the Bible. It's going to take all people to come together with the heart and mind, good heart and good mind. . . . We are going to make history in this new millennium. We are going to make a change for our children because our children and grandchildren are beautiful. As leaders today we need to connect. We need to help each other. In the Circle there is no one person higher than the other. It doesn't

matter what part of the world you are in. We are all being affected globally. That's why I really try to walk in prayer to help people understand what we are up against. We've got to be in spiritual unity."[30]

BUFFALO PROTECTOR—CYNTHIA HART

One of the first White Spirit Animal protectors I interviewed when I began this book was Cynthia Hart, a White Bison (Buffalo) protector whose own Lakota lineage includes her father's words to her on his deathbed.[31] Uriah White Buffalo told his daughter that she "would be a buffalo protector." Today, she is a keeper of a genetically pure, primarily white, bison herd.

During our discussions over several years, she told me that buffalo, while telepathic, are wild animals, yet "they come to know you and you them."

"It is very important to understand that these animals are not 'pets' and you should never turn your back on them, especially a male. . . . Don't be fooled into thinking these are domesticated cattle. The males especially can be very dangerous, and you have to be careful how close you get. If they put their head down and tail up, you have to know they are going to attack. They can get to forty-five miles per hour in a matter of seconds and they can jump a five-foot-high fence." She then said something especially insightful, "Animals," Hart explains, "react to our emotions, whether they are fear or joy, positive or negative. What they don't seem to understand is that we are afraid of them."

Cynthia Hart's sensitivities toward animals have their roots in her childhood.

"I was blind the first few years of my life," she said, explaining the origins of her inner vision, "and I would have animals and could see out of their eyes, and how they saw things. So there was this gift that I was given but I didn't know it until I was eight years old when I got my eyesight back. I retained the ability to connect with how animals see us today. When I put my hand on an animal, I can see through their eyes.

I can still do that today with animals and people." In the past, Hart was connected to circuses such as the Ringling Bros. and Barnum & Bailey through her dad, who worked for them as a healer and was also a caretaker for animals in the Buffalo Bill Wild West show.

"My great great grandfather was Sitting Bull and this was from my father's side, and my great great cousin, through marriage, was Buffalo Bill. So family members would tease me," Hart explained, "and call me

Fig. 6.9. Sitting Bull and Buffalo Bill.
Sitting Bull was employed by Buffalo Bill's Wild West show
from June to October 1885.
Courtesy of Cynthia Hart, family collection

Calamity Jane 'cause I could ride and shoot any target," adding "as long as it was not an animal. I won't shoot an animal."

Both Sitting Bull and Buffalo Bill have consequential histories. Sitting Bull (1831–1890) is best known as a Teton Dakota Indian chief and medicine man who united the Lakota tribes in their struggle for survival on the North American Great Plains. His vision before the Battle of Little Bighorn foretold and greatly inspired their victory against Custer, the battle being known as Custer's Last Stand (June 25, 1876). According to Kari Noren-Hoshal, White Bison Association director of education, "After that battle, Sitting Bull was named the chief of all the autonomous bands of Lakota, a position never before held by any Lakota chief. Sitting Bull, now the most famous Lakota of his nation . . . took his Hunkpapa band of about five thousand to live in Canada for four years between 1877 and 1881. In July 1881, after mass extermination of the buffalo caused near starvation of his people, Sitting Bull returned to the Standing Rock Agency that straddles the North and South Dakota border."[32] Standing Rock Reservation became his final home. In 1890, fearing Sitting Bull's support of the Native American Ghost Dance movement, the U.S. government attempted to have him arrested near Fort Yates, North Dakota. Sadly, in the process, Native reservation men employed by the U.S. government shot Sitting Bull to death on December 15th, 1890.

Thirty-four-year-old Major James A. Walsh, whom Sitting Bull knew by dint of their trying to negotiate treaties together, wrote of Sitting Bull the day after the chief's death:

> I am glad to hear that Bull is relieved of his miseries, even if it took the bullet to do it. A man who wielded such power as Bull once did, that of a King, and over a wild spirited people, cannot endure abject poverty . . . without suffering great mental pain, and death is a relief. I regret now that I had not gone to Standing Rock and seen him. Bull had been misrepresented. He was not the bloodthirsty man reports made him out to be. He asked for nothing but justice. He

was not a cruel man. He was kind of heart. He was not dishonest. He was truthful. He loved his people and was glad to give his hand in friendship to any man who was honest with him.[33]

Cynthia Hart comes by her persistence and belief in peace through genetics as well as via a soul affiliation with her great great grandfather, who she says "was a kindred soul seeking to preserve his way of life."

"My dad's teachings were all Native American. My mom's teachings were all Welsh, which was pretty interesting because a lot of their teachings were compatible." Cynthia did not know as a child that she was part Lakota. "Her father and his family felt that having no rights as 'Native blood,' it was best not to talk about these things." Hart laughed when describing how her blonde hair and green eyes made some people think that her "Indian-looking" dark-skinned, dark-haired father had kidnapped her.

Hart had an extraordinary childhood and young adulthood in animal care. "Some of the animals I worked with were rhinoceros, giraffe, zebras, lions, tigers, bears, exotic birds, water buffalo, yaks, longhorn cattle, and wild mustangs, which were brought in to be domesticated, and domestic horses, which were my best friends. My father was born into a family that did rodeo circus work, and grew up taking care of the animals for Barnum & Bailey and other circuses, as well as unwanted racetrack horses and greyhound dogs. There were also wild animals that found their way to our ranch, such as wild turkey and guinea fowl and pheasants. Finally, there were animals from zoos and exotic animals whose owners were unable to care for them correctly. They would come to my father's ranch and we would rejuvenate them and repatriate them to where they belonged in different preserves around the country and a few around the world. Some of them were sent back to their native lands, or into zoos where they would have some degree of freedom. Others that were more wounded, we would keep and doctor. I wasn't brought up with just domestic animals. I was with all types of animals.

Birds, hawks, eagles—all kinds of other animals. That was my life. I never knew anything else. My whole life has been with animals."

Having interviewed hundreds of animal enthusiasts and professionals, I have found that most share a rich childhood relationship with at least one animal, which leads to a lifetime of regard for our animal kin. Explaining that White Buffalo are not the only white-coated animals she is close to, Hart says, "It's funny how white animals have a tendency to come to me; white cats, white squirrels, and in Alaska, I was working with white wolves." (See plate 19 of Cynthia Hart.)

In 1988, when Hart was thirty-four years old, her father died of lung cancer. As mentioned earlier, he shared a very intimate and life-changing moment with his daughter before passing. As she describes, "He had a whole vision, and all the kids were standing around him and he gave my sister a prophecy and gave all the kids a turn, and then when it came to me he said, 'One day you will be protecting White Buffalo.'

"I looked at him and said, 'There's no such thing as White Buffalo. You mean like protecting the spirits of animals?'

"He said, 'No. White Buffalo Calf Woman is coming back to bring the herds to warn the people of the Earth changes that are coming.'

"So I asked him, 'How can I protect them?' And he said, 'You'll find the way. You are a buffalo protector and you will see many races and you will understand the world in a different way. Your job is to protect these animals because they are going to bring back love, honor, respect, integrity, and truth to all nations for world peace.'"

From that day until this one, Hart has honored her father's prophecy.

THE TRAIL OF THE WHITE BISON ASSOCIATION: A STORY OF PROPHECY AND SPIRIT

Describing her long odyssey with the buffalo, one sees how Spirit has woven in and out of their trail and how Hart listens to Spirit for guidance. Founded in March 2008, the White Bison Association now has twenty bison.

Wondering about Hart's own beginning on this journey, I inquired, "After you realized that this was your path and your destiny as your father had described in his dying vision, how did things unfold?"[34]

"This guy Barry called me when I was living in Sedona, Arizona, in late 2000," she began. "He said, 'We really need your help. There are some White Buffalo in South Dakota and they really need to come here, to Arizona.' And I said, 'White Buffalo, there are really White Buffalo? Is this a joke?' And he said, 'No, there is a small herd that needs to come here, due to the caretaker's health, from Custer, Dakota.'"

As she told the story I couldn't help but notice "Custer" in the buffalo's location name. It seemed to me that Sitting Bull, whose victory at Little Big Horn had been against General Custer, was passing on his lineage—in this instance, to his great great granddaughter.

Later, as her story reveals, Spirit apparently was present in what was happening. "I was sitting around and asked my friend Charles and some other friends at the time if they would help do a fundraiser with me [to bring the White Buffalo to Arizona] . . . . Together we raised the money and we gave it to Barry. . . . Almost a year later, before leaving for California with Charles on a vacation, we stayed an extra night in Sedona where we camped on the night of the blue moon."

"The next morning, November 1st, 2001, before leaving for California" Hart continued, "we were meditating. Suddenly, we both heard a voice telling us to go see the White Bison who had recently arrived. The deep man's voice said, 'You must go to the White Buffalo.' He told us to find them on 89A . . . to go up 89A toward the Grand Canyon. We followed these instructions and found three little White Bison and a few brown bison. We saw that they were safely settled, took a few pictures, and left." It was not until a few months later that Hart returned to see the bison she'd helped pay to transport to Arizona. That was the day she met the herd's original caretaker. He could see that Hart immediately knew how to handle the bison and he asked her right then and there if she would help care for the White Buffalo. Hart had a thriving business as a Grand Canyon guide and medical intuitive and counselor, but she accepted the position immediately. Her father's premonition had come true!

In 2008, after the original caretaker's death, Hart inherited Miracle Moon, Rainbow Spirit, Mandela Peace Pilgrim, and their parents, Big Momma and Willy Wonka—the founding members of the White Bison Association herd.

Fig. 6.10. Hiawatha of the White Bison Association herd
By Cynthia Hart

With Arizona as a starting point, in 2001, the next sixteen years were full of challenges and lessons dealing with the buffalo's purpose and the effort required by their human protectors.

In October 2015, Hart explained, a rancher, whose peace logo was the same as her organization's own symbol and who shared similar views about ecology and caring for animals, enabled their next move. "So, on Thanksgiving day 2015, we arrived in Upper Lake with the bison." Lake County, California, explains Noren-Hoshal, "was a good place for the White Bison . . . who are meant to be in ceremony, to be present when we teach ecological living, community building, and peace-making."

The destiny of the White Bison herd came into sharp focus between November 2015 and July 2017. While in Upper Lake at the ranch they were temporarily using, revered Lakota elder Grandfather Bosco, of the Crazy Horse lineage of the Oglala Lakota from South Dakota, visited and told of the prophecy about the return of bison to the Upper Lake area. Grandfather Bosco said that he had held a dance to pray for the return of bison to Upper Lake five years before, but he had never expected the bison that would come to the Pomo native land would be white.

In 2016, a mutual friend introduced Hart to Christopher Issa and Christopher Lindstrom of EarthStar Developments LLC who wanted to establish an eco-friendly historical and spiritual center near Serpent Mound and Amesville, Ohio. Synchronistically, Ohio is where Cynthia Hart lived her teenage years and into her twenties and Serpent Mound is where she received her first Lakota prayer pipe. Local Pomo Nation and Lakota descendants and others will be helping the White Bison Association move to a permanent sanctuary in Ohio where Hart grew up. "It's ironic," Hart said laughing, "that we had to move the White Bison [from Dakota to Arizona] to Oregon and finally California in order to find our way home to Ohio."

The White Bison herd will now become part of a private eco/spiritual village that allows them to be their authentic selves: Beings of Peace.

These kinds of migratory journeys reflect the lifestyle of a human guided by the voice of Spirit and by the animals' own intelligent communication. Even when using trans-species telepathy, though, there are not many people who have either the commitment or inner stamina for following the trail of Spirit.

RAINING PEACE AND OTHER BUFFALO CHARACTERISTICS

Buffalo are bringers of peace. They also have power, strength, and endurance. Like the bull of the heavens, Taurus, they are builders of the world. Buffalo are the quintessential Earth beings who bring people together into community, bring ideas of brotherhood into action, and lead us into our spiritual places of union so that we can come to know that this peace humans dream of is possible. Sitting Bull was renowned for having been a great warrior, then becoming a great peace-bringer through his tradition of prayer and nonviolent resistance. So too are the buffalo herd of one mind. They heed the council of their elders. They will protect members of their own herd and species by forming masterful circles. They will encircle the weak member of the herd that is in distress, thereby creating walls of buffalo around the focus of their protection. Despite what the species has endured—unimaginable slaughter on a scale unknown until the advent of factory farming—they remain present, and they are now asking for our care.

Like elephants, lions, and bears (and their marine counterparts, whales, dolphins, and porpoises), the buffalo taught our ancestors how to organize their own societies. Unlike our nation's European-born forefathers, the league of the Iroquois practiced a matriarchal society with women as landowners and arbitrators of tribal leadership issues. They also instituted representative lawmaking and the keeping of that law, which was copied directly from them by Thomas Jefferson, Ben Franklin, and John Adams. The Iroquois did not rule by the use of unbridled power but rather by consensus. This framework remains only in skeletal form today in the U.S. Congress, which has become primarily influenced by corporate and international power alliances and their moneyed interests.

Hart confirmed for me something the other mammals we have met also reveal. "The buffalo will surprise you; they are a matriarchal society and the female runs the herd and she sends her boys out to protect the herd. . . . We have Miracle Moon who is a peace-keeping momma, and is the firstborn White Bison of the herd. She makes the rules. People who have bison don't allow the males in with the babies. I walk with the girls, but never turn your back on a male or female buffalo." (See plate 20 of Miracle Moon and her calf.)

"At sunset, with a small herd [of sixteen]," she explains, "the males go to the four corners" [referring to the directions of the compass]. "Then the middle-aged females will push the little ones to come running with them in figure eights. Then the rest of the herd will join in. When they finally settle down for the night, the herd will watch the setting sun. They watch the stars rise in the evening sky. They are stargazers."

Hart says that during the day, "The females walk the fences. They each pick a direction and they have little males that follow them. Overall, other than a few young males too young to breed, the females stay clustered together as a female herd. You'll find a couple of the younger males sticking closer to the females, but they eventually get run off by the females to join the male groups they will be part of."

There are reasons humans also keep the males separate from the females. "This 'straining out' of the males helps to keep the breed lines clean. If young bulls are left in the enclosure with the females, they will try to breed with as many as possible. We can plan to put a certain bull in with a female. We know who the sire of a particular calf will be."

Buffalo show sentience and concern for others of their species. In personal correspondence, Hart describes how her herd's cows give birth, coming from all parts of their grazing acreage to participate in the birthing process. "One of the older ones, the grandmother or aunt to the new baby, will stand behind the mother and help her. When the baby comes out, the grandmother or the aunt will start cleaning the calf. One of them will lick it first. And then when the placenta comes out another of the older females will guide the mother to eat it for strength. Then the other females will come and start licking the calf until the mother comes to do the same thing. She will then move and nuzzle the baby around until it gets up on its feet. She will separate it from the placenta so that it can nurse. She encourages her calf, pushing it and rolling it until it finally gets up. This can happen as soon as a minute after being born."[35] Highlighting their natures in our interview she added, "They are a lot like goats—they like to climb to the top of the hills. And the males are always trying to knock each other off the top of the hill." (This calls to mind the game King of the Hill, a game we played as children.)

When a buffalo is wounded or old and unable to carry on, Hart explains how they will "go for the waters. Like in Yellowstone, they will go to the hot springs and lay in them until they die. They want to be warm. . . . Then, when one is about to die, all of the immediate family members of the dying bison come nearby to be with her, one by one, to say goodbye."

Now knowing the beautiful Lakota stories and prophecies about the return of Buffalo Calf Woman, and learning of Uriah White's deathbed vision about his daughter Cynthia's return to her people's ways and the arrival of White Buffalo, I asked Hart what the White Buffalo say the purpose of their return is. "That was my very first question to Miracle Moon. They are very telepathic. Miracle told me that they are here, and that they need to go into areas that need them the most. They are here for the time of change. For me they [her herd] are very Egyptian and have the mannerisms of Egyptian culture, and they are stargazers. These buffalo are not the typical buffalo that I can go and watch at Yellowstone. Right now, they are all around my RV [while continuing with our broadcast conversation]. They were watching the meteor showers the other night."

She describes how Miracle Moon will come to her and say, "We would like some water or we would like this or that." They can clearly communicate their needs. "Miracle seems to be the one [that is telepathic with Hart] ever since I met her in Arizona. Now, if I touch them, I can see how they see me. They tell me about events that are going to happen in the sky. Or that they need to stay here in Lake County, California, because they are going to help bring the rains here this winter," which they did in 2015."

"We've been to Montana, we've been to South Dakota and Arizona, we've been to Oregon, and to California. Everywhere these buffalo go they bring rain. So they are migrating . . . we are taking them where they want to go." Hart made a point of differentiating between her ideas and the buffalo's directives. Where they would go was decided on by listening to the animals' instructions.

As this odyssey demonstrates, animal protectors in the world give their lives entirely to the task of preserving the White Spirit Animals and their species, as Hart does with the twenty bison in her care.

WHAT BUFFALO TEACHES US

Cynthia Hart says she has learned important lessons from Buffalo: "Patience, humility, and to not take life too seriously. Regarding humans, everybody needs to slow down, everyone needs to come out of fear, come out of their guilt and shame, to get in touch with their own nature." Relating that, in addition, "Miracle keeps asking, 'Where are the people, why aren't they out here? Why are they inside their small buildings and why do they stay in there for hours?' There is a lot of confusion among the animals as to why the humans are not outside taking care of the forests. They [the buffalo] are very great guardians of nature."

Hart also believes that, as she puts it, "The herds being raised for meat consumption know they are going to be slaughtered and are terrified all the time." However, "Our herd knows it is not going to be killed." It is very clear to anyone who knows her that she means it when she says, "I will stand up to anything to protect them. The buffalo are definitely peace and prayer." (See plate 21 of Buffalo.)

For some reason when she said this I was reminded of a story recounted to me by Stephan Schwartz and written about in his book

The 8 Laws of Change, discussed more fully in the last chapter of this book.[36] In Gandhi's final interview before his death, Gandhi was asked by a BBC reporter "how he kicked the British out of India." Gandhi answered, "We did not kick the British out of India; they left." When asked why they left, he explained that it was because he and his fellow countrymen embodied the behavior they wanted to see in the world— or, in basic common parlance, by *walking their talk* they changed the course of history. This is also the way of the Lakota "living prayer." As Gandhi explained, it was not so much what they said (though that *did* matter) or how they said it (though that helps), it was that they became what they spoke of. What this means is that they did not respond to violence with violence but with nonviolent action instead.

In one correspondence, I asked Hart about the buffalo as peace makers: "Bison don't know anything about the concept of peace. If any of the herd is out of balance, the matriarch will stand up and get them back into balance. They are already in peace as their natural state. If a male sees that a female is being eyed by a predator or another male, he will fight or run. Bison know only peace, or reestablishing peace as their natural state of being. If a predator comes in to challenge a bull they will either take the challenge or walk away. They don't care to make peace or to make prayers, they are a walking prayer. They handle their issues right then and there. If one of the herd is in trouble they will stand or lay near her and support her silently. That energy goes to her senses and she then becomes peaceful."[37]

Miracle Moon, the matriarch of Hart's herd, passed away twenty minutes before thousands of buffalo began running at Standing Rock Reservation on October 28, 2016 (at 1:44 pm), as if in support of the protestors being arrested for opposing the ecosystem-destroying Dakota Access Pipeline. People there reported seeing a White Buffalo running among the thousands of her brown kin.

Buffalo teach us about the collective endeavor of peace over violence, even when violence at its most odious is used against them. Over time it is their enduring capacity of "being peace" that transforms the abuser—whether against human, animal, or ecosystem—into protector, just as we saw happening among the Maasai and the lions, the mahouts and the elephants, and the gypsies and the bears.

THE WHITE BUFFALO SPIRIT

While Lakota and other peoples regard Buffalo as guardian of this *Turtle Island* (the Native term for North America), buffalo are spiritually guardians of the soil and carriers of the peace that Spirit endows to the land itself. Where buffalo walk, peace follows in their wake and, evidently, so does rain. Chassidic Judaism views rain as the loving kindness of Creator, as an expansion, while snow is viewed as its polar partner of harshness, judgment, or contraction. That buffalo are at home in both environments is of interest relative to the fact that buffalo are peace beings who are adept at using both love and restraint. When the right and left hands are brought together in prayer we receive the greatest blessing Creator has made, and that is peace, within and without. Peace is the destiny for all Earth beings.

Before I knew of Cynthia Hart, Buffalo told me that buffalo's purpose is as peace-bringers.[38] Subsequently, it was important to have this telepathically received information confirmed by someone who lives among them. What the buffalo conveyed to me visually was that they were intended to be the center of our circle, the middle of the axis of the continents' well-being and of the heart of all people who live on Earth. They are respectful, self-reliant herbivores whose communal agreements are known but unspoken; generational herds of females, their offspring males and young bulls participating instinctively in their own circles. The buffalo's matrilineal society informed Native society of the ways to achieve the greatest well-being among themselves.

Not only was Buffalo the mainstay of the Native diet—along with the three sisters of corn, squash, and beans—but Buffalo provided furs for clothing and everything else the tribes needed to live. Having learned from Wolf how to hunt as a pack, Indians were very careful about which buffalo they chose to kill, trying to avoid the massive herd leaders and choosing ones that were less vital to the group. After killing a buffalo, the Indians performed ceremonies to celebrate the sacrifice Buffalo made. Among the Mandan people, the highest honor is when a woman of the tribe performs her role as White Buffalo Calf Woman in the buffalo ceremony. The buffalo woman is the bringer and keeper of holy peace.

WHITE SPIRIT BUFFALO LESSONS

White Buffalo are harbingers of Earth changes and Mother Earth's restoration. They call upon us to restore and invigorate the continental United States with our goodwill and the widespread introduction of buffalo onto wild lands. To increase their herds is to assure greater survival of humans during the coming Earth changes. As adaptable animals, buffalo are able to survive many changes other mammals cannot. Everyone who hears the buffalo's soul song dreams of a time when they may once again roam from state to state on ancestral lands.

They know their role as benefactor. They restore our spirit and the lands that our species has laid fallow or overused. As such, buffalo are land stewards and we are meant to be their protectors. No other animal in North America has been the spiritual epicenter of so many cultures as has the great buffalo. No other animal maintains a central visionary role in these times like the White Buffalo.

I have come to know the buffalo like a low rumbling humility, the moving sound of thunder that comes up from the center of the Earth. Their tremendous presence is knowable in one's pulse. It's a rhythm, like a subtle drumming, which one shares with Buffalo, from miles and miles away, as being of a single heart. Undisturbed by time and space, millions of hearts pounding to the same drumbeat—the same lull at rest, the same charging whirlwind of energy and dust when aroused. They are the drummers of nature on the skin of Earth's bowl.

Closing on a bright note, a recent treaty, the Northern Tribes

Buffalo Treaty, is designed to return wild buffalo to tribal lands "to perform again that species' cultural, spiritual, nutritional, and ecological role." As with the other preservationist models we have learned of for the White Spirit Bears, the White Elephants, the White Lions, and White Wolves, this treaty was spearheaded by a Native—in this case, a man named Leroy Little Bear who hails from the Blackfoot Confederacy in southern Alberta. "With support from the Wildlife Conservation Society he led the historic initial signing of the Treaty in Blackfeet territory in Browning, Montana, in September, 2014. It brought together members of the Blackfeet Nation, Blood Tribe, Siksika Nation, Piikani Nation, the Assiniboine and Gros Ventre Tribes of Fort Belknap Indian Reservation, the Assiniboine and Lakota Tribes of Fort Peck Indian Reservation, the Salish and Kootenai Tribes of the Confederated Salish and Kootenai Indian Reservation, and the Tsuu T'ina Nation. It was the first such treaty among those disparate tribes in over 150 years."[39]

As well, April 4, 2016, marked an historic day for the Blackfoot nation when ninety bison calves arrived at the nine-thousand acre Blackfoot Bison Ranch near Two Medicine River in Montana to form the source stock for future generations of buffalo that will be reintroduced onto larger landscapes in the Rocky Mountains.

As we have seen in the ecological crisis of every other apex animal, remedies are available and there are people who are focused on them. This is the world we are creating. This is the conservation, restoration, and preservation that Wolf taught me, and it's the simplest way to recall what it is we are all here to do. This is the peace building we can all be part of making: peace with our planet and her needs.

One of my last dreams of Buffalo was the shortest. In the dream, I was standing near thousands of buffalo when a medicine man came and placed his hands on each side of my face, embracing me. His hands were suntanned, hardened by weather and work but gentle in intention. In the way that Spirit speaks, in a clear and present greeting, he thanked me for doing what I could to support buffalo spirit.

It was the final dream, however, that I had of buffalo, in which the greatest teaching was shared.

The Greatest Love There Is

I was standing beside a single buffalo, as though standing with an elder friend. We were on a mountaintop plateau, overlooking an entire cosmopolitan city where their range used to be. The message was simple and clear. I was told when standing there with such a broadscale view that "When any one of us, human, animal, plant, or mineral, fulfills our purpose on Earth, we experience the greatest love there is."

Buffalo also told me that my favorite tree was also their own, the weeping willow, a sacred, lovely, whispering spirit tree that brings sweetness, shade, aroma, and water wherever she stands, a growing sentinel of the gentle and caressing Spirit that dances within us all, the Tree of Life, which the buffalo guard. Let us encourage the free-ranging movement of these brothers and sisters of ours, the free-ranging buffalo.

When I cannot sleep at night, I imagine myself lying down among six white buffalo that are part of a larger herd, but who gently hum as I fall asleep among their wide berth of fur and their snores of pleasure. They bring my heart to calm; a cedar-and-sweet-grass-scented feeling of being one with Mother Earth. Like a walking prayer, Buffalo is arising and guiding us toward peace.

7
The Signs

Giants, White Dragons, and Other Stories of Extinction and Restoration

One day the absurdity of the almost universal human belief in the slavery of other animals will be palpable. We shall have then discovered our souls and become worthier of sharing this planet with them.

MARTIN LUTHER KING

ALL OF THE WHITE SPIRIT land mammals with whom we have become familiar share a concern for the future. Indigenous communities that revere these beings tell how these animals speak about profound climate and Earth changes and how they have arrived to help humanity survive another time of upheaval, which today we are clearly beginning to experience. All human cultural traditions in which these mammals are treasured share similar prophecies. As legend recounts, their animal equals, the White Spirit Animals and their species, have helped restore life on Earth through trans-species telepathy—yet another aspect of the White Spirit Animal story that has been shared with humanity.

THE UNIVERSE'S CYCLICAL CATASTROPHES

The White Spirit Animals depicted in these pages are great spirit beings who are understood to be messengers from the Ice Age. They are here to remind us of our innate ability to change, adapt, and survive, as is witnessed in the cyclical rise and fall of civilizations over time. Historically, civilizations as we know them have been upended and, in many instances, radical changes in landscapes have occurred in a matter of days or hours. These events change the weather dramatically across generations of time much like comets have done when they strike the Earth. If, during these unstable episodes, one species fails to thrive, others take their place. This is the perspective that I heard from Matata, the great matriarch bonobo that readers met at the beginning of our journey. She is a member of an endangered species herself (*Pan paniscus*). In one of our many shared discussions, mind-to-mind, heart-to-heart, Matata described calamitous Earth changes and their associated meteorites and comets as a way in which, in the past, the "sky gods" helped eliminate the carnivorous prehistoric bipedal giants who dominated the planet.

Graham Hancock, author of *Magicians of the Gods,* describes how almost thirteen thousand years ago, comet fragments a "mile wide approaching at more than 60,000 miles an hour" hit the Earth and generated "huge amounts of heat which instantly liquidized millions of square kilometers of ice, destabilizing the Earth's crust and causing the global Deluge that is remembered in myths all around the world." There were, he continues, "a second series of impacts, equally devastating, causing further cataclysmic flooding, [which] occurred 11,600 years ago, the exact date that Plato gives for the destruction and submergence of Atlantis." All of this shows that "beyond reasonable doubt that an advanced civilization that flourished during the Ice Age was destroyed in the global cataclysms between 12,800 and 11,600 years ago."[1]

In 1997 paleoanthropologist Timothy White unearthed the skeletal remains of *Homo sapiens* outside the Ethiopian village of Herto. They belonged to two adult males and one child dating back 165,000 years.[2] The 1974 findings by paleoanthropologist Donald Johanson, of a skeleton subsequently named Lucy, was dated at 3.2 million years old. Lucy was named such because the team of researchers that excavated her body listened to the Beatles' song "Lucy in the Sky with Diamonds" repeatedly and very loudly while doing their work. Michael Cremo and Richard Thompson, Ph.D., also present data in their book *Forbidden Archeology: The Hidden History of the Human Race* that proves humans and other technology-savvy civilizations have existed on this planet not just for tens of millions of years but billions of years, in keeping with Vedic teachings on the issue.

As discussed earlier, Tom Van Flandern, Ph.D., an American astronomer and author who specialized in celestial mechanics, provides another layer of possibilities of sentient history by looking at other past civilizations beyond Earth such as those on Mars.

> We've shown conclusively that at least some of the artifacts on the surface of Mars were artificially produced, and the evidence indicates they were produced approximately 3.2 million years ago, which is when Planet V exploded. Mars was a moon of Planet V, and we speculate that the Builders created the artificial structures as theme parks and advertisements to catch the attention of space tourists from Planet V (much as we may do on our own Moon some day, when lunar tourism becomes prevalent), or perhaps they are museums of some kind. Remember that the Face at Cydonia was located on the original equator of Mars.
>
> The Builders' civilization ended 3.2 million years ago. The evidence suggests that the explosion was anticipated, so the Builders may have departed their world, and it produced a massive flood, because Planet V was a water world. Is it a coincidence that the face on Mars is hominid, like ours, and the earliest fossil record on Earth of hominids is the "Lucy" fossil from 3.2 million years ago? There have been some claims of earlier hominid fossils, but Lucy is the earliest that is definite.[3]

Van Flandern leaves us with yet another provoking idea. "So I leave you with the thought that there may be a grain of truth in

The War of the Worlds, with the twist that WE are the Martians."[4]

Rudolph Steiner (1861–1925), the great Austrian seer, scientist, architect, esoteric visionary, and educator, writes about the various planetary phases of old Saturn, the old sun, the old moon, and our current Earth phase as stages of our cosmos' development over billions of years. Conscious life is part of cosmic evolution and activity shifts from planet to planet depending on galactic changes. In his description of the incarnations of the solar system and our evolution, Steiner suggests that there will be a new Venus and new Vulcan phase, which when added to our past, make up what he calls the Earth incarnations in our development.[5] Planets have incarnations too.

This recalls Ingo Swann's claims of life elsewhere in our solar system, when he was forced, by clandestine military agents who kidnapped, hooded, and then, like in a great spy film, took him to an underground location to remote view the moon. From there he saw naked human-like beings involved in some sort of lunar mining operation. Swann's book about this experience, called *Penetration,* is worth reading no matter what your beliefs are. If what Swann saw is evidence of other humanoid-like beings active today on the moon, then what Steiner perceived about our evolutionary future is more understandable.

If cosmic impacts to the Earth have happened before, and the data certainly suggests that this is so, then what happened? Where did everyone, in recent Earth history, go? More than three-fourths of the large Ice Age mammals died out thirteen thousand years ago, yet the mammals we have met in this book were part of the landscape more than *200 million years before that.* At one point scientists thought overhunting may have caused the extinctions of the large mammals, but there is a growing consensus that it was due to extraplanetary events. We see the cyclical nature of life at a smaller scale in our own lifetimes. History is not linear, progressing from more primitive to more modern societies *ad infinitum,* rather it is cyclical in what appear to be ascending and descending stages. The "Sleeping Prophet" Edgar Cayce (1877–1945) adds another dimension to past civilization's ruination. He spoke of

Atlantis and its people's mastery of natural forces, and that there was a kind of "star wars," which figured as a significant factor, leading to Atlantis's eventual destruction.

The shamans and animals we have met show us that advanced civilizations had off-planet collaborators, having everything to do with the Earth's welfare, particularly before and after global catastrophes. After the comet struck and the subsequent tsunamis, earthquakes, and sudden melting of ice sheets occurred, there was global flooding. By 8000 BCE the climate became very much like ours has been for the past ten thousand years, but this is now changing in measureable ways.

GIANTS AND OTHER "DISAPPEARING ACTS"

Another interesting derivative of the White Spirit Animals and the stories about them is that their Ice Age lineages are reflected in some of our own bipedal records of *Homo varius* (a term I "coined" for any unknown or known species that is similar to *Homo erectus*). Another unusual history lesson that Matata taught me concerns giants and giant animals. Compared to our present sizes, these beings were huge. When looking at the size of life-forms from an evolutionary perspective, life on Earth is getting smaller both in terms of the scale of species and the number of species, except for *Homo sapiens*. My own hypothesis, that the animals agree with when asked, is that as sentient life re-ascends the ladder of light, starting from a dense material state and moving into a less dense state over the coming millions of years, smaller life-forms will likely make the transition most readily. Perhaps these extinction cycles lessen the physical mass on Earth in order to prepare our DNA and life systems for existence as light bodies. These light bodies would replace the denser vessel that we currently occupy temporarily, which we call our body. This transformation allows a return to our origins as spiritual beings of light. On the other hand, decreasing our scale may also facilitate space travel, which some futurists say is how Earth remnants will survive the coming changes.

Some extinctions go entirely unnoticed by subsequent generations. *Homo varius* was once proportionate to the woolly mammoth in size, much in the same way as we are to today's wolves and bears. Matata claimed that human evolution continued during the Ice Age, when giants lived. The White Spirit Animal species were able to survive these giants. "When the waters were gone and humans went down into the valleys, ape and human went their own ways," as Matata put it, "no longer mating and living with bonobo."[6]

During our ninth recorded session in 2012, Matata related that her "people were not there when the first giants were on Earth—no people were."[7] She said, "Bonobo and human come after first giants. Then new giants who liked human and mated made new giants. These mixed giants were helpful to humans and liked humans but the parent giants (the purebred giants as they thought of themselves) were like gods—they were in charge and the new giants who were part human threatened their position." When I asked her to explain further, she told me that her "Council of Elders" said, "There was war and most giants were eliminated by the big giants and bigger animals they had under their control." [This suggests that there was mind control of these colossal animals]. "And then there were the Earth changes. . . . Then most all giants gone—gods of sky killed them, and some humans too but not on purpose. Sky Gods leave and we are left, bonobo, human, other creatures too."* Much of this, she said, was completed by 11,000 BCE.

For many readers, it may seem that bonobo telepathic communication is not only unprovable but also absurd. I can appreciate this skepticism. It is always healthy to question what we learn from others. But I

---

*Matata was saying what the Hebrew Bible attests to in Genesis 6:4: "There were giants (nephilim) on the Earth in those days; and also after that, when the sons of God came in unto the daughters of men, and they bore children to them, the same became mighty men which were of old men of renown."

can confirm that the information has a consistent pattern, which upon receipt is significantly different from my own thoughts. It is this difference, this distinction, which I have come to learn signals its authenticity and that it does indeed derive from outside my own issuance. The simplest way to say it is that "Animals say the darndest things." In conversations with domestic animals and wildlife, they tell you what they want you to know. They are very direct and will say things that I had not thought of before or ever imagined on my own. In these instances, I am a spectator to their story much like an English-speaking foreign film viewer when everything in audio is in a foreign language, but the subtitles (in these instances the telepathic messages) are relayed in English. My own experiences are resonant with ancient indigenous traditions that have relied on being able to hear and understand the spirits and the animals.

When I told my husband about Matata's version of history—one that featured giants—he left the room for a moment and then returned with a book that he handed to me. I was about to find out that Matata the bonobo, who had shared such amazing stories with me telepathically from 885 miles away and at different times of day and night, was correct. Her accounts agreed with those in the history book about giants. Regardless of how fanciful it may seem, we "had some talk" indeed.

The book that my husband handed to me was *The Ancient Giants Who Ruled America* by Richard J. Dewhurst. It is a fantastic exposé of various races of giants who once roamed North America. "Long before the so-called 'discovery of America,' this land was populated by very ancient peoples," Dewhurst writes, "some of whom were of enormous size, as attested to by the numerous reports of giant finds."[8] This history was deliberately covered up by the Smithsonian Institution shortly after the American Civil War. There was an intentional and successful effort to wipe any trace of giants, dwarfs, and other anomalous creatures from the historical anthropology, archaeology, and geology literature despite the fact that farmers, tribal people, and developers constantly unearthed these remains and newspapers reported candidly about them without censure up until the early 1900s.

Many Native Indian stories exist about their people's history of killing the carnivorous giants. Giants found in Anderson, Indiana, who were part of a series of unearthed mounds, were nine feet tall. Discovered November 25, 1892, by farmer John Beal while digging a hole in his field, the local newspaper, the *Goshen Daily News,* told the story without edit the following day. These unearthed creatures may seem large to us, but they are not as large as those dug up elsewhere in North America, Peru, and France. Just as Matata described to me, others measured twenty-five to thirty-six feet tall, the tallest being comparable to a three-story building.

News reports before the cover-up make it clear that in the nineteenth century such finds were common knowledge around the country. When carbon dating became available, age estimates of remains went from five thousand to fourteen thousand years old, "linking some of those early, magnificent humans with mastodons. . . . Not surprisingly, many finds indicate that the giants were royal beings."[9] But reports ceased by the 1920s as if on cue. This cessation caused irreparable harm to our knowledge about ourselves and Earth history.

Archaeological bone and fossil remnants, such as the eighteen giant skeletal remains found on May 4, 1912, near Lake Delavan, Wisconsin, were described in a *New York Times* May 14, 1912, article as corresponding to body heights that "ranged between 7.6 feet and 10 feet." A February 5, 2003, *National Geographic* exposé described Cyclops skeletons with skulls having only one eye socket that were found in Greece and that stood fifteen feet tall.[10]

Giants are typically described as cannibalistic and proved to be formidable enemies of smaller bipedal beings such as *Homo sapiens,* Neanderthals, and bears. On November 28, 1897, the Fort Wayne, Indiana, *Sentinel* reported that a cemetery of giants had been found. In their words, a "prehistoric battlefield with the skulls of 100,000 'Giant Neanderthals' (*Homo* genus from 300,000 years to 20,000 years ago)—

some with two rows of teeth and others with red hair still attached, all with arrow points in them—were found near Wichita, Kansas, in Redlands near the Choctaw Indian reservation."

Archaeologist Edwin Walters, discoverer of the thirty-acre site, believed that a battle had been fought between the "Mound Builders and the Maya Toltec race from Yucatan that were trying to take over the Mississippi Valley" twenty thousand years ago. The archaeologists found some three thousand skeletons. Bones were literally "dug out by the carload" and "each skull was found with one to five arrow heads sticking into it. Some of the skeletons were dwarfish while others were gigantic, and they were all buried in circles in a sitting position, just like the ones found in Anderson, Indiana."[11]

Numerous articles of this sort appeared in the 1800s. These burial mound findings of ancient races of giants attest that more than one variant or species of giants existed, some being as tall as thirty-two feet. Evidence of intact skeletons prove this. Why, we might ask, like the information concerning the Face on Mars, is this fascinating part of history on Earth passed through a "knowledge filter"? Processes such as peer review and status quo journals and institutions like the Smithsonian, and government agencies and their contractors that are supposed to uphold truth, in fact, have historically distorted and hidden it.

Why? The simple reason is that giants and other phenomena simply do not conform to the story line considered necessary to uphold the governing power elite. This was the very case regarding the "disappearing giant act" that the Smithsonian helped to perpetrate. The truth up-ended their scientific story line of evolution and threatened to derail their agenda of control. As a result, our present culture does not appreciate that extinctions do happen, those of other species and that of our own.

Who knows what future generations will report about *us*? What species will be remembered that even we do not know about, which are now becoming or have already vanished in our lifetimes, this past year, or even today?

DRAGON TALES

In addition to fascinating tales about ancient giants, another very interesting idea to contemplate is the existence of White Dragons. Indeed, Lion reported to me that lions had once lived alongside ice age White Dragons. Dragons? That was my response too. One repeated dream I had was that three cave beings used to share the lands: the White Lion, the White Bear, and the White Dragon.[12]

The White Dragon is part of many cultures, including the Chinese culture. Chinese rulers used the dragon as an emblem of imperial power. The dragon is believed to have the ability to see into the future, bring good luck, and provide ferocious protection. They were powerful, ice-savvy prehistoric reptiles, despite the popular mainstream claim that dragons exist only in myths. But myths are not very different from scientific stories; ways of telling history as narratives that can be easily preserved orally for generations. Why are myths any less real than scientific narrative?

Mythologies about dragons and specifically the White Dragon are a good example of how extinction may actually entail transformation. Today's Komodo dragon, native to Indonesia, grows up to ten feet and weighs one hundred fifty pounds. They are certainly reminiscent of the enormous legendary flying dragons but at a much reduced scale. The historic dragon, whose wingspans were said to have been as great as twenty-five feet, are well represented by skeletal remains of an extinct sea bird, *Pelagornithid*. It was found in 1983 when the Charleston International Airport in South Carolina was undergoing expansion. The skeletal remains were so enormous that they had to be dug out with a backhoe. These great birds (or flying dragons), to whom the condor is related, lived 25 to 28 million years ago. (See plate 22 of a White Dragon.)

Of course there were flying dragons—every child will tell you this is so. Accounts of flying dragons are endemic to many ancient cultures of the world. Today these huge, fire-breathing dragons remain in our psyche and are reflected in modern films and cartoons, but there is no question in my mind that there were dragons on Earth and that their relatives exist today on the physical plane in smaller forms. They too were part of the great species extinctions and transformations when new species emerged and others went extinct. Some scientists suggest we are presently living in an interglacial period that is still part of the Pleistocene, which leads others to conclude that we are due for another ice age. All of this is consistent with White Spirit Animal prophecies. The current instability of our climate and the fact that we are losing species every day of the year provides confirmatory evidence of this.

CONSERVATION AND EXTINCTIONS

Along with these colossally scaled humans were huge historic mammals. Consider the forty-four hundred pound giant Ice Age bison who flourished millions of years ago, and their smaller progeny, at a thousand pounds less, who came on the scene two hundred fifty thousand years ago. Then, twenty to thirty thousand years ago, the Wisconsin glaciations took place, and the smaller *Bison occidentalis* became extinct. Today we have the beloved American bison, the buffalo, who weigh two thousand pounds. So from the vantage point of time, these cycles seem more about changing the scale of life-forms than ending all life on Earth.

Every epoch is marked by civilizations, each with its own expressed form. If, as ancient mystery traditions teach, all things are related in octaves of similars, then a two-ton animal of any kind is still related to its smaller version, who may weigh less than a thousand pounds. Scientists have mapped dinosaur offspring species that carry some of their genetic signature and thereby contribute to the gene pool in this way. Some Ice Age fish and other wildlife from that time period have survived. Big Foot (also called "Yeti" and "Sasquatch"), Chessie of the Chesapeake Bay waters, and Scotland's Loch Ness monster may be examples of the few that have endured. Only 5 percent of America's wilderness remains, but our oceans are full of life-forms we know nothing of and have never seen. It is also true that the seas may be a repository of survivors from the last ice age. So too do cryptozoologists (those looking for lost or hidden animals) routinely discover ancient or new and amazing species in the great rain forests and other unexplored regions of the world. However, today's Sixth Extinction, which has been caused by human activity, has accelerated the pace of species' die-off in unprecedented ways.

WE ARE IN THE SIXTH EXTINCTION: THE ANTHROPOCENE

The Center for Biological Diversity asserts that "Our planet is now in the midst of its sixth mass extinction of plants and animals—the sixth wave of extinctions in the past half-billion years. We're currently experiencing the worst spate of species die-offs since the loss of the dinosaurs 65 million years ago. Although extinction is a natural phenomenon, it occurs at a natural 'background' rate of about one to five species per year. Scientists estimate we're now losing species at 1,000 to 10,000 times the background rate, with literally dozens going extinct every day." This conclusion is startling, with as many as "30 to 50 percent of all species possibly heading toward extinction by mid-century." Approximately three hundred species of one sort or another perish every week.[13] The National Wildlife Federation reports that "Every day, an estimated 100 plant and animal species are lost to deforestation. . . . A conservative estimate of the current extinction rate indicates that about 27,000 species a year are being lost."[14]

Elizabeth Kolbert, writing in her book *The Sixth Extinction, An Unnatural History,* makes clear that in Charles Darwin's (1809–1882) *On The Origin of Species,* Darwin "drew no distinction between man and other organisms. As he and many of his contemporaries recognized, this equivalence was the most radical aspect of his work. . . . At the heart of Darwin's theory, as one of his biographers put it, is, 'the denial of humanity's special status.'"[15] It is interesting that to Darwin the science of love was one of his passionate interests and his acknowledgment that humans differ from animals only in our cultures has been misrepresented by scientific guilds and overlooked by subsequent generations. Darwin never said that we are better, bigger than, or deserving of a position of domination that is embodied by a status quo of the world sciences and religions—quite the reverse.

The extent to which modern humans have changed the planet's life systems has merited the moniker of what scientists call "the Anthropocene." It is defined as the period of time when human impacts on the planet began to dominate. As Dutch chemist Paul Crutzen suggests in his essay "Geology of Mankind,"[16] the "geological scale changes, people have effected: transforming a third and a half of the land surface of the planet; damming or diverting most of the world's major rivers; producing more nitrogen by fertilizer plants than is fixed naturally by terrestrial ecosystems; removing more than one-third of the primary product of the ocean's coastal waters; and pointing out that humans use more than half of the worlds readily accessible fresh water run off." It was Paul Crutzen's collaborative work on ozone-depleting compounds that earned him the Nobel Prize.

He shows that we have altered the composition of the atmosphere and this will have impacts for centuries to come. "For the past three centuries the effects of humans on the global environment has escalated. Because of these anthropogenic emissions of carbon dioxide, global climate may depart significantly from the natural behavior for many millennia to come. It seems appropriate to assign the term *Anthropocene* to the present, in many ways human dominated, geological epoch, supplementing the Holocene—the warm period of the past twelve millennia." The Anthropocene "started in the latter part of the eighteenth century when analysis of air trapped in polar ice showed the beginning of the growing global concentration of carbon dioxide and methane."

A Solution from the Future

In a telepathic communication with Lion, I was shown hollow metal poles that were six stories high and twelve to sixteen inches wide. They were to be inserted into space, acting like pumping pogo sticks of many miles' range, for helping us address ozone-impacting elements. How they work or what they do exactly was not something I learned in the dream. White Lion showed me a solution from the future. It was a dream that followed weeks after another lion instruction in which I was told that if we are to choose only one first step in restoring our ecosystem overall, it needs to be addressing the ozone hole that opens each spring over Antarctica. This hole is caused by ozone-depleting compounds and exposes all life on Earth to too much ultraviolet radiation—impacting marine ecology, crops, animals, and humans with some specifically noted damage to eyes (cataracts), skin (cancer), and immune system depletion overall.

It seems that the odds facing us in the decades ahead are insurmountable. Some believe that the Earth's ecosystem is too far out of balance to regain its harmonic wellness. Paul Crutzen speaks of the challenge for bioengineers and others to create controlled environments, enclosed cities, and rural settings, much like those envisioned by research meditators who, in the early 1980s, asked participants to look at the future—into the twenty-first and twenty-second centuries. As I described in *The Future of Human Experience*, they saw not only domed cities in the twenty-first century but also survival cities of war-like behaviors and more peaceful golden cities of people working together for their survival and rebuilding.[17] But to stabilize ecosystems now requires the greatest efforts to preserve rain forests, apex animals worldwide, and the natural environments upon which we all depend. In the decades if not centuries to come, people will wonder how things deteriorated so much, given the level of scientific and technological achievement in our society. They will ask what happened. How will this question be answered?

All of the White Spirit Animals in this book have come to declare this reality. Rather than this being a story of being banished from the Earth, the story of the White Spirit Animals is a tale of lifesaving efforts, beginning with the reclamation of our purpose, followed by the restoration, conservation, and preservation of our planet.

To me there is no other choice but to move forward by embracing the old ways when we lived in harmony and respect with other animals. Intentional respect between humanity and nature has been the major thread that has run all through my life's work. I am certainly not alone in cherishing these values. There is no other dream as important as this potential of restored well-being. It is a theme that resonates down through time and calls each of us to action—all ages, all generations. Everything and anything that we each do at any time, which is life-affirming and compassionate, is important work for the world. But are there ways we can act *collectively* that can make a vital contribution to the planet's restored health in a more quantum way, which we may not even imagine is possible now?

PRESERVING OUR OWN SPECIES

If we retrace our travels from British Columbia to South Africa, from India to Montana, we find an honest record of suffering and hope. Overcoming the tendency to dissociate from the pain that we cause ourselves and others of any species or life-form is a vital part of restoring the Earth. Our ability to respect and listen to these animal stewards is also imperative, as is showing forgiveness for what we have done. Forgiveness elevates the spirit and opens the heart to new possibilities, to new ways of relating to others and the world. It lessens everyone's suffering. The Buddhic elephants and great chiefs of medicine, bears, teach that this is so. Our lion leaders remind us that it is our role to protect the entire world in the same way that buffalo do.

When we consider the cosmic roles of these spirit animals in the universe's star systems, we see that they are signatories of Creation—shape-shifters who connect millions of years of life on Earth with other civilizations in the galaxy and beyond. Their interpreted roles as guardians of Spirit (Bear), the world (Lion), the Milky Way road (Elephant), the continuum of life and death (Wolf), and the soil of Earth herself (Buffalo) help all of us with wise advice. The teachings that we have learned from these beings on this journey provide guidance for the roles that each of us must play.

THE NEED FOR CULTURAL RESTORATIONS

One of the strongest messages our capstone guardians share with us deals with how our society is structured. These five mammals govern vast territories of Earth and their precious ecosystems of the grasslands, woods, fields, forests, mountains, rivers, lakes, and the snow-filled Arctic. The waters have their guardians too among the sea mammals: whales, sharks, porpoises, and dolphins who, like the bear, lion, elephant, and buffalo, are matrilineal societies. Their offspring and females are placed at the center of society in recognition of their need for protection and how precious they are to the society and to Earth. This attitude and social geometry is quite the reverse of the human patriarchy and its distorted sense of power and entitled domination. It has led to the enslavement, abuse, and diminishment of human men, women, children, and nature for thousands of years.

The White Spirit Animals illustrate how our survival depends on transforming from a patriarchy to a matriarchy. This understanding is not political feminist philosophy, nor is it a sociological invention. Rather it reflects a profound appreciation for how all mammalian species best organize themselves *prosocially*—to educate their young, to breed healthy children and families, to respect the ecosystem in which one resides. In short, it creates the greatest happiness and well-being for life overall, for cultivating an *ethic of care*. At the heart of the community is a love and regard for equal status among all its members—animals and humans, both male and female.

We do not need a global law of proclamation to enact this transformation. Such a change occurs each time any one of us is unwilling to accept the shackles of any dominating philosophy or activity that excludes certain people or animals from the rights and entitlement that all beings are due. Equality is not a philosophy, it is an inherited birthright that comes with the first breath of life. Jacques Cousteau points out that freedom is not something we can actually bestow on others, it is only something humans can take away. Therefore, we must not deny the birthrights of equality and freedom to ourselves or others. When our species or another is handicapped by oppression, aberrations of all sorts develop. When these conditions and behaviors become chronic, the abuse becomes acceptable and normative.

As healers say, post-traumatic stress is "a natural response to unnatural conditions." The essential freedom, the sovereign entitlement to rule over one's own body and mind, is innate and is the root of each being's life expression. As stated previously, this natural freedom is the axis mundi around which all Native Earth-based traditions derive their authority: the divine right of the individual to be self-governed by proper laws of decorum. Each person knows this truth through communion with the Earth and Earth's guardians and its Creator, with an inward knowing through one's own self-cultivation, through our heart and life experience.

THE NEED TO PRIORITIZE A LIFE ECONOMY

All of the White Spirit Animals and their associated prophecies speak of coming destabilization and record-breaking weather events. Limiting our own impact on Earth's meta-systems, such as ceasing all fracking as a gas extraction method, is imperative. The United States Geological Survey (USGS) has already noted the increased frequency of sinkholes and earthquakes as a result of this process, which creates poisonous effluence and waste. Fracking also has a deleterious effect on local water supplies and wells and on local roads and bridge infrastructure. In my home state of Maryland, fracking was banned in 2017, joining two other East Coast states (New York in 2015 and Vermont, which was the first state to ban fracking in 2012) in the prohibition of this life-impacting, ecosystem-destroying process.

Common sense dictates that all nuclear plants and facilities should be closed as well. They pose inherent, unacceptable risks by posing what constitutes the *reckless endangerment* of life for centuries to come given their capacity for leaking, exploding, or cracking open due to earthquakes, terrorism, or accident.

The end of all fossil fuel extraction and use is mandatory if we, and life on Earth, are to survive and if our carbon imprint is to be reduced enough to stave off entire planetary collapse. Exchanging soft, sustainable technologies for poisonous ones is a critical mandate and one that we should apply national and world talent to in the same way we have done for other issues—with a green emergency national jobs plan and focus. What emerges depends on our intentions, our actions, and our economic will.

RESTORING THE EARTH'S SOIL, PRESERVING HER SEEDS, AND CONSERVING HER WATER

Another emergent solution for the planet worldwide is topsoil enrichment with nonpoisoning agriculture using natural, organic, and other well-tested restorative systems like biodynamic farming. Russia has started down this path by replacing chemical agriculture with organic farming. Healthier soil means healthier bio-life: healthier water, air, and human and animal well-being overall. Outlawing GMOs worldwide is another step toward agricultural transformation. GMOs are a serious death economy lynchpin, undermining agriculture and food sustainability wherever they are planted and subsidized. Preservation tells us to guard the planet's sustaining heirloom seeds for ecological, animal, and human health, enriching all localized croplands and seed banks globally. Reprioritizing the least impactful distribution of food is vital to addressing our carbon imprint and minimizing localized food dependency on foreign welfare. Produce grown in each country should feed its own people and animals as a priority, and enrichment of the soil should be part of that local restoration. Both Buffalo and Elephant have shown how important this is for the preservation and enrichment of all ecosystems.

Chemical fertilizer has released so much nitrogen into the meta-systems and these chemicals, like many plastics, cannot be transformed. Stopping this practice alone would be an immense benefit to the world. Modern farming is a by-product of chemical warfare science and has impacted health worldwide by poisoning every bio-system on Earth in the mineral, plant, animal, and human communities. This war against the Earth with deadly chemicals and genetic engineering needs to end and be replaced with systems that support biotic life and produce more nutritious and beneficial plant life, including the restoration of our forests and plains. Regeneration has the added benefit of decreasing global warming. The White Bear of the temperate rain forests shows this fundamental wisdom of preserving pristine land, with respect for the overall improvement of the world's bio-systems.

Today's industrial agriculture and proliferation of GMO crops has not increased food production as once hoped for and has instead been detrimental to all life systems it impacts. The United States is the only Western nation that continues to promote GMO agriculture and its products. The rest of the world has outlawed or is in the process of outlawing their use, having seen the harm done to the animal consumers (cows regularly abort their young when fed a steady diet of GMO grain) and, naturally, to the health of human consumers as well as to our air, water, and soil. At the very least, consumers are demanding that any food that has a GMO ingredient be labeled as such. The right to know what is in our foods is a fundamental necessity for human health. Industry giants continue to resist this change, already knowing that labeling decreases the sale of their GMO products.

GMO seeds are sterile synthetic hybrids that can have poison inserted into their genetic structure. They require the application of even more chemical poisons than comparable natural crops grown with herbicides. This has a long-term effect of breeding new kinds of insects and molds or fungi impervious to the chemical warfare used against them. Significantly, from an irresponsible and unsustainable perspective, it epitomizes all that is wrong with our current death economy. Farmers are unable to save seed from their own harvests to plant the following year. The seed is sterile and the plants cause ill effects everywhere that they are planted and consumed.

If this is allowed to continue, then grains, fruits, and vegetables in each country, which currently feed billions of people and animals, could be eliminated in the timeframe of several generations. All food would be not only substandard nutritionally, but in the hands of global corporations instead of the free individual who farms the land for their own family as their forebears have done before them, utilizing seed variants passed down through generations of farming. From an organic farmer's point of view, the contamination of cultivated soil by the GMO seeds renders the farm useless. The monolithic Monsanto often levies lawsuits against these victims of "drift warfare" for having stolen their "patented" seeds. Knowing that no organic farmer would deliberately invite destruction of their crop, land, and livelihood, these actions are nothing more than corporatized terrorism.

The late Christopher Bird (1928–1996) was a dear friend to both my husband and me. He was concerned about the issue of topsoil regeneration and wrote about this and related ecosystem issues and their relationship to human consciousness in his books. He is the coauthor of *The Secret Life of Plants* and *Secrets of the Soil* and the author of *The Divining Hand,* which chronicles five hundred years of the history of dowsing. Christopher was a "bear" of a man. He used to stride down the sidewalk outside his Georgetown home in the winter, singing a robust version of "The Bear Went Over the Mountain," wearing no shoes and clad in nothing more than pants and a shirt—which wasn't even buttoned to keep him warm. Chris also liked to sing "Ol' Yeller," a song he wrote about his dog. On these occasions, my husband would join in, the two of them serenading the neighborhood.

Chris Bird was not alone on this issue of topsoil regeneration as a simple solution to an issue of such enormous scale. He also maintained that our planet-wide soil erosion precipitates an ice age. Dust bowls and soil acidification combined with vast forest fires are a serious situation. It is a lesson that we learned in the 1930s, for by 1934 it was estimated that 100 million acres of farmland had lost all or most of their topsoil to the winds. On Sunday, April 14, 1935, called "Black Sunday," huge dust storms hit the North American Great Plains, literally swallowing up whole towns in miles-high dust waves. "The cloud that appeared on the horizon that Sunday was the worst. Winds were clocked at 60 mph. Then it hit."[18] The dust was so pervasive that ropes had to be tied between homes, barns, and outhouses in order for people to find their way. Inhaling the dust led to many people's deaths, especially children. Overall it was the final cause of the great migration west away from the American Plains. (See plate 23 for an image of a ferocious dust bowl storm.)

The devastation caused by the great dust bowl would not have occurred if the crop rotation system had been maintained. If synthetic agriculture had never been introduced for the purposes of massive wheat production subsidized by the U.S. government with taxpayer dollars, and if the buffalo had still roamed, there would have been no dust bowl. Topsoil blew away because cost-saving mono-crop seeding had replaced diversified crop rotation and intensive chemical fertilizer and herbicides were amply applied. Also these larger farms often removed perennial trees, shrubs, and vines to create open, empty tracts of land for annual seed planting. With the genocide of the buffalo, the soil had lost its number one ally who could increase the micro-organic health of the soil. We are seeing this pattern repeated today.

As of 2015, tree ring analyses show that California recently experienced the worst drought since the sixteenth century. Conditions prompted tribal and other peoples to perform blessings and rain dances for the suffering land and its beings. Further north there were forest fires in Edmonton, Canada, during the late spring of 2016 that were unprecedented in scale. Fire, drought, and dust bowls all lead to potential famine. Global hunger is already increasing and the shared global food banks have only a seventy-six day capacity. This is a sobering reality that seems entirely shortsighted and reckless. In this day and age it is hard to understand or believe and yet it is so.

The flip side of drought, of course, is flooding, landslides, and torrential rains. As sea levels rise and moisture becomes more available over land from the upper atmosphere, storms are dropping unprecedented amounts of rain in short periods of time over areas already saturated by overflowing rivers, streams, oceans, and other bodies of water. How much of this weather mayhem stems from the impact of classified geoengineering of the climate is a topic seldom discussed. Western nations, however, are deeply engaged in trying to control weather systems for warfare and things as unessential as sporting events. The long-term damage these experiments are doing to the upper atmosphere, oceanic patterns, and land mass destabilization (as occurs from underground detonations and liquid and gas extraction of all sorts) needs to become part of the public discussion.

Both drought and oversaturation wash away precious topsoil, but there are well-proven solutions that allow the restabilization of healthy land and forests. For example, when glacial rock dust was sprayed on the soil of the dying Black Forest in Germany, the soil and then the trees were successfully restored. Ecologist Donald Weaver, geologist John Hamaker (1914–1994), and glaciologist Joanna Campe of Remineralize the Earth have been teaching this successful restoration and preservation practice around the world.[19]

Remineralizing the soil is not only life-enhancing, it is climate changing because it stimulates plant growth, which is needed to alleviate excess carbon dioxide and methane gas that is being released into the atmosphere. It is carbon reducing, in other words. This is why remineralizing the soil and forests worldwide with pulverized glacial rock dust, volcanic ash, and other rich elemental source materials is such a logical and simple step and one that can be taken everywhere—in our world's forests and in our own backyards.

Countries such as Brazil and Cuba are beginning to include soil remineralization as part of their agricultural practices, and various farms—ranging in size from several hundred to several thousand acres—have put this restorative soil practice into place.* Joanna Campe mentioned a recent meeting she knew of with a company in China responsible for 70 percent of the remediation of farmland there. "That would be an opportunity on a huge scale to sequester carbon." She further explains that "a lot of the farmland there is so contaminated" that recent laws prescribe ecofriendly methods in lieu of more synthetic chemical agriculture.[20]

With useable cropland shrinking, China has begun buying up huge swathes of land in others countries such as the Ukraine. As well, with China's purchase of the large company Smithfield Foods for 4.7 billion dollars, it also received over one hundred thousand acres of farmland in Missouri, Texas, and North Carolina.

Ecologist Don Weaver, who co-authored with John Hamaker *The Survival of Civilization*, has been promoting remineralization of the soil, as shared in their book, since the 1980s. Another champion of soil restoration is Gary Zimmer, known as the father of biological farming. He details a discussion of this topic in his two books, *The Biological Farmer* and *Advancing Biological Farming*. Gary also agrees

---

*Remineralization is the practice of adding rock dust to soil to restore vital nutrients crucial to the growing of crops, forests, and any other plant-based ecosystem. Many of the soil nutrients have been lost due to conventional agricultural practices, such as overuse of the land and the application of synthetic chemicals. In a major forward stride for sustainable agriculture, the country of Brazil has enacted legislation that includes soil remineralization as part of its agricultural policy.

that remineralizing the soil is the primary foundational solution to the restoration of the Earth planet wide, accompanied by the elimination of all toxic agricultural practices.

Donald Weaver emphasizes that "If we want to regenerate, we regenerate from the soil up . . . for the forest, for the crop land, for human health at the same time. Human health is not separate from soil health and planetary health and they all go together."[21] He points out that while we figure out all the particulars of what to do in the various impacted meta-systems, we can "plant billions of trees which will reduce the carbon dioxide load Earth wide and help us put nutrients back into the soil." His point, like that of Joanna Campe, is that the science has been done and some basic solutions are clear.

"Saying that a crop is organic," Gary Zimmer adds, "simply means what has been withheld during its production. But if the soil itself has been depleted of nutrients from runoff, contamination, floods, droughts, and so on, then remineralizing is the simplest restorative process there is" and it is virtually foolproof.[22]

Another perspective I find compelling and elegant is Mark Shepard's approach to farming. Shepard is an expert practitioner of permaculture on his 106-acre New Forest Farm in Wisconsin. Perennial crop farming rather than planting monoculture seed annuals is the wisest use of water, land, and sun. He reminds us that farmers are actually solar collectors. Perennial farming that features fruit and nut trees, berry bushes, and fruit-growing vines, among other perennial species, not only supports humans without destructive impacts on our soil, it also reduces the farm labor required to plant seeds and support the farm's ecosystem, which includes its animals. This is not to say local farmers shouldn't grow food crops derived from annual seed planting, but as we derive food from fewer and fewer resources, it makes much more sense to grow more foods that replenish themselves naturally every year: our fruits, nuts, berries, mushrooms, and such.

Restoration agriculture, which includes the ethical principles and practices of permaculture, follows the balanced course of nature, which is to nurture the biome in layers, as occurs naturally worldwide. With the canopy, understory, and forest floor, a forest is an integral whole that teaches us how to think about perennial farming. "It's not flat, it's multidimensional," Shepard shows us. "Annual agriculture," which since World War II also applies billions of tons of pesticides a year, has overall only been used in the last ten thousand years.[23]

"Today," Shepard shares, "twenty tons of topsoil blow away a year" due to our agricultural practices, which include the mismanagement of the animals' role in managing ecosystems properly. "Penning up grazing herbivores [cattle, sheep, goats, and buffalo] who do a magnificent job of managing the grasslands and undergrowth, has, rather than a positive impact on their environment, a negative one, relegated to being overbreeders and polluters." Shepard underscores the problem with our food system being so dependent on the one-season crop-planting method that is used worldwide today. "Every culture in which this practice of annual seed crop dominance has been utilized has disappeared," he says.

The ethical foundation of permaculture consists of "Earth care, people care, and equitable distribution and recirculation of resources." These principles help guide everyone into making choices that elevate the life around us, the directive given at the start of my journey with the White Spirit Animals. There are such simple but ancient and proven restoration methods: remineralize our soil everywhere we can and plant trees wherever and whenever we can, including our perennial food-producing bushes and trees, which are sustainable food sources.

It is calculated that of the planet's biome overall, one-third goes to supporting human life and two-thirds to animals being raised for human food. Only 5 percent of that animal percentage is made up of animals in the wild or domestic pets.

Joel Salatin describes decades of experience with his polyface farming methods. Salatin proves that livestock can be part of a farm's overall culture and well-being, but not factory farmed as is done today worldwide. "Raising livestock," he claims, "is doable, without doing harm to animals, ecosystem, or human nature."[24] His farm animals are all integrated in one cohesive, supportive system, demonstrating how the peasant farm of only a few hundred years ago functions so well. As our food goes, so goes our humanity. In short, the idea is to support our local farmers and encourage community-based agriculture, co-ops, and other locally managed food-related networks, as they all encourage us to do. These solutions and others have been popularized and discussed in the extraordinary magazine *Acres U.S.A.*, begun by Charles Walters Jr. (1926–1990) in 1970 and continued today by his son Fred Walters. It is the only national monthly magazine that has, during all these decades, devoted itself to nontoxic and sustainable commercial-scale agriculture.

Our civilization is not powerless to change long-established habits, patterns, and subsidized ways of doing things. Our rather dire circumstances of shrinking agricultural resources, polluted natural meta-systems, and centralized power should not throw us into total despair, for all is not lost. One obvious solution to world hunger, as well as a way to decrease our carbon footprint, which is needed to alleviate global warming: farming and food distribution should be done at the local and regional levels.

Decentralizing food growing and distribution makes all parts of the world more resilient and fosters community building. Strengthening local communities is a natural outcome of following nature's lead for practical scale economies and agricultural processes. Stable networks of products and services, able to deliver locally and regionally, become important factors in emergencies and Earth challenges. Local economies that thrive also result in land usage being better designed for the local community's needs, leading to greater harmony and health overall. It's important for all of us to add to the welfare of our local communities, where we each live. We can be globally aware but we must also be locally active.

All together, from every place on Earth, we can elevate the world around us in this fashion. Life asks us to do our part, to be resilient, and to make the land resilient as well by rebuilding its foundation and following nature's lead in making deliberate choices. We are asked to make a difference in the best ways we each can. If we all take this lesson to heart, pitching in and serving each other, our communities, animals, wildlife, and the ecosystem, then the world will improve radically. This is completely predictable, knowable, and true. It is an expression of love. Love, which the animals show us, is not an emotional state of being; it is energetic rapport that is established in respectful relations between all sentient lives. "Love," as buffalo said to me in the final dream I had of them while writing this book, "is what we experience when each of us fulfills our soul's purpose."

THE 8 LAWS OF CHANGE

In his magnificent book *The 8 Laws of Change,* Stephan Schwartz explains what the abolitionist, civil rights, women's vote, public education, and public health movements, as well as Greenpeace, share in common. A few Quakers who wanted to improve the world for others began all of these movements. Schwartz discovered eight basic laws that appear to govern the Quaker philosophy and that were applied in these instances but are not exclusive to them.

Schwartz asked the question, "How does a small group of people actually change the world?" He spent almost two decades searching for the answers. Mohandas Gandhi and Martin Luther King and their hundreds of thousands of supporters did it. They instigated successful change against tyranny. How? By making a conscious effort to embody the qualities they wanted to see in the world and, unlike the American revolutionaries who also seized freedom from oppression, these movements were all done by foreswearing any and all violence. Schwartz found eight principles that these historic group efforts were guided by, successfully changing laws and the behavior of individuals. These principals are in complete alignment with those of countless spiritual communities across the ages, as well as with the basic nature of the animal communities we have now spent time with, and the societies that revere them.

Here are the eight laws of change:

First Law. The individuals, individually, and the group, collectively, must share a common intention.

Second Law. The individuals and the group may have goals, but they may not have cherished outcomes.

Third Law. The individuals in the group must accept that their goals may not be reached in their lifetimes and be okay with this.

Fourth Law. The individuals in the group must accept that they may not get either credit or acknowledgment for what they have done and be authentically okay with this.

Fifth Law. Each person in the group, regardless of gender, religion, race, culture, must enjoy fundamental equality, even as the various roles in the hierarchy of the effort are respected.

Sixth Law. The individuals in the group must foreswear violence in word, act, or thought.

Seventh Law. The individuals in the group and the group itself must make their private selves consistent with their public postures.

Eighth Law. The individuals in the group and the group collectively must always act from the beingness of life-affirming integrity.[25]

As the author points out, groups of people all over the world have undertaken positive change using these principles. Perhaps they did not identify them in the same way, but in essence they embodied them in their own culturally unique ways. If we remind ourselves of these guidelines, we will be less frustrated with the pace of change and more likely to have hope and appreciate the rewards of our efforts, which will extend beyond our own lifetimes.

NONLOCAL CONSCIOUSNESS, PRAYER, AND OTHER LIFESAVING TOOLS

At the start of this book I shared the primary experiences that many people have had with psi phenomena. These are the same kinds of phenomena that shamans and other animal communicators experience. Cross-culturally, these communicators and the White Spirit Animals and the species to which they belong participate in what is called "nonlocal consciousness." As we have learned, this refers to our ability to experience phenomena that happen outside normal constraints of time and space.

Each of us is born with all of these supersensible capacities. The cultures that the White Spirit Animals bless with their presence use all of these and other faculties in their personal and communal lives. As mentioned earlier in this book, skills such as farseeing (remote viewing); knowing things before they occur (premonition); understanding what any person, animal, or other life-form needs by hearing or seeing their own images (telepathy); being contacted by someone who has died; recalling other lives (regressive memory); being able to see nature spirits (clairvoyance); hearing spiritual messages (clairaudience); experiencing ourselves as outside of our own bodies (astral projection); and knowing the future (prophecy) are just a few of the practices and qualities that we possess. All of these modalities of communication and experiences are examples of senses we have but which are not always nurtured or cultivated. Yet learning to rely on our intuition, our "hunches," is another vital skill to practice.

Prayer is another powerful tool for the "speaking human." Research shows that prayer does change matter, and so does our attention. As established earlier, *the observer effect* demonstrates that anything any of us looks at is changed by our presence, whether it is a microbe or a city. Our observing something with awareness activates some aspect of its life system, which, by coming into rapport with the observer's consciousness, is affected by the observer's own attention and intention. In my prior three books, *The Kabbalistic Teachings of the Female Prophets, The Sanctuary of the Divine Presence,* and *The Future of Human Experience,* I describe the kinds of prayers that have proven most effective. Prayer is one of humanity's greatest tools for problem solving and peacemaking. Generally, prayers that are nongoal directed have the biggest outcome. Decades of research by Spindrift Research, founded by father and son Christian Scientists Bruce and John Klingbeil, examined the difference between goal-directed prayer and nongoal-directed prayer. They discovered that when we pray for the restored well-being of any living entity, and have an attitude of "thy will be done," the target's state of existence is changed in a better way than if we pray for a specific outcome.[26]

We also know that prayer is reciprocal: praying for someone else has a positive effect on the one doing the praying. Try to think of this as shared light. We are each at one moment the emanator of the light and at another moment, the receiver. This light energy that we share is the "spirit" that fills all life. When we tap into it through our awakened heart, with life-affirming intentions, we are not the creator of the energy, we are a point in its distribution network. Once humanity appreciates the power of collective prayer to draw down this creative spirit power, we will have added yet another tool to our bear medicine bag.

TELEPATHY IN EMERGENCIES

As we move into the age of unity consciousness, we will come to know better the power of our thoughts, our words, and our deeds. We will learn to collectively shift weather systems to save lives and to help others, who are in desperate need, from afar. We will discover telepathic communication and understand that it's a way for everyone, everywhere, to work together harmoniously, without the need for technology. Humans have the *inner technologies* to do everything we are copying in our material world with machines (cell phones, faxes, telescopes), which may fail to operate in the future due to extraplanetary events or local ones. This is one reason why improving our individual and collective intuition and nonlocal consciousness skills is so vital. But primarily, by doing so, we can all experience more fully our human potential, which shamans and medicine men and women have displayed throughout the ages.

Animals, we now know, are anxious to help us, warn us, and guide us to safety when they are able. Here is one example from my own experience to illustrate how the animals can do this to help us in the future. It demonstrates that when animals broadcast their own form of universal signaling to anyone tuning in, it can be heard. (I was tuned in but I didn't know the meaning of what I'd heard.)

In 2011, just as I began to expand my conversations at a distance with animals in the wild and wild animals in captivity, animals of all kinds began to screech inside my head. Birds were cawing, lions roaring, snakes hissing—it was a genuine cacophony of chaos. The level of noise that was streaming through my nonphysical ears was very loud and full of agonized screams such as are emitted during traumatic encounters. I wondered if my inner receiver was getting tuned in to some "animal suffering channel" or moving around the channels like tuning into a station on a shortwave radio. Before finding just the right station, one hears all kinds of static and conversation in foreign languages. I wondered if I was moving up and down the bandwidth of various animals. I commented to my husband, Bob, that if this was what this work would be like, I wouldn't be able to do it.

Initially the frenzy was way over the top. It was entirely distracting and alarming to listen to creatures in such pain and fear. In addition I thought that if all the animals were going to communicate at once and scream in my head, how could I be of any help? This went on sometimes during the day and sometimes as I tried to fall asleep at night—layer upon layer of animal voices echoed inside my head. Almost two weeks later, on March 11, 2011, an 8.9 magnitude earthquake and the Tohuku tsunami, with waves as high as 133 feet, hit Japanese shores as far inland as six miles. The explosive impact caused the worst ongoing nuclear disaster in world history and continual leaking of the Fukushima nuclear plant into the Pacific Ocean. But at the same time, I got relief. Whatever telepathic channel I had been tuned into stopped broadcasting.

This experience could be described as psychic or telepathic hearing of a warning siren from those who knew Spirit before Spirit had acted. Animals hear things way before they happen. In 1999, during the civil war in Yugoslavia between Croatians and Serbians, people at the Belgrade Zoo (Belgrade Good Hope Garden) witnessed animals aborting fetuses, screaming, breaking out of cages, and, when they could, devouring their young. The zoo animals could hear the war planes long before they arrived with their bombs, before the siege began. The quieter we become, the more we still our minds, the more we will hear as a result. This also requires faith that this is true—and, in this case, that animals are speaking to us and that they are reaching out to help.

THE DREAMS OF CHILDREN

The dreams and visions of children are important as well. Children's perceptions of their own future, their purpose, and what they say about the world and the world's future should not be belittled or diminished. The imagination is one of the most powerful gifts we have and as history shows us, what seems imaginary in one century is manifest form in the next. What I have found in interviewing so many wonderful men and women whose life work has required opposing the status quo in their fields of expertise is that they were exposed to more than a single culture as a child. And they usually had a mentor of some sort, whether a parent or a teacher, who encouraged their exploration. Most had unusual experiences with the paranormal or psi phenomena.

In Western culture these anomalous phenomena haven't been

talked about or encouraged since the end of the matriarchal lineages among humans. Today, however, in Native cultures, they are not only talked about and encouraged, they are acknowledged as being great gifts to the community. Let us all encourage children to dream themselves and the future richly. What children talk about or what they seem to recall from some other time or vision should not be discounted as make-believe.

Until the age of four and as late as ten, most children are still very much in touch with the nonmaterial realms of existence that are part of our lives when we, as adults, choose to pay attention. Children do so naturally until that door to the essential inner life gets closed by social pressure or a lack of nurturance. But it can open again at some point as it often does during a time of crisis. Many prophecies teach that this is a time on Earth when all of our inner talents need to be awakened and developed and that the outcome will be the talked-about mystical state of unity consciousness. Many traditions also speak of this time as an age of prophecy by women and children.

With Earth changes and the new term "climate change refugee" now formally in our vocabulary, it is clear that a destabilized world will pose challenges to all living forms. Animal displacement will bring animals into closer proximity with humans everywhere. They can warn us of impending disaster and council us on what steps to take to nurture the Earth. For the animals' survival, collaborative efforts are necessary. This can be enhanced with trans-species telepathy. When we listen, animals will tell us what is needed, as they do in our dreams and waking visions or what are sometimes called "daydreams." It is they who called *me* to council in order to share their wisdom teachings. I did not assemble *them*.

The writing of this book has been an amazing journey for me, a humbling experience that has brought fountains of tears for the vast suffering of sentient life. But knowing that we can imagine and create a better future on Earth has also produced an abiding sense of hope and joy. The journey with the White Spirit Animals has been wondrous. It is a great honor to be their student and their advocate, and gaining a better understanding of each species' purpose, physically and spiritually, has changed my life. Dreaming with them has brought me into a deeper feeling of rapport and closeness with them.

As I set out to prove to myself, this journey has demonstrated that dreaming is one way of communicating in any relationship and that the spiritual soul of all species is commingled in its unitary root, The All, from which every aspect of Creation ushers forth. We can dream with the Earth and discover what she needs from us anywhere and at any time. Such supersensible access is a vital field in which all life is connected. Dreams like the telepathic communication services are free and available to everyone. We can all make the effort to access them.

ANIMAL LESSONS

Each of the White Spirit Animals and their species teach us important lessons about our own evolution and our relationship to off-planet neighbors who have helped humanity over the course of billions of years and who still continue to help us today. They guide us in our inner development as well as our way of being in the world. Awakening to the presence of the voice of Spirit is what animals teach us by being exactly who they are and by doing exactly what we are here to do together, which is, in short, to have a respectful relationship with all life.

The lessons gleaned from our five prophets of the wild are quite simple:

1. **Bear,** Chief of Medicine, guardian of Spirit, the Pole Star, and the North, teaches us how to heal the Earth and ourselves by displaying patience and nonviolence as well as a mastery over dreamtime as an important gift of Spirit. Being large or powerful does not equate with being brutal. It means finding ways to make peace through self-restraint, sharing resources, and planning ahead. Bear

is ascetic in lifestyle and oriented around the raising of its young. Mother Bear teaches us how to align our lives with nature and how to be stewards of the Spirit in all of life.

2. **Lion** shows us how to be a protector as both male and female, how to lead with a noble heart even when we face insurmountable odds. Lions are visionaries who see far ahead and provide clues to what is approaching before it arrives. They teach us how to find collaborative solutions. They show us that nobility is a state of consciousness that reveres all life with pride. The "heart of gold" is the central sun within each person from whence the light of love and courage shines.

3. **Elephant** is our noble spiritual teacher of compassion, showing us modesty, humility, and the power to love all of Creation. Elephants teach enduring attention and nurturance of the young and old (as being most precious) by the entire community. They demonstrate that matrilineal wisdom keeps mammalian species healthy and safe. Enlightenment, they show us, is by right action in our daily lives. As the manifestation of Buddhic awareness they remind us to achieve equanimity in mind and heart, to treasure water wherever it is, and to forgive the aggressor within ourselves as well as those aggressors around us. They who stir the Milky Way remind us that we are co-creators in the universe just as they are agents of Creation from outer to inner space.

4. **Wolf** guides us in the seamless web of life and death and between all species. Wolf shows us that everyone has a role to play in restoring the world and that collaboration is a sustainable and regenerative process. Wolves also remind us that male and female are equal partners in rearing our young, though each gender has its own necessary leaders. They also teach us that those who are "not here now" are all around us in spirit, that we are all "undying stars." As escort of thresholds, Wolf as an intradimensional shape-shifter par excellence teaches us that we function in multidimensions simultaneously.

5. **Buffalo** is the perfect guide for all Earth beings to walk the Red Road—the road of the Earth, to protect and restore our soil. Buffalo show group consciousness at work over long periods of time and over vast landmasses. "We will come again" is their message, reminding us that we should never give up our hope for conservation, preservation, and restoration. It can take one hundred years, or longer in some cases, to see the change we hope to see. Peace, they teach us, is the heart of our purpose and our planetary calling. It is our soul's most blessed prayer. Buffalo ignite in us a longing for peace within ourselves and in our communal lives.

IN CLOSING

We now see that preserving apex guardian animals, mammals often targeted for annihilation by humans, is a practical and directly measureable way to keep ecosystems in balance, not only by preserving them but by helping to enrich them. We need to do this for our sea mammals as well. By such reciprocal care, we assist in making them more resilient to change.

Each of us should know that our own inner personal development is key to Earth's well-being as well as our global community's. Becoming individually self-aware is the cornerstone to a healthy and peaceful existence. Self-development can lead to having a more compassionate heart, mindful flexibility, and spiritual openness. Practicing nonjudgmental attitudes awakens our psi talents. Our guides also make clear that we must focus on the well-being of our women and children and nurture our culture so that we are guardians of it rather than dominators. "Save as many of us as you can" was their earliest exhortation to me after they first arrived in 2013. We now know why we must. For each of the animals featured in this book, examples of progressive efforts to restore their species in their natural habitats have been showcased, along with stories of the animal's human champions and the animal's historic roles in human society.

It is a wonderful blessing to close this wilderness journey with these beautiful prophets of the wild by witnessing another hopeful, synchronous sign of Lakota prophecy being fulfilled. The buffalo are the Earth's ancient caregivers. The Lakota White Buffalo Calf Woman is the bringer of the prayer pipe tradition, of naming and marriage ceremonies, of sweat and smoke medicine—a bringer of peace between all nations. Having respect for buffalo and enabling their reemergence speaks to the spirit that renews the heart, encourages forgiveness, and blesses humility. Their reappearance in national consciousness illustrates what is taking place worldwide; strong and life-elevating bonds between peoples and other kin species are being nurtured.

Over one hundred years after William T. Hornaday stopped the complete annihilation of the buffalo with the aid of then President Theodore Roosevelt, on May 9, 2016, President Barack Obama signed the National Bison Legacy Act into law, officially making the American bison the national mammal of the United States. This majestic animal joins our indigenous bald eagle as the official symbol of America, and much like the eagle, it is part of our conservation legacy. This elevated position signifies the renewal and arising of the buffalo, which was prophesized long before today. This is a sign of human awakening. The migratory freedom of the buffalo is essential to the restoration of the soil and the uplifting of our communal spirit. As one of the apex guardians, the buffalo offers us peace and assistance.

As I have experienced in my telepathic exchanges with animals and then in the writing of this book, and using dreams as a place of communication between us, the kingdom of life speaks among its members—the mineral, plant, animal, human, and spiritual realms. The call of the wild, like the voice within, are the intelligent hearts of each one of us and of nature. There is no Babel, only a loving and purposeful exchange in the unity of the sacred. (See plate 24 of the author with a few of her dogs.)

Now we can listen to our animal kin. Now we can hear the howl of wolves across the world drum, the purr of nursing bear cubs, the lion's roar of belonging, the trumpeting elephant announcing her place to all, and the sound of buffalo hooves turning over the soil. This is the call of the wild to *all of us*. This is the call to find a place of balance within ourselves, where we are at one with nature and where we live in loving communion with all of life, taking part in the blessings of Creation with respect and gratitude. This is the hope of the White Spirit messengers, ambassadors from the animal kingdom, calling us home to celebrate our reunion.

Notes

INTRODUCTION. WHITE SPIRIT ANIMALS

1. Cerretani, "The Contagion of Happiness."
2. Dorje, *Interconnected,* 238–39.

CHAPTER 1. DREAMING SHAMANS

1. Byrd, "Positive Therapeutic Effects," 826–29; https://en.wikipedia.org /wiki/Princeton_Engineering_Anomalies_Research_Lab.
2. Walton et al., "Lowering Cortisol and CVD risk," 211–15.
3. Maharishi University of Management, www.mum.edu/about-mum /consciousness-based-education-subpages/tm-research/maharishi-effect (accessed May 23, 2017); Dillbeck et al., "Test of a Field Model of Consciousness," 457–86; Mudd, "Research Shows Group Meditation Can Reduce Crime."
4. McMoneagle, *Ultimate Time Machine,* 21.
5. Smith, *Reading the Enemy's Mind,* 128–29; McMoneagle, *Memoirs of a Psychic Spy,* 110.
6. Bem, "Feeling the Future," 407–25; Morse et al., "Childhood Near-Death Experiences," 1110–14; Morse et al., "Near-Death Experiences in a Pediatric Population," 595–600.
7. Moody, *Life After Life.*
8. Personal correspondence with the author, September 5, 2016.

9. Ibid.

10. Krippner, interview by Zohara Hieronimus, *21st Century Radio,* July 12, 2015.

11. Krippner and Rock, *Demystifying Shamans,* 6, 23.

12. Ibid., 69.

13. Ibid., 70.

14. Ibid., 3.

15. "Obedience: Milgram (1963)," www.intropsych.com/ch15_social/milgram _1963_obedience.html (accessed May 23, 2017); McLeod, "The Milgram Experiment."

16. Bradshaw, interview by Zohara Hieronimus, *21st Century Radio,* August 2, 2015.

17. Bradshaw, "Advocating for the Souls of Animals."

CHAPTER 2. BEAR

1. https://grahamhancock.com/magicians/ (accessed May 23, 2017).

2. Transcript excerpt of conversation with Matata, January 17, 2012.

3. Hieronimus, *Future of Human Experience,* 26.

4. R. E. Green et al., "Draft Sequence of the Neandertal Genome," 710–22.

5. First People—The Legends, www.firstpeople.us/FP-Html-Legends/Cherokee _Medicine_Man-Cherokee.html (accessed May 23, 2017).

6. Ibid.

7. Tallwing, interview by Zohara Hieronimus, *21st Century Radio,* November 23, 2014.

8. Wasco Tribe, "Coyote, Wolves, and Bears."

9. Hieronimus, *Future of Human Experience,* 33–38.

10. http://en.wikipedia.org/wiki/Pole_star. A wonderful source on the lore and origin of star names is *Star Names: Their Lore and Meaning* by Richard H. Allen.

11. An excellent book on the influence of Artemis as the modern-day activist is *Artemis: The Indomitable Spirit in Everywoman* by Jean Shinoda Bolen.

12. Human Trafficking Facts & Stats, www.f-4-c.org/slavery/facts.asp (accessed May 23, 2017).

13. Gimbutas, *Language of the Goddess,* 116.

14. Spencer, "Southern Ute Bear Dance."

15. Encyclopedia Britannica Advocacy for Animals, "The Dancing Bears of India."

16. Ibid.

17. World Animal Protection, www.worldanimalprotection.us.org/bear -sanctuaries (accessed May 23, 2017).

18. Kavoussi, "Asian Bear Bile Remedies."

19. www.animalsasia.org.

20. http://bcspiritbear.com/spirit-bear-facts/.

21. Levi-Strauss, "The Story of Asdiwal."

22. Russell, interview by Zohara Hieronimus, *21st Century Radio*, June 8, 2014.

23. Russell, *Spirit Bear*, 9.

24. Ibid., 79.

25. McGrady, interview by Zohara Hieronimus, *21st Century Radio*, April 13, 2014.

26. Nature Conservancy, "Canada: Great Bear Rainforest."

CHAPTER 3. LION

1. Michell, *Sacred Center*.

2. Queen of Heaven, "Asherah, Part III: The Lion Lady," https://thequeenofheaven .wordpress.com/2010/11/16/asherah-part-iii-the-lion-lady (accessed June 7, 2017).

3. www.goddessaday.com/african/nomkhubulwane.

4. Peterson, *Out of the Blue*.

5. Mutwa, *Zulu Shaman*.

6. www.december212012.com/articles/phenomenon/5.htm (accessed June 7, 2017).

7. Ibid.

8. Martin, "Great Zulu Shaman."

9. R. G. Haliburton, *New Materials for the History of Man*, 8.A.

10. Ibid.

11. Mother Nature Network, www.mnn.com/earth-matters/animals/blogs /how-many-lions-are-left-in-the-wild.

12. WWF Living Planet Report 2014, www.worldwildlife.org/pages/living -planet-report-2014.

13. Kevin Richardson, www.lionwhisperer.co.za/conservation.php (accessed July 28, 2017).

14. Kevin Richardson, www.lionwhisperer.co.za/wild-life.php (accessed July 28, 2017).

15. www.lionguardians.org.

16. Ghose, "'Presentiment' Study."

17. Four Eagles, *Making of a Healer,* 17; Four Eagles, interview by Zohara Hieronimus, *21st Century Radio,* December 27, 2014.

CHAPTER 4. ELEPHANT

1. "Hanno (elephant)," https://en.wikipedia.org/wiki/Hanno_(elephant) (accessed May 24, 2017).

2. "Ninety-Six Elephants," www.96elephants.org/chapter-1 (accessed May 24, 2017).

3. "Buddhist Studies," www.buddhanet.net/e-learning/buddhism/pbs2 _unit02.htm (accessed May 24, 2017).

4. "Gautama Buddha," https://en.wikipedia.org/wiki/Gautama_Buddha (accessed May 24, 2017).

5. "Buddha Biography.com," www.biography.com/people/buddha-9230587#the -buddha-emerges (accessed May 24, 2017).

6. "Guide to Buddhism A to Z," http://buddhisma2z.com/content.php?id=123 (accessed May 24, 2017).

7. Ibid.

8. Ibid.

9. Ibid.

10. "Zen guide: Principles," www.zenguide.com/principles/sutras/content .cfm?t=lotus_sutra&chapter=1 (accessed May 24, 2017).

11. Before It's News, "It's No White Elephant."

12. NPR Staff, "The Biggest Thing Out of Thailand."

13. Bradshaw, interview by Zohara Hieronimus, *21st Century Radio,* August 18, 2011.

14. Sheldrick, "Elephant Emotion."

15. Ibid.

16. "Wild Elephants Gather Inexplicably, Mourn Death of Elephant Whisperer," http://delightmakers.com/news/wild-Elephants-gather-inexplicably-mourn -death-of-Elephant-whisperer (accessed May 24, 2017).

17. Bryant, "Seismic Communication in Elephants."

18. RSPCA, "Live Hard, Die Young," 5.

19. UNHCR, "Worldwide Displacement."

20. Cattaneo, "How Does Climate Change Affect Migration?"

21. Bradshaw, "From Agony to Ecstasy."

22. Ibid.

23. Elephant Aid International, "Compassionate Elephant Care," https://elephantaidinternational.org/about/compassionate-elephant-care (accessed May 24, 2017).

24. Steyn, "African Elephant Numbers Plummet."

25. Steyn, "Report Estimates Enormous Economic Value."

26. Cruise, "More African Elephants May Be Sold to China."

27. Steyn, "Largest Wildlife Census in History."

28. Ibid.

29. Ibid.

30. Platt, "Elephants Are Worth."

31. Krippner, interview by Zohara Hieronimus, *21st Century Radio,* July 12, 2015.

32. Ford, "Ringling Bros. Elephants."

CHAPTER 5. WOLF

1. Song, interview by Zohara Hieronimus, *21st Century Radio,* July 26, 2015.

2. Hieronimus, *Future of Human Experience,* 255–62; https://en.wikipedia.org/wiki/Tom_Van_Flandern.

3. "The Giza Pyramids . . . and the Constellation of Orion," www.bibliotecapleyades.net/piramides/esp_piramide_8.htm#Thepercent20Orionpercent20Mystery (accessed May 24, 2017).

4. Private conversation with Tamarack Song, August 5, 2015.

5. Song, *Entering the Mind,* 3.

6. Lamplugh, interview by Zohara Hieronimus, *21st Century Radio,* January 4, 2015.

7. Tulleners, interview by Zohara Hieronimus, *21st Century Radio,* February 1, 2015.

8. Rueness et al., "The Cryptic African Wolf."

9. Brown, "DNA Proves It."

10. Kinver, "Study Shows Canid Is 'Wolf in Jackal's Clothing.'"
11. Bangs, "Potential Impact of Wolf Predation."
12. "Wolf Myths of the Middle Ages," www.Wolfcountry.net/information /myth_stories/middleages.html (accessed May 24, 2017).
13. "Medicine of the Wolf," www.kickstarter.com/projects/645287247/medicine -of-the-wolf (accessed May 24, 2017).
14. "A Wolf's Role in the Ecosystem—The Trophic Cascade," www.missionWolf .org/page/trophic-cascade (accessed May 24, 2017).
15. Lamplugh, interview by Zohara Hieronimus, *21st Century Radio,* January 4, 2015.
16. Bradshaw, interview by Zohara Hieronimus, *21st Century Radio,* August 2, 2015.
17. Lopez, *Of Wolves and Men,* 133.
18. Song, off-air interview by Zohara Hieronimus, *21st Century Radio,* August 4, 2015.
19. Russell, interview by Zohara Hieronimus, *21st Century Radio,* June 8, 2014.
20. "Werewolf," https://en.wikipedia.org/wiki/Werewolf (accessed May 24, 2017).
21. Holz and Holz, *Secrets of Aboriginal Healing,* 13.
22. Song, off-air interview by Zohara Hieronimus, *21st Century Radio,* on August 4, 2015.
23. Red Star, interview by Zohara Hieronimus, *21st Century Radio,* February 1, 2015.

CHAPTER 6. BUFFALO RISING

1. Hollenhorst, "Study."
2. Ibid.
3. Ibid.
4. Ibid.
5. "Miracle: White Buffalo of Prophecies Born in Wisconsin," www.kstrom .net/isk/arvol/whitbuff.html (accessed May 24, 2017).
6. "American Bison Society News and Updates," www.wcsnorthamerica.org /Wildlife/Bison/American-Bison-Society-News-and-Updates.aspx (accessed May 24, 2017).
7. Roca et al. "Elephant Natural History," 139–67.

8. Erdoes, *Lame Deer,* 130.

9. Hornaday, *Extermination of the American Bison,* 377.

10. Ibid., 390.

11. Ibid., 391.

12. "William Temple Hornaday: Saving the American Bison," http://siarchives.si .edu/history/exhibits/stories/william-temple-hornaday-saving-american -bison (accessed May 24, 2017).

13. Hornaday, *Extermination of the American Bison,* 396.

14. Ibid.

15. "William Temple Hornaday," https://en.wikipedia.org/wiki/William _Temple_Hornaday (accessed May 24, 2017).

16. "The Descent of Civilization: The Extermination of the American Buffalo," www.pbs.org/wnet/frontierhouse/frontierlife/essay8_3.html (accessed May 24, 2017).

17. "William Temple Hornaday," https://en.wikipedia.org/wiki/William _Temple_Hornaday (accessed May 24, 2017).

18. "Buffalo & Native Americans," www.buffalofieldcampaign.org/about-buffalo /buffalo-and-Native-americans (accessed May 24, 2017).

19. Hornaday, *Extermination of the American Bison,* 377.

20. Ibid., 379.

21. "About Hornaday," Wildlife Conservation Society Library & Archives, http://hornadayscrapbooks.com/about_hornaday (accessed May 24, 2017).

22. Hornaday, *Extermination of the American Bison,* 369, 521.

23. "Buffalo Field Campaign: History," www.buffalofieldcampaign.org/aboutus /camphist.html (accessed May 24, 2017).

24. Seay, interview by Zohara Hieronimus, *21st Century Radio,* April 24, 2016.

25. "Inter Tribal Buffalo Council: Who We Are," http://itbcBuffalo.com /node/3 (accessed May 24, 2017).

26. "Chief Arvol Looking Horse Speaks of White Buffalo Prophecy." www .youtube.com/watch?v=PHqVdZmpRgI. Transcribed by Kari Noren-Hoshal, White Bison Association.

27. "White Buffalo Calf Woman," http://kstrom.net/isk/arvol/buffpipe.html (accessed May 24, 2017).

28. "The White Buffalo," www.merceronline.com/Native/native05.htm (accessed May 24, 2017).

29. "White Buffalo Calf Woman," http://kstrom.net/isk/arvol/buffpipe.html (accessed May 24, 2017).

30. "Chief Arvol Looking Horse Speaks of White Buffalo Prophecy." www .youtube.com/watch?v=PHqVdZmpRgI. Transcribed by Kari Noren-Hoshal, White Bison Association.

31. Hart, interview by Zohara Hieronimus, *21st Century Radio,* on February 2, 2014; August 16, 2015; March 13, 2016.

32. Personal correspondence, August 14, 2017.

33. "Sitting Bull," www.historynet.com/sitting-bull (accessed May 24, 2017).

34. Hart, interview by Zohara Hieronimus, *21st Century Radio,* on February 2, 2014; August 16, 2015; March 13, 2016.

35. Personal correspondence, August 26, 2016.

36. Schwartz, interview by Zohara Hieronimus, *21st Century Radio,* October 18, 2015.

37. Private correspondence with the author, August 29, 2016.

38. Author's exchanges with the buffalo during the month of August 2015.

39. Locke, "Pledge to Restore Wild Buffalo."

CHAPTER 7. THE SIGNS

1. http://grahamhancock.com/magicians (accessed May 24, 2017).

2. Roach, "Oldest *Homo Sapiens* Fossils."

3. "Tom Van Flandern," https://en.wikipedia.org/wiki/Tom_Van_Flandern (accessed May 24, 2017).

4. Ibid.

5. https://sites.google.com/site/waldorfwatch/planets (accessed June 12, 2017).

6. Transcript excerpt of conversation with Matata, January 21, 2012, 2:58 to 3:15 p.m. ET.

7. Ibid.

8. Dewhurst, *Ancient Giants,* 1.

9. Ibid., 2.

10. Mayell, "Cyclops Myth."

11. "Has the Smithsonian Hidden Evidence of Ancient Giants on Earth," http://dcxposed.com/2013/10/28/deep-conspiracy-has-the-smithsonian -hidden-evidence-of-ancient-giants-on-Earth (accessed May 24, 2017).

12. Dreams of author in late October of 2015.

13. "The Extinction Crisis," www.biologicaldiversity.org/programs/biodiversity
/elements_of_biodiversity/extinction_crisis (accessed May 24, 2017).

14. "Problem: Extinction of Plant and Animal Species," www.webofcreation
.org/Earth%20Problems/species.htm (accessed May 24, 2017).

15. Kolbert, *Sixth Extinction,* 69.

16. Crutzen, "Geology of Mankind," 23.

17. Hieronimus, *Future of Human Experience,* 51–53.

18. "The Dust Bowl," www.livinghistoryfarm.org/farminginthe30s/water_02
.html (accessed May 24, 2017).

19. See more at http://remineralize.org and www.carbon-negative.us/soil
/bruck.htm.

20. Campe, interview by Zohara Hieronimus, *21st Century Radio,* June 19, 2016.

21. Weaver and Zimmer, interview by Zohara Hieronimus, *21st Century Radio,*
June 19, 2016.

22. Ibid.

23. Shepard, interview by Zohara Hieronimus, *21st Century Radio,* August 28,
2016.

24. Salatin, interview by Zohara Hieronimus, *21st Century Radio,* August 28,
2016.

25. Schwartz, *The 8 Laws of Change,* 18.

26. See www.zoharaonline.com/sweets-treats-the-spindrift-years.

Bibliography

Alexander, Shana. *The Astonishing Elephant*. New York: Random House, 2000.

Allen, Richard H. *Star Names: Their Lore and Meaning*. Mineola, N.Y.: Dover Publications, 1963.

Anthony, Lawrence. *The Elephant Whisperer: My Life with the Herd in the African Wild*. New York: Thomas Dunne Books, 2009.

———. *The Last Rhinos*. New York: Thomas Dunne Books, 2012.

Anthony, Lawrence, and Graham Spence. *Babylon's Ark: The Incredible Wartime Rescue of the Baghdad Zoo*. New York: Thomas Dunne Books, 2007.

Bangs, Ed. "Potential Impact of Wolf Predation in the Greater Yellowstone Area." www.forwolves.org/impact.html (accessed May 24, 2017).

Bauval, Robert, and Adrian Gilbert. *The Orion Mystery*. New York: Random House, 1994.

Before It's News. "It's No White Elephant in Thailand's Herd." March 13, 2015. http://beforeitsnews.com/middle-east/2015/03/its-no-white-Elephant-in -thailands-herd-2469408.html (accessed May 24, 2017).

Beery, Yitzak. *The Gift of Shamanism, Visionary Power, Ayahuasca Dreams, and Journeys to Other Realms*. Rochester, Vt.: Destiny Books, 2015.

———, ed. *Shamanic Transformations: True Stories of the Moment of Awakening*. Rochester, Vt.: Destiny Books, 2015.

Bem, Daryl J. "Feeling the Future: Experimental Evidence for Anomalous Retroactive Influences on Cognition and Affect." *Journal of Personality and Social Psychology* 100, no. 3 (March 2011), 407–25.

Bird, Christopher. *The Divining Hand: The 500-Year-Old Mystery of Dowsing*. New York: E. P. Dutton, 1979.

Bird, Christopher, and Peter Tompkins. *Secrets of the Soil: A Fascinating Account of Recent Breakthroughs—Scientific and Spiritual—That Can Save Your Garden or Farm.* New York: Harper and Row, 1989.

———. *Secrets of the Soil: New Solutions for Restoring Our Planet,* rev. ed. Anchorage, Alaska: Earthpulse Press, 1998.

Bolen, Jean Shinoda. *Artemis: The Indomitable Spirit in Everywoman.* New York: Conari Press, 2014.

Boone, J. Allen. *Kinship with All Life.* New York: Harper Collins, 1976.

Braden, Gregg. *Secrets of the Lost Mode of Prayer: The Hidden Power of Beauty, Blessings, Wisdom, and Hurt.* Carlsbad, Calif.: Hay House, 2006.

Bradshaw, G. A. *Carnivore Minds: Who These Fearsome Animals Really Are.* New Haven, Conn.: Yale University Press, 2017.

———. *Elephants on the Edge: What Animals Teach Us About Humanity.* New Haven, Conn.: Yale University Press, 2010.

———. "From Agony to Ecstasy: An Interview with Carol Buckley on Elephant Trauma Recovery." *Psychology Today* (December 18, 2015). www.psychologytoday .com/blog/bear-in-mind/201512/agony-ecstasy.

Bradshaw, Gay. "Advocating for the Souls of Animals: An Interview with Gay Bradshaw." *MOON Magazine.* http://moonmagazine.org/advocating -souls-animals-interview-gay-bradshaw-2015-01-03.

———. "Interview with Gay Bradshaw." By Zohara Hieronimus. *21st Century Radio* (August 14, 2011; August 2, 2015). http://hieronimusdb.com /guestcenter/showguest.asp?ID=2253.

Brown, Eryn. "DNA Proves It: African 'Golden Jackal' Is Really a Golden Wolf." *Los Angeles Times,* August 3, 2015. www.latimes.com/science/sciencenow /la-sci-sn-golden-jackal-wolf-20150731-story.html.

Brown, Lester R. *Full Planet, Empty Plates: The New Geopolitics of Food Scarcity.* New York: W. W. Norton and Company, 2012.

Brunke, Dawn Baumann. *Dreaming with Polar Bears: Spirit Journeys with Animal Guides.* Rochester, Vt.: Bear & Company, 2014.

Bryant, Astra. "Seismic Communication in Elephants." Stanford Neuroblog, July 8, 2013. http://web.stanford.edu/group/neurostudents/cgi-bin/wordpress /?p=4037.

Byrd, R. C. "Positive Therapeutic Effects of Intercessory Prayer in a Coronary Care Unit Population." *Southern Medical Journal* 81, no. 7 (July 1988): 826–29.

Campe, Joanna. "Interview with Joana Campe." By Zohara Hieronimus. *21st*

Century Radio (June 19, 2016). http://hieronimusdb.com/guestcenter/showguest.asp?ID=617.

Cattaneo, Cristina. "How Does Climate Change Affect Migration?" November 23, 2015. www.weforum.org/agenda/2015/11/how-does-climate-change-affect-migration (accessed May 24, 2017).

Cerretani, Jessica. "The Contagion of Happiness: Harvard Researchers Are Discovering How We Can All Get Happy," https://hms.harvard.edu/news/harvard-medicine/contagion-happiness.

Clow, Barbara Hand. *Awakening the Planetary Mind: Beyond Trauma of the Past to a New Era of Creativity.* Rochester, Vt.: Bear & Company, 2001, 2011.

Cremo, Michael A., and Richard L. Thompson. *Forbidden Archeology: The Hidden History of the Human Race.* San Diego, Calif.: Bhaktivedanta Institute, 1993.

Croke, Vicki Constantine. *Elephant Company.* New York: Random House, 2014.

Cruise, Adam. "More African Elephants May Be Sold to China This Year." *National Geographic,* January 1, 2016. http://news.nationalgeographic.com/2016/01/160101-zimbabwe-elephants-china-export-zoos-conservation-jane-goodall.

Crutzen, P. J. "Geology of Mankind." *Nature* 415, no. 6867 (January 2002): 23.

Dewhurst, Richard J. *The Ancient Giants Who Ruled America.* Rochester, Vt.: Bear & Company, 2013.

Dillbeck, M. C., C. B. Banus, C. Polanzi, G. S. Landrith III. "Test of a Field Model of Consciousness and Social Change: Transcendental Meditation and TM-Sidhi Program and Decreased Urban Crime." *The Journal of Mind and Behavior* 9, no. 4 (1988): 457–86.

DiPietro, Vincent, Gregory Molenaar, and John Brandenburg. *Unusual Martian Surface Features.* 4th ed. Glenn Dale, M.D.: Mars Research, 1988.

Dorje, Ogyen Trinley (the Karmapa). *Interconnected: Embracing Life in Our Global Society.* Somerville, Mass.: Wisdom Publications, 2017.

Dossey, Larry. *One Mind: How Our Individual Mind Is Part of a Greater Consciousness and Why It Matters.* New York: Hay House, 2014.

———. *The Power of Premonitions: How Knowing the Future Can Shape Our Lives.* New York: Dutton, 2009.

Encyclopedia Britannica Advocacy for Animals. "The Dancing Bears of India: Moving Toward Freedom." December 17, 2007. http://advocacy

.britannica.com/blog/advocacy/2007/12/the-dancing-bears-of-india-moving-toward-freedom/.

Erdoes, Richard. *Lame Deer, Seeker of Visions*. New York: Simon and Schuster, 1972.

Four Eagles, Russell. "Interview with Russell Four Eagles." By Zohara Hieronimus. *21st Century Radio* (December 27, 2014). http://hieronimusdb.com/guestcenter/showguest.asp?ID=2494.

———. *The Making of a Healer: Teachings of My Oneida Grandmother*. Wheaton, Ill.: Quest Books, 2014.

Ford, Dana. "Ringling Bros. Elephants to Get an Early Retirement." CNN, January 11, 2016. www.cnn.com/2016/01/11/us/ringling-bros-elephants.

Gaubert, Philippe, Cécile Bloch, Slim Benyacoub, Adnan Abdelhamid, Paolo Pagani, Chabi Adéyèmi Marc Sylvestre Djagoun, Arnaud Coulous, and Sylvain Dufour. "Reviving the African Wolf *Canis lupus lupaster* in North and West Africa: A Mitochondrial Lineage Ranging More than 6,000 km Wide." *Plos One* 7, no. 8: e42740. http://journals.plos.org/plosone/article?id=10.1371/journal.pone.0042740.

Ghose, Tia. "'Presentiment' Study Suggests People's Bodies Can 'Predict Events,' But Scientists Skeptical." *HuffPost*, November 2, 2012. www.huffingtonpost.com/2012/11/05/presentiment-bodies-predict-future-skpetical_n2075632.html.

Gimbutas, Marija. *The Language of the Goddess*. New York: Thames and Hudson, 1989.

Green, R. E., J. Krause, A. W. Briggs, T. Maricic, U. Stenzel, M. Kircher, N. Patterson et al. "A Draft Sequence of the Neandertal Genome." *Science* 328, no. 5979 (May 7, 2010): 710–22.

Haliburton, R. G. *New Materials for the History of Man* (1863). Reprinted in Toronto, Canada: Royal Astronomical Society, 1920.

Hancock, Graham. *Magicians of the Gods: The Forgotten Wisdom of Earth's Lost Civilization*. London: Coronet, 2015.

Hart, Cynthia. "Interview with Cynthia Hart." By Zohara Hieronimus. *21st Century Radio* (February 2, 2014; August 16, 2015; March 13, 2016). http://hieronimusdb.com/guestcenter/showguest.asp?ID=2421.

Hieronimus, J. Zohara Meyerhoff. *The Future of Human Experience, Visionary Thinkers on the Science of Consciousness*. Rochester, Vt.: Inner Traditions, 2013.

———. *Kabbalistic Teachings of the Female Prophets: The Seven Holy Women of Ancient Israel*. Rochester, Vt.: Inner Traditions, 2008.

———. *Sanctuary of the Divine Presence: Hebraic Teachings on Initiation and Illumination*. Rochester, Vt.: Inner Traditions, 2012.

Hieronimus, Robert. *America's Secret Destiny: Spiritual Vision and the Founding of a Nation*. Rochester, Vt.: Destiny Books, 1989.

———. *Founding Fathers, Secret Societies: Illuminati, Free Masons, Rosicrucians, and the Decoding of the Great Seal*. Rochester, Vt.: Destiny Books, 2006.

Hieronimus, Robert, and Laura Cortner. *The Secret Life of Lady Liberty: Goddess in the New World*. Rochester, Vt.: Inner Traditions, 2016.

Hollenhorst, John. "Study: 'Pure' Herd of Bison Living in Utah." KSL.com. December 16, 2015. www.ksl.com/?sid=37798442&nid=1288&fm=home _page&s_cid=toppick3.

Holz, Gary, and Robbie Holz. *Secrets of Aboriginal Healing: A Physicist's Journey with a Remote Australian Tribe*. Rochester, Vt.: Bear & Company, 2015.

Hornaday, William T. *The Extermination of the American Bison*. Washington, D.C.: American Government Printing Office, 1889.

———. *Our Vanishing Wildlife: Its Extermination and Preservation*. New York: New York Zoological Society, 1913.

Horowitz, Joshua. *War of the Whales*. New York: Simon and Schuster, 2014.

Ingerman, Sandra, and Lyn Roberts. *Speaking with Nature: Awakening to the Deep Wisdom of the Earth*. Rochester, Vt.: Bear & Company, 2015.

Johnson, Buffy. *Lady of the Beasts: Ancient Images of the Goddess and Her Sacred Animals*. New York: Harper and Row, 1988.

Kavoussi, Ben. "Asian Bear Bile Remedies: Traditional Medicine or Barbarism?" *Science-Based Medicine,* March 24, 2011. https://sciencebasedmedicine .org/asian-bear-bile-remedies-barbarism-or-medicine.

Kinver, Mark. "Study Shows Canid Is 'Wolf in Jackal's Clothing.'" BBC News, January 28, 2011. www.bbc.com/news/science-environment-12298337.

Kolbert, Elizabeth. *The Sixth Extinction: An Unnatural History*. New York: Pocador Books, 2014.

Krippner, Stanley. "Interview with Stanley Krippner." By Zohara Hieronimus. *21st Century Radio* (July 12, 2015). http://hieronimusdb.com/guestcenter /showguest.asp?ID=1406.

Krippner, Stanley, and Adam J. Rock. *Demystifying Shamans and Their World: A Multidisciplinary Study*. Charlottesville, Va.: Academic, 2011.

Krippner, Stanley, and P. Welch. *Spiritual Dimensions of Healing: From Native Shamanism to Contemporary Healthcare.* New York: Irvington, 1992.

Krupp, E. C. *Skywatchers, Shamans and Kings: Astronomy and the Archaeology of Power.* New York: Wiley and Sons, 1977.

Lamplugh, Rick. "Interview with Rick Lamplugh." By Zohara Hieronimus. *21st Century Radio* (January 4, 2015). http://hieronimusdb.com/guestcenter /showguest.asp?ID=2461.

Laszlo, Ervin. *Science and the Akashic Field: An Integral Theory of Everything.* 2nd ed. Rochester, Vt.: Inner Traditions, 2007.

Laszlo, Ervin, and Kingsley L. Dennis. *Dawn of the Akashic Age: New Consciousness, Quantum Resonance, and the Future of the World.* Rochester, Vt.: Inner Traditions, 2013.

LaViolette, Paul A. *Earth under Fire: Humanity's Survival of the Apocalypse.* Alexandria, Va.: Starlane Publications, 1997.

Levi-Strauss, Claude. "The Story of Asdiwal." http://web.sbu.edu/theology /bychkov/asdiwal.pdf.

Locke, Harvey. "Pledge to Restore Wild Buffalo Unites First Nations of North America." *National Geographic,* August 18, 2015. http://voices.nationalgeographic .com/2015/08/18/the-power-of-a-wild-animal-to-help-people-two-more -first-nations-sign-historic-treaty-to-bring-wild-buffalo-back-to-tribal-lands.

Lopez, Barry Holstun. *Of Wolves and Men.* New York: Scribner, 2004.

Martin, Rick. "Great Zulu Shaman and Elder Credo Mutwa on Alien Abduction & Reptilians: A Rare, Astonishing Conversation." September 30, 1999. www.metatech.org/wp/aliens/reptilians-africa-zulu-shaman-elder-credo -mutwa-alien-abduction-reptilians-1 (accessed June 7, 2017).

Mayell, Hillary. "Cyclops Myth Spurred by 'One-Eyed' Fossils?" *National Geographic News,* February 5, 2003. http://news.nationalgeographic.com /news/2003/02/0205_030205_cyclops.html.

McGrady, Tim. "Interview with Tim McGrady." By Zohara Hieronimus. *21st Century Radio* (April 13, 2014). http://hieronimusdb.com/guestcenter /showguest.asp?ID=2428.

McLeod, Saul. "The Milgram Experiment." *SimplyPsychology* (2007). www .simplypsychology.org/milgram.html (accessed May 23, 2017).

McMoneagle, Joseph. *Memoirs of a Psychic Spy: The Remarkable Life of U.S. Government Remote Viewer 001.* Newburyport, Mass.: Hampton Roads, 2002, 2006.

———. *The Ultimate Time Machine.* Newburyport, Mass.: Hampton Roads, 1998.

Metzner, Ralph. *Green Psychology: Transforming Our Relationship to the Earth.* Rochester, Vt.: Park Street Press, 1999.

Michell, John. *The Sacred Center: The Ancient Art of Locating Sanctuaries.* Rochester, Vt.: Inner Traditions, 2009.

Moody, Raymond. *Life After Life: The Bestselling Original Investigation That Revealed "Near-Death Experiences."* New York: HarperOne, 2015.

Moody, Raymond, and Paul Perry. *Reunions: Visionary Encounters with Departed Loved Ones.* New York: Random House/Villard Books, 1993.

Morse, M. L., P. Castillo, D. Venecia, J. Milstein, and D. Tyler. "Childhood Near-Death Experiences." *American Journal of Diseases in Children* 140 (1986): 1110–14.

Morse, M. L., D. Conner, and D. Tyler. "Near-Death Experiences in a Pediatric Population. A Preliminary Report." *American Journal of Diseases in Children* 139, no. 6 (1985): 595–600.

Moss, Robert. *Dreaming the Soul Back Home: Shamanic Dreaming for Healing and Becoming Whole.* Novato, Calif.: New World Library, 2012.

Mudd, Mimi. "Research Shows Group Meditation Can Reduce Crime Rates." *Liberty Voice,* April 1, 2014. http://guardianlv.com/2014/04/research -shows-group-meditation-can-reduce-crime-rates (accessed May 23, 2017).

Mutwa, Credo Vusamazulu. *Zulu Shaman: Dreams, Prophecies, and Mysteries.* Rochester, Vt.: Destiny Books, 2003.

The Nature Conservancy, "Canada: Great Bear Rainforest." www.nature .org/ourinitiatives/regions/northamerica/canada/placesweprotect/great -bear-rainforest.xml (accessed May 23, 2017).

Nerburn, Kent, ed. *The Wisdom of the Native Americans.* New York: MJF Books, 1999.

NPR Staff. "The Biggest Thing Out of Thailand: An Elephant Orchestra." August 3, 2013. www.npr.org/2013/08/03/208338182/the-biggest-thing -out-of-thailand-an-Elephant-orchestra (accessed May 24, 2017).

O'Regan, Brendan, and Caryle Hirshberg. *Spontaneous Remission: An Annotated Bibliography.* Petaluma, Calif.: Institute of Noetic Sciences, 1993.

Pearce, Joseph Chilton. *Spiritual Initiation and the Breakthrough of Consciousness: The Bond of Power,* rev. ed. Rochester, Vt.: Park Street Press, 2003.

Petersen, John L. *Out of the Blue—Wild Cards and Other Big Future Surprises:*

How to Anticipate and Respond to Profound Change. Arlington, Va.: Arlington Institute, 1997.

Pitchford, Jeannine A., and Daniel B. Pitchford, eds. *Stanley Krippner: A Life of Dreams, Myths, and Visions.* Colorado Springs, Colo.: University Professors Press, 2015.

Platt, John R. "Elephants Are Worth 76 Times More Alive Than Dead: Report." *Scientific American.* October 8, 2014. https://blogs.scientificamerican.com /extinction-countdown/elephants-are-worth-76-times-more-alive-than -dead-report.

Pritchard, Evan. T. *Bird Medicine: The Sacred Power of Bird Shamanism.* Rochester, Vt.: Bear & Company, 2013.

Rabhi, Pieerel. *As In the Heart, So in the Earth: Reversing the Desertification of the Soul and the Soil.* Rochester, Vt.: Park Street Press, 2006.

Red Star, Nancy. "Interview with Nancy Red Star." By Zohara Hieronimus. *21st Century Radio* (February 1, 2015). http://hieronimusdb.com/guestcenter /showguest.asp?ID=2339.

Roach, John. "Oldest *Homo Sapiens* Fossils Found, Experts Say." *National Geographic News,* June 11, 2003. http://news.nationalgeographic.com /news/2003/06/0611_030611_earliesthuman.html.

Roca, Alfred L., Yasuko Ishida, Adam L. Brandt, Neal R. Benjamin, Kai Zhao, Nicholas J. Georgiadis. "Elephant Natural History: A Genomic Perspective." *Annual Review of Animal Biosciences* 3, no. 1 (2015): 139–67.

Ross, T. Edward, and Richard D. Wright. *The Divining Mind: A Guide to Dowsing and Self-Awareness.* Rochester, Vt.: Destiny Books, 1990.

———. *The Healing Mind: The Way of the Dowser.* Danville, Vt.: American Society of Dowsers, 2014.

RSPCA. "Live Hard, Die Young—How Elephants Suffer in Zoos." www.idausa .org/wp-content/uploads/2013/05/Satellite-1.pdf (accessed May 24, 2017).

Rueness, E. K., M. G. Asmyhr, C. Sillero-Zubiri, D. W. Macdonald, A. Bekele, A. Atickem, et al. "The Cryptic African Wolf: *Canis aureus lupaster* Is Not a Golden Jackal and Is Not Endemic to Egypt." *PLoS ONE* 6, no. 1 (2011): e16385. http://journals.plos.org/plosone/article?id=10.1371/journal .pone.0016385.

Russell, Charles. "Interview with Charlie Russell." By Zohara Hieronimus. *21st Century Radio* (June 8, 2014). http://hieronimusdb.com/guestcenter/showguest .asp?ID=2437.

———. *Spirit Bear: Encounters with the White Bear of the Western Rain Forest.* Ottawa, Canada: Key Porter Books, 2002.

Russell, Charles, and Maureen Enns. *Grizzly Heart: Living Without Fear among the Brown Bears of Kamchatka.* Toronto: Random House, 2002.

———. *Grizzly Seasons: Life with the Brown Bears of Kamchatka.* Toronto: Random House, 2003.

Sachs, Robert. *The Ecology of Oneness: Awakening in a Free World.* Bloomington, Ind.: IUniverse, 2016.

Salatin, Joel. "Interview with Joel Salatin." By Zohara Hieronimus. *21st Century Radio* (August 28, 2016). http://hieronimusdb.com/guestcenter/showguest .asp?ID=2542.

Schoch, Robert M., and Robert Aquinas McNally. *Voices of the Rocks: A Scientist Looks at Catastrophes and Ancient Civilizations.* New York: Harmony Books, 1999.

Schwartz, Stephan A. *The 8 Laws of Change: How to Be an Agent of Personal and Social Transformation.* Rochester, Vt.: Park Street Press, 2015.

———. "Interview with Stephan Schwartz." By Zohara Hieronimus. *21st Century Radio* (October 18, 2015). http://hieronimusdb.com/guestcenter /showguest.asp?ID=988.

———. *Opening to the Infinite: The Art and Science of Nonlocal Awareness.* Langley, Wash.: Nemoseen Media, 2007.

Seay, Stephany. "Interview with Stephany Seay." By Zohara Hieronimus. *21st Century Radio* (April 24, 2016). http://hieronimusdb.com/guestcenter /showguest.asp?ID=2518.

Shanor, Karen Nesbitt, and Jagmeet Kanwal. *Bats Sing, Mice Giggle: The Surprising Science of Animals' Inner Lives.* London: Totem Books, 2009.

Sheldrake, Rupert. *Dogs That Know When Their Owners Are Coming Home: And Other Unexplained Powers of Animals.* New York: Three Rivers Press, 2000.

———. *Morphic Resonance: The Nature of Formative Causation.* 4th ed. Rochester, Vt.: Park Street Press, 2009.

Sheldrick, Daphne. "Elephant Emotion." www.sheldrickwildlifetrust.org/html /Elephant_emotion.html (accessed May 24, 2017).

Shepard, Mark. "Interview with Mark Shepard." By Zohara Hieronimus. *21st Century Radio* (August 28, 2016). http://hieronimusdb.com/guestcenter /showguest.asp?ID=2543.

———. *Restoration Agriculture: Real World Permaculture for Farmers.* Austin, Tex.: Acres U.S.A., 2013.

Smith, Paul H. *Reading the Enemy's Mind: Inside Star Gate America's Psychic Espionage Program.* New York: Forge Books, 2005.

Snow, Chet B. *Mass Dreams of the Future.* New York: McGraw-Hill, 1989.

Song, Tamarack. *Becoming Nature: Learning the Language of Wild Animals and Plants.* Rochester, Vt.: Bear & Company, 2016.

———. *Entering the Mind of the Tracker.* Rochester Vt.: Bear & Company, 2013.

———. "Interview with Tamarack Song." By Zohara Hieronimus. *21st Century Radio* (July 26, 2015; April 24, 2016). http://hieronimusdb.com/guestcenter /showguest.asp?ID=2499.

Spencer, Tanya. "Southern Ute Bear Dance, Sun Dance and Pow Wows." March 30, 2011. https://tanyaspencer.wordpress.com/2011/03/30/southern-ute -Bear-dance-sun-dance-and-pow-wows (accessed May 23, 2017).

Stewart, Pete. *The Spiritual Science of the Stars: A Guide to the Architecture of the Spirit.* Rochester, Vt.: Inner Traditions, 2007.

Steyn, Paul. "African Elephant Numbers Plummet 30 Percent, Landmark Survey Finds." *National Geographic,* August 31, 2016. http://news .nationalgeographic.com/2016/08/wildlife-african-elephants-population -decrease-great-elephant-census.

———. "Largest Wildlife Census in History Makes Waves in Conservation." *National Geographic,* January 4, 2016. http://news.nationalgeographic.com/2016 /01/160104-great-elephant-census-vulcan-paul-allen-elephants-conservation.

———. "Report Estimates Enormous Economic Value of Living Elephants." *A Voice for Elephants,* October 17, 2014. http://voices.nationalgeographic .com/2014/10/17/report-estimates-enormous-economic-value-of-living -Elephants.

Sweet, Bill. *A Journey into Prayer: Pioneers of Prayer in the Laboratory: Agents of Science or Satan?* Bloomington, Ind.: Xlibris Publishing, 2007.

Talbott, David, and Wallace Thornhill. *Thunderbolts of the Gods.* Portland, Ore.: Mikamar Publishing, 2005.

Tallwing, Judy. "Interview with Judy Tallwing." By Zohara Hieronimus. *21st Century Radio* (November 23, 2014). http://hieronimusdb.com/guestcenter /showguest.asp?ID=2457.

Temple, Robert. *Oracles of the Dead: Ancient Techniques for Predicting the Future.* Rochester, Vt.: Destiny Books, 2005.

———. *The Sirius Mystery: New Scientific Evidence of Alien Contact 5,000 Years Ago.* Rochester, Vt.: Destiny Books, 1998.

Tiller, William. *Science and Human Transformation: Subtle Energies, Intentionality, and Consciousness.* Walnut Creek, Calif.: Pavior Publishing, 1997.

Tucker, Linda. *Mystery of the White Lions: Children of the Sun God.* New York: Hay House, 2010.

Tulleners, Lois. "Interview with Lois Tulleners." By Zohara Hieronimus. *21st Century Radio* (February 1, 2015). http://hieronimusdb.com/guestcenter/showguest.asp?ID=2460.

UNHCR. "Worldwide Displacement Hits All-Time High as War and Persecution Increase." June 18, 2015. www.unhcr.org/news/latest/2015/6/558193896/worldwide-displacement-hits-all-time-high-war-persecution-increase.html (accessed May 24, 2017).

Vennum, Thomas. *Lacrosse Legends of the First Americans.* Baltimore, Md.: Johns Hopkins University Press, 2007.

Walton, K. G., J. Z. Fields, D. K. Levitsky, D. A. Harris, N. D. Pugh, and R. H. Schneider. "Lowering Cortisol and CVD Risk in Postmenopausal Women: A Pilot Study Using the Transcendental Meditation Program." *Annals of the New York Academy of Sciences* 1032 (December 2004): 211–15.

Wasco Tribe. "Coyote, Wolves, and Bears." www.wwu.edu/skywise/legends.html (accessed May 23, 2017).

Weaver, Donald, and Gary Zimmer. "Interview with Donald Weaver and Gary Zimmer." By Zohara Hieronimus. *21st Century Radio* (June 19, 2016). http://hieronimusdb.com/guestcenter/showguest.asp?ID=308.

Zimmer, Gary F. The Biological Farmer: *A Complete Guide to the Sustainable and Profitable Biological System of Farming.* Austin, Tex.: Acres U.S.A., 2000.

Index

Numbers in *italics* indicate illustrations.
Numbers in *italics* preceded by *pl.* indicate color insert plate numbers.

Abul-Abbas, 121, 123

Adams, John, 256

Adamson, George, 105

Adamson, Joy, 105

adrenal glands, 32

Africa, 43

afterlife communication, 201

Agra Bear Rescue Facility, 55–56

Ainu people, 40

alchemy, *pl. 9*, 94–95

All Halloween, 99

All Souls Day, 99

Alnitak, 176

Alrai, 48

American bison, 222–25

American Bison Society, 219, 235–36

Ancient Giants Who Ruled America, The, 271–72

animalcide, 31, 154–55, 194–95

animal communication, 26

animal exploitation, 57

animals, commonality with humans, 32–34

Animals Asia, 57

Anthony, Lawrence, 144–45

Anthropocene, 276–80

Anubis, 180–83, *182*

apex animals, 193, 235, 300

Arcas, 49–50

Argentina, 43

Artemis, 50

Artio, 53

as above, so below, 46, 178

Asdiwal, 68–69

Asherah, 87, 89

Aslan, 100–101

astral body, 67

Atlantis, 266

attention, 26

authority figures, 28

Baum, L. Frank, 105

Bauval, Robert, 176

Beal, John, 272

Bear, 35–73, 58–59

    basic facts, 58–59

cross-cultural perspectives of,
39–40

cultural portrayals of, 35–39, *36, 38*

Great Bear Initiative, 78–79

horrors endured by, 56–57

Ice Age factor, 40–43, *41*

legend of, 70–71

lessons of, 79–81, 298–99

man who walks with bears, 70–77

medicine dreams, 62–66

phenomenology of, 65–67

roots of Western dissociation, 49–52

symbolism in heavens, 46–49, *46*

value of ecotourism, 77–78

veneration of she bears, 52–54

White Spirit Bear, *pl. 6, pl. 7,* 9, 42,
58–59, 67–69, 70–71, 79–81

Bear Dance, 54–56

beauty, 3

beef production, 106–7

Bekoff, Marc, 155

Bella (dog), 16

Berenstain Bears, 37

Bergin, Patrick, 162

Big Dipper, 46

Big Foot, 40, 275–76

Biggest Bear, The, 60

bile, bear, 56–57

bilocation, 15–16

biomind superpowers, 4

Bird, Christopher, 284–85

bison, 222–25

Black Diamond (buffalo), 240–43,
242

Blackfoot, 174, 263

blood lust, 51

blue moon, 20

bonding, 170

Bonobo Hope, 18

bonobos, 43

Boo-Boo Bear, 37

Boone, J. Allen, 146

Born Free, 105

Bosondjo (bonobo), 17–18

Bouba Ndjidah National Park,
154–55

Bradshaw, Gay, *pl. 5,* 30–31, 138–41,
150, 195

brain, 5, 31

bridge walkers, 62

British Columbia, 67–68

British Isles, 43

Bronx Zoo, 219–20, 229, 235

Brown, Lester, 107–8

Brunke, Dawn, 65–66

Buckley, Carol, *pl. 14,* 150–53

Buddha, 127–29

Buddhism, 127–32

Buffalo, *pl. 21,* 45, 207–64

Black Diamond, 240–43, *242*

characteristics of, 256–59

constellations and, 220–22

extermination of, 232–37

finding a missing horse, 207–14

great American bison, 222–25

history of, 215–20, *216, 218*

lessons of, 259–64, 300

mismanagement of current herds,
237–40, *238*

Native Americans and, 232–37

official meeting with white man,
225–28, *228*

protector of, 248–56

White Buffalo Calf Woman,
243–48

Buffalo Bill, 249–50, *249*

Buffalo Field Campaign (BFC),
238–39

buffalo head nickels, 241, *241*

bullying, 32–33

Callisto, 49–50

Campe, Joanna, 286

Canada, 43

Cancer, 84

canned camps, 109–11

cascade trophic china model, 193

catastrophes, 265–69

Catholic Church, 23–24, 177

Catlin, George, *pl. 4,* 25

cattle, 106–7, 189, 217–18, 239

Cayce, Edgar, 268–69

cell phones, 111

Cepheus, 48

change, 291–92

Charlemagne, Emperor, 121–22

Chase, Mike, 154

Chasing Horse, Joseph, 245

Chatterjee, Keya, 107

Cherokee, 44–46, 169–70

Chessie, 275–76

children, dreams of, 296–98

Chile, 43

China, 157

circuses, 164

clairaudience, 293

clairvoyance, 293

Cleveland, Grover, 232–37

collateral damage, 29

collective unconscious, 165–66

compassion, 11, 165–66

computers, 111

concern, 80

conservation, 3, 275–76

constellations, 83–84, *84,* 172–75,
173

Cook Report, The, 110

cooperation, 171

Copper Top (horse), 208–14

courage, 171

Cousteau, Jacques, 281

Coyote, 179

Creation, 4–5, 33, 111–13, 199

Creation of the Big Dipper, 47

Creek, 169–70

Cremo, Michael, 267

Crow Dog, Leonard, 246

cruelty, 32–33

crush cages, 57

Crutzen, Paul, 277–78

cultural restoration, 280–81

Cybele, 89

dancing, 146–47

dancing bears, 55–56

Darwin, Charles, 276–77

David, King, 85

David Sheldrick Wildlife Trust,
143

dead, rituals for, 145–47

defense mechanisms, 28–29

Demystifying Shamans, 22–23

detachment, 30–31

Dewhurst, Richard J., 271–72

dissociation
   domination and, 52
   impact and remedy for, 30–31
   modern plague of, 28–30
   roots of, in Western culture, 49–52
divine feminine, 52–54
divine soul, 2–3
Divining Mind, The, 208
DNA, 187
Dogon people, 97, 174
dogs, 168–69, 178
domination, 8–9, 32–33, 51–52, 109
dragons, *pl. 22,* 274–75
Dreaming with Polar Bears, 65–66
dreams and dreaming, 23–28,
   157–64, 187–88, 296–98
dreamtime, 64–66, 201
drumming, 146–47
Durga, 87
dust bowl, *pl. 23,* 285–86
du Toit, Johan, 216–17

Earth, 282–91
Earth Organization, 144
ecosystems
   damage to, 29–30
   restoring, 282–91
ecotourism, 77–78
8 Laws of Change, The, 260, 291–92
Elephant, *pl. 13,* 45, 121–66
   author's dreams with, 157–74
   census of, 155–57
   cross-cultural perspectives of,
      126–27
   disposition of, 125–26
   extinction threat, 137–43

famous ones in history, 121–25, *122*
lessons of, 299
mankind's abuse of, 147–55, *148,
   152*
meeting Buddhist White Elephant,
   127–32
pictured, *pl. 15*
rituals for the dead, 145–47
situation today, 133–37
trans-species telepathy and, 144–45
White Elephant, 9, 127–32,
   132–33, 165–66
Elephant Aid International, 153
Elephants on the Edge, 30–31
Elephants Without Borders, 154
Elk Island National Park, 218
Elsa (lion), 105
Elykia (bonobo), 19
emotional body, 67
Endangered Species Act (ESA), 192
endurance, 171
Entering the Mind of the Tracker, 186
entitlement, 51–52
ethic of care, 280–81
eugenics, 18
Europa, 220–22
exploitation, 8–9
extinction, 275–80
extinction threats, 194–95, 202–3,
   232–37

fear, 10, 95
Feld Entertainment, 164
fertilizers, 283
fight-or-flight impulse, 3, 32
fishing, 106

Fool Bull, *63*
forgiveness, 125
Four Dignities, 79–80
Four Eagles, Russell, 117
Fox, 179
Franklin, Benjamin, 256
freedom, 234
Future of the Human Experience, The, 47–48

Gabriel, Peter, 17
Ganesh, 126
Ghost Bear, 72
giants, 269–73
Gilbert, Adrian, 176
Gimbutas, Marija, 53
GMOs, 282–84
Goldilocks, 35–36
Goodall, Jane, 30
Goode, George Brown, 233–34
Great Bear, 52
Great Bear Initiative, 78–79
Great Council of the Pawnee, 196–97
Great Elephant Census, 156
Great Pyramid, 174–75, 176–77
Great Sphinx, 83
Great Spirit, 7, 96
Gregory XIII, Pope, 177
group meditation, 13

habitat loss, 106
hair, uncut, 111–12
Haliburton, R. G., 98–99, 100
Hamaker, John, 287–88
Hancock, Graham, 41–42, 266
Hanno (elephant), 123–25, *124*

harmony, 109
Hart, Cynthia, *pl. 19,* 218–19, 248–56, 261
Hart, Mickey, 24–25
Hathor, 221
Healing Mind, The, 208
health, 170–71
Hebrew prophets, 5
Hennepin, Louis, 226
Hera, 50
Hercules, 85, 87, 100
Hiawatha (buffalo), *254*
Hieronimus, Bob, 5
Hieronimus, J. Zohara Meyerhoff
    conversations with Matata, 15–20
    dreams of, 62–66, 157–64, 171–72, 178–79, 204–5, 263–64, 278
    introduction to Bear, 60–62
    pictured, *pl. 1, pl. 24, 27*
highly sensitive person, 7
hope, 80
Hopi people, 97
Hornaday, William, 226–31, *230,* 235, 237, 301
howls, 167–68
Huffman, Julia, 192
human-animal telepathy, 9
humanitarian aid, 29
humans, commonality with animals, 32–34
human trafficking, 51–52, 138, 149
humility, 131, 158, 208, 259
hunting, 106, 181
hypnosis, 24–25, 32
hypothalamus, 32

Ice Age, 9, 19, 40–43, *41*
Iceland, 42–43
Ideal Toy and Novelty Company, 37–39
Iliad, 172
Inanna, 87
incubated dreams, 7
India, 100
infanticide, 102
inner technologies, 294–96
intelligence, 170
intention, 26
interaural time differences (ITD), 147
Interconnected: Embracing Life in Our Global Society, 11
International Union for the Conservation of Nature (IUCN), 156
Intertribal Bison Association (ITBC), 240
In the Temple of Wolves, 186
intuition, 11, 170
invention, 3
Iranian hostage crisis, 14
Iroquois, 169–70, 256
Isaac the Jew, 121, 123
Ishtar, 87, *88*
Isis, 87
Issa, Christopher, 255
ivory, 138, 155, 156–57

jackals, 182, 187–88
Japan, 194–95
Jefferson, Thomas, 256
Jewel (elephant), 162–64, *163*
Jewel in the Crown, The, 163–64

Johanson, Donald, 266–67
joy, 10
Jung, C. G., 157–58

Kabbalah, 1–2, 33
Kalandar people, 55–56
Kanzi (bonobo), 17–18
Kerulos Center, 30–31
Kimba (lion), 105
Kinship with All Life, 146
Klingbeil, Bruce, 294
Klingbeil, John, 294
knowledge, 3
Kolbert, Elizabeth, 276–77
Krippner, Stanley, *pl. 3,* 15–16, 20–27, 28–29, 158
Kruetzmann, Bill, 24–25

Lady of the Lions, 87
Lakota, 7, 232, 240, 245–46, 251
Lame Deer, John Fire, 223, 246–47
Lamplugh, Rick, 186, 194–95
land appropriation, 106
LaViolette, Paul, 47–48, 92
left hemisphere, 5
Lenape, 169–70
Leo, 83–84, *84*
Leo X, Pope, 123
Lewis, C. S., 100–101
lexigram boards, 17
liberation, 160
life economy, 281–82
Lincoln, Abraham, 121
Lindstrom, Christopher, 255
Lion, *pl. 10, pl. 11, pl. 12,* 45, 82–120
  cultural histories of, 85–90, *86*

in the heavens, 83–84, *84*

lessons of, 117–20, 299

lions of today, 101–6, *103*

listening for language of creation, 111–13

Maasai Lion Guardians, 113–14

Pleiades and, 97–101

points of alignment, 82–83

species decline accelerating, 106–8

symbologizing, 115–16

teachings of Credo Mutwa, 93–97

White Lion, 9, 82, 90–92, 95–97, 109–11, 117–20

Zulu shamanism, 92–93

Lion King, 105

literacy, 107–8

Little Bear, 52

Little People, 44–46

Little Red Riding Hood, 189–90, *190*

Little Thunder, Rosalie, 238–39

Loch Ness monster, 275–76

Looking Horse, Arvol, 243–45, 247–48

Lopez, Barry Holstun, 196–97

Lotus Sutra, 127, 131–32, 160

Louis XIV, King, 226

love, 10, 94

low magic, 200

loyalty, 171

Lucy, 266–67

lycanthropy, 199–200

Lycaon, 49

Maasai, 113–14

Mageba, King, 108–9

magic, 20–23

Magicians of the Gods, 41

Maharishi Effect, 13

Maisha (bonobo), 19

Manuel I, King, 123

Mars, 175, 267–68

Matata (bonobo), *pl. 2,* 15–16, 42, 43, 269–71

materialism, 29–30

matriarchal societies, 12, 52–54, 280–81

McCartney, Paul, 17

McGrady, Tim, 77

meaning, 3

Medicine Man Performing His Mysteries over a Dying Man, pl. 4, 25

Medicine of the Wolf, 192

medicine people, 4, 15

Meese, Mike, 238–39

Michell, Jon, 82–83

Michtom, Morris, 37

Michtom, Rose, 37

Middle Bronze Age, 48

Milgram, Stanley, 28

Milky Way, 174

Miracle (buffalo), 245

Miracle Moon (buffalo), *pl. 20,* 257, 260

Mission: Wolf, 193–94

Moody, Raymond, 14–15

mothering, 80

Mound Builders, 273

multiverses, 13–16

musth, 134

Mutwa, Credo, 93–97, 112–13

Narasimha, 100
NASA, 116
National Wildlife Federation, 276
Native Americans, 232–37. *See also*
    specific tribes
nature, 11, 20
Neanderthals, 43
near-death experiences, 14, 20
Nemean lion, 85, 87
New Materials for the History of Man,
    98–99
New Order of the World Mother, 20
Nile River, 94
Nomkhubhlwane, 90
nonlocal consciousness, 3–4, 293–94
Northern Tribes Buffalo Treaty,
    262–63
Nyota (bonobo), 19

Obama, Barack, 156
Obedience, 28
objectivity, 30–31
O'Connell-Rodwell, Caitlin, 147
Of Wolves and Men, 196–97
Ojibwa, 169–70, 197

pagan worship, 115
Panbanisha (bonobo), 19
pantheism, 115
patience, 131, 259
Pawnee, 196–97
peace, 260–61
Penetration, 268
permaculture, 288–90
Perrault, Charles, 189
pets, 26

phajaan, 150–52
Plains Indians, 233
Planet V, 267–68
Plato, 266
play, 170
Pleiades, 97–101
Pliny the Elder, 126, 199–200
poaching, 106
Pole Star, 42, 47–48, 177
prayer, 293–94
predictions, 15
premonition, 4
premonitory physiology, 14–15
presentiment, 116
preservation, 279–80
prophecy, 293
Psychology Today, 150
psychosis, 27
PTSD, 13, 30, 32, 281

quantum physics, 13–16

rain forests, 69–70, 106–7
Rama IV, King, 121
rape, 51–52
red hawk, 204–5
Red Star, Nancy, 205
reiki, 14
remineralization, 286–87
remote viewing, 4, 14
responsibility, 131
restoration, 3, 280–81
restoration agriculture, 288–89
Richardson, Kevin, 110–11
right action, 11
right hemisphere, 5

Ringling Bros., 164
Roberts, Carter, 108
Robinson, Jill, 57
Rock, Adam J., 22–23
Roosevelt, Theodore, 37–39, *38,* 219, 301
Rose, Charlie, 161–62
Ross, Terry Edward, II, 208
Ruscombe Mansion Community Health Center, 7
Russell, Charlie, *pl. 8,* 70–77, 192, 198

Sacred Center, 82–83
sacred centers, 82–83
sacred societies, 176–77
Sadat, Anwar, 180
Sadat, Jehan, 180
Salatin, Joel, 289–90
Sanctuary of the Divine Presence, 22
Sasquatch, 40
Savage-Rumbaugh, Sue, 16, 17
Schwartz, Stephan, 259–60, 291–92
Seay, Stephany, 239–40
seeds, 282–91
Sehkmet, 87, 89
Selene, 87
self-sacrifice, 40
service, 158
sexual assault, 51–52
Shaka, King, 113
shamans and shamanism, 4, 15, 22
    dreaming, 23–28
    Lion shamanism, 108–9
    White Wolf shamanism, 197–200
    Zulu shamanism, 92–93, 112
shape-shifting, 15, 66–67, 199–200

Sheldrake, Rupert, 145–46
Sheldrick, Daphne, 142–43
Shepard, Mark, 287–88
Shoshone, 170
Siddartha, 127–29
sinkholes, 281–82
Sirius, 97, 172–75, *173,* 176–78, 180–83
Sitchin, Zecharia, 89
Sitting Bull, 249–50, *249,* 256
Sixth Extinction, 99, 276–80
Skidi tribesmen, 170
sky gods, 42
slavery, 51–52, 149
sleep, 24
Smokey Bear, 36
social ecology, 29–30
Solomon, King, 85
Song, Tamarack, *pl. 18,* 168, 179–80, 186, 198, 201–2
soul retrieval, 33
South America, 106–7
species entitlement, 9
Spirit Bear Lodge, 77
Standing Rock Agency, 250
Stanford Research Institute (SRI), 14
star ancestors, 97–101
Star Gate Project, 14
Steiff Company, 37–38
Steiner, Rudolph, 268
strength, 171
Sultzer, David, 137
Swann, Ingo, 4, 14, 268

Tallwing, Judy, 45–46
Targ, Russell, 14

Taurus, 220
technology, 111
Teddy Bear, 37–38
Teko (bonobo), 19
telepathy, 4, 9, 25–26, 97, 294–96
television, 111
Thai Elephant Orchestra, 137
Thailand, 132–33
Thompson, Richard, 267
Thuban, 48
Thula Thula Private Game Reserve,
    144–45
Timbavati, 82–83, 90
Toltecs, 273
topsoil enrichment, 282–91
tracking, 186–88
traditions, 104–5
trans-species telepathy, 4, 17–20, 31,
    97, 144–47
Tree of Life, 33
trees, 107–8
trophy business, 109–11
Tsavo East National Park, 143
Tsimshians, 68–69
Tucker, Linda, 83
Tulleners, Lois, 186–87
Turner, Jeff, 72
Turner, Sue, 72

Umvelinqangi, 92
understanding, 3
United States Department of
    Agriculture, 36
United States Geological Society
    (USGS), 281–82
universal love, 94

Unkulunkulu, 92
Ursa Major, 46–49, *46*
Ute people, 54–56

Van Flandern, Thomas, 175,
    267–68
Viking 1, 175
Virgin Mary, 53
Vishnu, 100
visions, 15
vitriol, 94–95

waking visions, 8
Walsh, James A., 250–51
Walters, Charles, Jr., 290
Walters, Edwin, 273
Ward, Lynd, 60
Warner, John, 161–63
warp speed, 116
water, 282–91
Weaver, Donald, 286, 287–88
whales, 10
White, Timothy, 266–67
White Bison Association, 218–19,
    252–56
White Buffalo, *pl. 20,* 9, 220–22,
    252–59. *See also* Buffalo
  lessons of, 259–64
White Buffalo Calf Woman, 243–48,
    301
White Dragon, *pl. 22,* 274–75
White Elephant, *pl. 13,* 9. *See also*
    Elephant
  Buddhism and, 127–32
  lessons of, 165–66
  Thailand and, 132–33

White Lion, 9, 82, 90–92, 109–11.
    See also Lion
    lessons of, 117–20
    origin story, 95–97
White Spirit Animals, about, 1–8
White Spirit Bear, *pl. 6, pl. 7,* 9, 42,
    67–69. *See also* Bear
    basic facts, 58–59
    legend of, 70–71
    lessons of, 79–81
White Witch, 100–101
White Wolf, *pl. 16,* 9, 197–200,
    205–6. *See also* Wolf
White Wolf Sanctuary, 186–87
Wildlife Conservation Society
    (WCS), 219–20, 229
Wind Cave National Park, 218
wisdom, 3, 80
Wolf, *pl. 16, pl. 17,* 45, 167–206
    Anubis and star system Sirius,
        180–83, *182*
    constellations, 172–75, *173*
    cosmic name game, 178–80
    end of the Japanese Wolf, 194–95
    families of, *pl. 17,* 183–85, *185*
    history of, in North America,
        188–94, *190*

lessons of, 299
magic of, 200–205
relationship with humans, 167–72,
    169
shamanism and the White Wolf,
    197–200
tracking Anubis, 186–88
unhooking humanity from celestial
    markers, 176–78
Wolf Star, 174
Wonderful Wizard of Oz, The, 105
Worldwatch Institute, 107–8
World Wildlife Fund (WWF),
    106–7
Wright, Richard, 208

Yellowstone National Park, *pl. 17,*
    pl. 21, 39, 186, 193–94, 218,
    237–40
Yeti, 40–44
Yogi Bear, 36–37

Zeus, 49–51, 87, 220, 234–35
Zimmer, Gary, 287–88
Zishwezi, 97
zoos, 147–49, 153–54, 155
Zulu people, 90, 92–93, 108–9

BOOKS OF RELATED INTEREST

The Future of Human Experience
Visionary Thinkers on the Science of Consciousness
by J. Zohara Meyerhoff Hieronimus, D.H.L.

Power Animal Meditations
Shamanic Journeys with Your Spirit Allies
by Nicki Scully
Illustrated by Angela Werneke

Speaking with Nature
Awakening to the Deep Wisdom of the Earth
by Sandra Ingerman and Llyn Roberts

Animal Messengers
Oracles of the Soul
by Regula Meyer

Bird Medicine
The Sacred Power of Bird Shamanism
by Evan T. Pritchard

Shapeshifting
Techniques for Global and Personal Transformation
by John Perkins

Psychic Communication with Animals for Health and Healing
by Laila del Monte

Animal Voices, Animal Guides
Discover Your Deeper Self through Communication with Animals
by Dawn Baumann Brunke

INNER TRADITIONS • BEAR & COMPANY
P.O. Box 388 • Rochester, VT 05767
1-800-246-8648
www.InnerTraditions.com
Or contact your local bookseller